POMP AND PIETY

POMP AND PIETY

EVERYDAY LIFE OF THE ARISTOCRACY IN STUART ENGLAND

BEN NORMAN

AMBERLEY

In loving memory of Anna Norman
She would have made a fine gentlewoman.

First published 2023

Amberley Publishing
The Hill, Stroud
Gloucestershire, GL5 4EP

www.amberley-books.com

ISBN 978 1 3981 1017 5 (hardback)
ISBN 978 1 3981 1018 2 (ebook)

British Library Cataloguing in Publication Data.
A catalogue record for this book is available from the British Library.

1 2 3 4 5 6 7 8 9 10

Typesetting by SJmagic DESIGN SERVICES, India.
Printed in the UK.

CONTENTS

AUTHOR'S NOTE

Keeping track of the information that forms the background to this book has been a bit like attempting to tame a wild beast. Nevertheless, every effort has been made to ensure that names, places and dates appear correctly throughout, and are presented with some level of consistency. Any oversights, errors, or inconsistencies identified are entirely the fault of the author.

Spelling and grammar within primary material has been modernised at the author's discretion, where he has deemed it appropriate. Contemporary sources containing odd phrasing, spelling, use of punctuation, or use of capitalisation have likely kept their original form.

ACKNOWLEDGEMENTS

There are no two ways about it: writing a book is challenging. On this, my second literary outing, I was under the erroneous impression that the process might be somewhat easier to navigate. In fact, the very knowledge that I had already completed one book somehow rendered the act of finishing another much more difficult. If this line of thinking makes little sense to the reader, rest assured it makes even littler sense to the author. Perseverance, periods of reflection, a determination to enjoy what I was doing, and black coffee eventually saw this title come together, and it is with a fair amount of relief that I say I am more or less pleased with the outcome.

Researching and writing are largely solitary activities, but a few words of gratitude here are necessary. My thanks go, of course, to Amberley for showing an interest in my idea and agreeing to publish. I would also like to thank Rebecca for kindly reading through the finished manuscript, Hannah for accompanying me to Berry Pomeroy Castle in Devon, Nathan for tolerating my obsession with 'book work', and Sam for his constant encouragement. It is all very much appreciated.

INTRODUCTION

> Mr Hastings, by his quality, being the son, brother, and uncle to the Earls of Huntingdon, and his way of living, had the first place amongst us. He was peradventure an original in our age, or rather the copy of our nobility in ancient days in hunting and not warlike times; he was low, very strong and very active, of a reddish flaxen hair, his clothes always green cloth, and never all worth when new five pounds.[1]

Thus, we are introduced to the intriguing character of Henry Hastings, a country gentleman who lived at his Dorset estate of Woodlands Park in the latter years of the Tudor regime and the first half-century of the reign of the Stuarts. That we know so much about this colourful individual is thanks to Hastings' neighbour and evident admirer, Anthony Ashley Cooper, 1st Earl of Shaftesbury. The ill-fated earl appears to have been quite taken with his contemporary's quotidian surroundings and routine. The house at Woodlands was 'perfectly of the old fashion', he noted in the 1630s, set in acres of verdant parkland that housed deer, rabbits, fish ponds, and 'great store of wood and timber'. There was also a bowling green pockmarked with ridges and uneven sections, and a 'banqueting-house' built in a nearby tree.

Coexisting with the deer and rabbits kept in the park were 'all manner of sports-hounds' bred specifically for hunting, this being an adored pastime of Henry's and, by all accounts, the centre of his eccentric world.

The interior of the house confirmed Hasting's obsession with chasing animals. The Earl of Shaftesbury, quite bluntly, observed that the great hall was nothing short of a complete mess. The room was 'strewed with marrow bones', he related, 'full of hawks' perches, hounds, spaniels, and terriers, the upper sides of the hall hung with the fox-skins of this and the last year's skinning, here and there a polecat intermixed, guns and keepers' and huntsmen's poles in abundance'. The parlour, large, long, and sufficiently furnished, appeared slightly less filthy. We are told that the dogs settled down in here from time to time and dozed on a brick hearth built into one of the walls, while nestled in two great chairs could often be found furry litters of newborn kittens, staring bleary-eyed into the foreign expanses around them. The space was not dark, featuring large windows that allowed Henry to see what he was eating at mealtimes. The general clutter of the property extended into the parlour, albeit in small ways: weapons were placed for easy access in the welcome recesses created by the room's windows, corners were filled with hunting and hawking poles, and at the upper end were tables and a solitary desk groaning with the weight of biblical texts, old hats turned inwards to hold eggs, used tobacco pipes, and more hunting equipment.

Dining was an interesting experience at Woodlands. Both dinner and supper were taken in the parlour, but not before the Dorset gentleman had first helped himself to a selection of fresh oysters eaten at an 'oyster-table at the lower end'. Although Hastings was famous for his signature offering of 'beef pudding and small beer', according to the Earl of Shaftesbury at any rate, in reality the food and drink you might be expected to consume at his table was wide-ranging and plentiful. Beef, mutton, venison, gammon, and fish freshly caught from Poole were all staples of the generous diet at Woodlands Park, together with sweet and savoury pies, 'strong' beer – sometimes stirred 'with a great sprig of rosemary' – and wine, which was to be drunk in moderation. In typical quirky fashion, Hastings kept his provisions cool by storing them in a disused chapel adjoining the parlour, in the bowels of a redundant pulpit. To make doubly sure that the hungry cats joining him at the dinner table avoided the grave error of pinching food that did not belong to them, he armed himself at every meal with a 'little white round stick of fourteen inches long'.

For a country gentleman inhabiting a sleepy part of England, Henry Hasting's character and personal life were markedly explosive. He was a notorious womaniser in Dorset, with Shaftesbury suggesting that there was 'not a woman in all his walks of the degree of a yeoman's wife or under, and under the age of forty, but it was extremely her fault if he were not intimately acquainted with her'. Probably to the disbelief and incredulity of many, Hastings managed to get away with such promiscuous behaviour by befriending the male intimates of the women he courted, including their unwitting husbands. The man's passionate temperament was not limited to female lovers, however. Sexual fervour seemed all too easily to morph into aggression where Henry was concerned, and it was his domestic attendants who were to bear the brunt of their master's wrath when it materialised. 'He was well natured, but soon angry,' Shaftesbury summarised, '[and] called his servants bastard and cuckoldy knaves.'[2]

The unforgettable Mr Henry Hastings, along with Anthony Ashley Cooper, 1st Earl of Shaftesbury, belonged to a distinguished segment of English society known broadly as the aristocracy. As in other epochs before and after, the aristocracy dominated both the national and local stages in Stuart England, coming in just below the royal family in the country's social hierarchy. Within their gilded ranks existed two basic groups, the nobility and gentry. While the nobility technically outranked the gentry in that the former either inherited noble titles or were gifted them by the sovereign, both parties occupied an exalted position in the seventeenth and early eighteenth centuries, sharing not only status and prestige but more specifically wealth, high offices, coats of arms, and significant lands and property. The increasingly blurred – or indeed invisible – line between the nobility and gentry in seventeenth-century England was eloquently articulated by Margaret Cavendish, Duchess of Newcastle, who, in recalling her late father's standing in an autobiographical text, noted that he was 'a gentleman, which title is grounded and given by merit'. More pertinently, she went on to write almost defensively, 'and though my father was not a peer of the realm, yet there were few peers who had much greater estates or lived more noble therewith.'[3] In talking about peers of the realm, Margaret was referring to the nobility. Under this pennant were assembled, in order of precedence, the dukes, duchesses, marquesses, marchionesses, earls, countesses, viscounts, viscountesses, barons, and baronesses of the land, together with their immediate families. Beneath the standard of the gentry, on the other hand, were gathered in full force baronets, knights, esquires, gentlemen, and their respective wives and close kin. It was possible for a member of the gentry to slip into the category of the nobility in his or her lifetime, through marriage or a newly acquired noble title.

The aristocracy living under the Stuart dynasty, which ran from the accession of King James I in 1603 to the death of his great-granddaughter Queen Anne in 1714, are best recalled in the twenty-first century through their austere oil portraits, imposing church monuments, the complex and subservient relationships they cultivated with the ruling monarch of the day, and their legendary roles in high politics, particularly the English Civil War and the Glorious Revolution of 1688. Lady Brilliana Harley, for instance, is forever remembered as the heroine of Brampton Bryan Castle in Herefordshire, valiantly defending the fortress and its inhabitants against besieging royalist troops in 1643, until her health finally failed her in the autumn. John Churchill, 1st Duke of Marlborough, is likewise immortalised through his involvement in a string of game-changing political developments: including but not limited to the defeat of the Monmouth

Rebellion in 1685, the deposition of King James II three years later in 1688, and the infamous relationship he and his wife, Sarah, crafted with the impressionable Queen Anne in the early eighteenth century.

Although the aforementioned events were undoubtedly important details in the lives of Brilliana Harley and John Churchill, this book aims to look beyond recognised civil war bravery and remote portraiture, to consider instead the everyday lives of such influential men and women. What did Lady Brilliana Harley wear to bed every night? How did the Duke of Marlborough treat his maids and footmen? What did they both do for fun in those quiet moments when there was no politics, no royalists knocking on the castle door, and no Queen Anne to entertain? These are the kinds of questions that will be posed and, hopefully, sufficiently answered over the course of the following chapters. Beginning first with a perusal of the lifecycle of a typical aristocrat, topics cover the experience of privileged children, houses and gardens, the types and role of servants, clothing and appearance, food and drink, pets and amusements, travel, illnesses and treatments, and of course religion. In focusing on the day-to-day experiences of Stuart England's dukes and viscountesses, its baronets and esquires, it is anticipated that an understanding can be acquired of them as living, breathing, sentient human beings, as folk who harboured inconsequential hopes and fears, who had unique mannerisms and routines, who fell out and made up again, who loved and lost, and, finally, as individuals we might be able to recognise from our vantage point in the modern era.

Henry Hastings provides a perfect example of how rewarding and valuable an endeavour it can be to shine a light on the habitual activities of members of the Stuart aristocracy. One almost feels as if one knows Henry personally after learning about the condition of his house in Dorset, from the marrow bones littering the floor to the spaniels and terriers curled up on the brick hearth in the parlour. There is something deeply gratifying about imagining the kittens packed together haphazardly on the great chairs, and, truthfully, it is difficult not to smile at the thought of Hastings choosing to keep his fresh produce in an old pulpit and the creases of inverted hats. His is an eccentric example, but as will become evident, small delights like these are to be found in the everyday lives of a great many of our aristocratic forebears.

I

CEREMONIES AND CELEBRATIONS

Personal ceremonies and celebrations punctuated the lives of aristocrats residing in Stuart England. Often constituting significant milestones or episodes in the aristocratic lifecycle, they included christenings, weddings, funerals, and in the case of annual celebrations, Christmases, New Years, Easters, and birthdays. Between christenings and weddings, but of course much closer to weddings, there was also the quasi-ceremony of matchmaking. The latter was a peculiar rite wholeheartedly embraced by the nobility and gentry and always taken very seriously, particularly by close relatives who had a vested interest in the outcome of negotiations. Matchmaking could either become a protracted affair spanning years or conclude alarmingly quickly, sometimes resulting in the shepherding of two very youthful individuals down the aisle to be married, who could be as young as twelve or thirteen.

The christenings, weddings, and funerals of the Stuart aristocracy were commonly tinged with at least some element of grandiosity, the general trend seeming to be that ostentation increased with the maturity of ceremonial participants. Therefore, while christenings might be relatively low-key occasions, it was not unusual to witness an aristocratic funeral that sailed perilously close to unnecessary extravagance. As the Stuart era progressed and the early eighteenth century beckoned, the funeral ceremonies of the nobility and gentry lost much of their resplendence in line with religious doctrine and changing tastes, although many continued to rely on pomp and pageantry into the reign of Queen Anne.

The annual celebrations of Christmas, New Year, and birthdays were observed with much feasting, drinking, and merrymaking by the aristocracy, a proclivity that, unlike the grandeur exhibited at funerals, was left well enough alone throughout the period. At the coming of spring and Easter week, however, the focus shifted conspicuously from revelry to piety. It is a given that beneath every ceremony and celebration lay the fundamental foundation of religion, but Easter was noteworthy for its total absence of any real commemoration beyond prayer and attending church. In fact, the majority of aristocratic sources from the seventeenth and early eighteenth centuries barely mention this Christian festival, save for a brief acknowledgement of its yearly occurrence. In 1706, for instance, the future baronet Sir Walter Calverley of Esholt in Yorkshire merely noted in his diary on Easter Day that 'Samuel Hemingway made the tenders of the modus's for tythe corn and tythe hay as usual, in Otley church, but nobody received them.'[1] Christmases and New Years were recorded in much greater detail.

Christenings

No aristocrat would ever remember their first religious ceremony in Stuart England. Even so, christenings carried enormous significance in this pious period, being the point at which a newborn baby was officially admitted into the Christian church and bathed in God's love and protection. The christenings of aristocratic infants tended to be small, intimate occasions attended by close family and friends only, including the godparents of the child. Lady Anne Clifford, then wife of the 3rd Earl of Dorset, commented on the birth of her cousin's son in Chiswick in January 1619, who was 'christened in the church privately and was named Francis'. Many years later in April 1694, Sir Walter Calverley was a guest at the quiet christening of a child of the esquire Robert Baynes in Yorkshire, noting that he had 'stood godfather' alongside Sir William Lowther, with a woman named Mrs Fairfax acting as godmother. It was traditional for guests to reward the women who had been involved in the mother's pregnancy and postnatal life at this unassuming ceremony. Thus, at the christening of Mr Baynes' son, Calverley gave the midwife a guinea for the baby's safe delivery, along with ten shillings apiece to the nurse and housekeeper for their subsequent good work. In August 1646, a lavish £4 was given by the Earl and Countess of Bath to the midwife of Mary Vere Fane, Countess of Westmorland, which was presented to the female attendant at the christening of the noblewoman's son, Harry.[2]

Elegant presents or handsome sums of money were similarly bestowed on the infant being christened and his or her immediate family. William Russell, 5th Earl of Bedford, spent £147 on 'fine lace for several childbed suits' in 1671, which he gave as a gift to his granddaughter Anne on the day of her christening. Evidently thinking this was not enough for so near a relation, he parted with an additional £85 'for 15½ yards of rich broad gold, silver wire, [and] pearl lace'. Nine years on, in 1680, Russell's generosity continued unabated, for he arrived at the christening of his grandson with sixteen congratulatory guineas to give to the child's father, another William Russell.[3] In the opening decade of the seventeenth century, we have a very good record of the various presents Roger Manners, 5th Earl of Rutland sent to aristocratic families when a baby was baptised. A 'guilt standing cup and cover' weighing 46 ounces was presented to Sir Arthur Gorges upon the christening of his son in early 1606, along with twenty shillings each for the midwife and nurse. As gifts to mark the christening of his niece in August 1603, however, Manners had been slightly more profligate and purchased 'a silver basen and ewer, and a pair of lyvery pottes, all guilt', which in total weighed 122 ounces. On this occasion the midwife and nurse were given £4 between them.[4]

Some aristocratic christenings in Stuart England were inevitably grand affairs. In December 1661, William Rumbold, Comptroller of the Great Wardrobe and a relation of the future Rumbold baronets, had his son baptised in London in a manner that greatly impressed the diarist Samuel Pepys, who referred to it as a 'great christening' adorned with 'courtiers and pomp, which I wonder at'.[5] Certainly, christenings could be followed by a respectable feast, in much the same way as weddings and funerals were. Rachel Bourchier, Countess of Bath, was the recipient of an excitable letter from Oxfordshire in 1651, in which her sister Elizabeth wrote with undisguised pride that almost everybody invited to her son's christening dinner had attended. 'My dining room was filled from one end to the other all with the best sort of company,' she gushed.[6] Gracing such dinners was considered a privilege and an honour by the majority of guests, but for some it appeared quite the chore, no matter how splendid the spread on offer. In 1692, Anne Pye related to her cousin Lady Abigail Harley that she had recently been 'forced to go to a gentlewoman's christening to whom I have been much obliged'. She continued sullenly, 'I sat at a table with nineteen more, and nigh twenty dishes of meat first and last and all "gentile" ones, and three tables more, most fresh dishes for them.'[7]

Matchmaking and weddings

Once aristocratic offspring had developed sufficiently in the eyes of their watchful parents and extended families, it was time to begin entertaining the idea of marriage. The process of elite matchmaking was ritualised enough in this period to sit comfortably as a kind of abstract rite preceding the wedding ceremony. When considering suitable spouses for their relatives, the things that mattered most to the nobility and gentry were vigorously underpinned by self-interest, which stemmed from an ancient instinct to survive. As a consequence, money on the table, a touch of good looks, and ensuring that the child in question avoided marrying below their station were all musts.

In a series of letters to her son Thomas Wentworth, 3rd Baron Raby, who by this time was well into his thirties and in Berlin, Lady Isabella Wentworth exemplified the pressure aristocratic parents placed on their successors when it came to matchmaking in the early eighteenth century. She made sure to jot down the following remark on 3 April 1705: 'I wish you a good wife before next Easter. I have found out a match that will please you I am sure very much; she has 4000 a year and very pretty, but what will please you most is – she is but four years old.'[8]

It is disturbing to contemplate a middle-aged man marrying a four-year-old girl, however large her dowry, but it is probable that the real value of the match lay in the certainty that Lady Wentworth's son would not have to go anywhere near the child for many years to come. Two and a half years later, in November 1707, the determined woman was still trying. This time, she had decided to promote a betrothal that would profit from a recent tragedy. Admiral of the Fleet Sir Cloudesley Shovell and his two stepsons had been drowned off the Isles of Scilly at the end of October, leaving a daughter who was set to inherit a fortune. When Baron Raby dismissed the candidate his mother had put forwards for him once again, she fought on unperturbed, and in October 1710 wrote emphatically: 'Pray my dear, why will you let Lady Mary [Villiers go], she is young, rich, and not unhandsome, some say she is pretty; and a virtuous lady, and of the nobility, and why will you not try to get her?'[9]

Unsurprisingly, nothing came of this match either. Baron Raby seems to have taken matters into his own hands in the end, opting for the daughter of a successful shipbuilder and Member of Parliament. Anne Johnson brought with her an amiable character and pleasing physical features, along with a rumoured dowry of £60,000 from her parents, which was more than enough to satisfy Lady Wentworth.

On those frequent occasions in Stuart England when aristocratic relatives, especially fathers, were more unbending in terms of their preferred choice of a match, it was at least customary to allow the intended couple to meet each other before any firm decisions were made. This, according to Roger North, was a logical step to take. Writing to his nephew the 6th Baron North on a match that was put to him in 1696, the man advised, 'I think it becomes your Lordship to say, that before you engage, you desire to see the lady and that she may see you; for, if you should not like her, a prior engagement, though in honour only, would be a great difficulty to your Lordship.'[10] The benefits of a preliminary introduction were made all too clear in a comical example taken from the middle of the seventeenth century. In 1649, the father of the heiress Lady Theodosia Ivie was keen that his daughter should take Anthony Brown of Weald Hall in Essex for her second husband, duly organising a meeting, as was the aristocratic custom, to see if the pair would hit it off. Unfortunately for the eligible gentlewoman, both of them 'fell to drinking' upon their indiscreet rendezvous, perhaps as a way to steady the nerves and make the situation less awkward. If this was indeed the intention, it failed miserably. When Anthony finally plucked up the courage to court Theodosia, he proceeded to be sick in her lap instead. With good reason, Theodosia refused to see him again.[11]

Matchmaking might sometimes cause tempers to fray in the family. Sir John Reresby walked headfirst into an unfolding drama at Welbeck Abbey in 1686, the Nottinghamshire seat of the Duke and Duchess of Newcastle. He was 'extremely surprised', he recounted in his memoirs, 'to find a great disorder in the family by reason of so great a falling out between the duke and duchess that they were parted from bed and board'. The cause of the rift was a difference in opinion on the terms of one daughter's betrothal and the identity of the suitor of another. The duchess, Frances Cavendish, wanted to enlarge the dowry that was to be given to the 12th Earl of Shrewsbury upon his theoretical marriage to Margaret Cavendish, suggesting a sum that the

Duke of Newcastle found wholly unacceptable. In the case of their youngest daughter, the duke wished for her to be engaged to 'Fitzroy, the King's natural son', presumably the illegitimate child of Charles II, Henry FitzRoy; his wife, however, is said to have argued against such a match, stating 'she should never marry a papist and a bastard.' The two girls sided with their mother in both controversies, enraging the Duke of Newcastle to such a degree that he burned his will and 'made another settlement, not at all to the advantage of those daughters'.[12]

Given the aggravation formal matchmaking could incite, and its obvious constraints, an aristocratic individual might wriggle free of the ritual altogether and set about organising a marital alliance independently. Taking this path could lead to questionable propositions in unorthodox settings, as was seen at Althorp House in 1671. In residence as part of a social gathering were the recently widowed Elizabeth Percy, Countess of Northumberland, and the courtier Henry Savile, who, encouraged by adoration and sexual attraction, had decided that he must have this noblewoman for himself. In the early hours of the morning, having tricked the Earl of Sunderland – Althorp's owner at the time – into giving him a key that would open every door in the building, the daring Henry took his chance to woo her. Gaining access to Elizabeth's bedchamber in nothing more than a shirt and nightgown, Savile crept to her bedside and whispered, 'Madam, I am come with great confusion of face to tell you that now which I durst not trust the light with, the passion with which I serve and adore you.' This act understandably did not go down well with the noblewoman. Instead of extending her arms and welcoming him into bed to begin their union, as no doubt the courtier hoped she would, Elizabeth immediately rang the bell in the room and ran horrified and barefoot into the gallery.[13]

Two youngsters who were firmly caught in the teeth of the matchmaking beast in Stuart England, and who had no choice in their engagement at all, were Ralph Verney of Middle Claydon, future baronet, and the eligible heiress Mary Blacknall. In the late 1620s, the helpless pair, unable to stop what was happening to them, were brought together to be married by their respective families when Ralph was only fifteen and his betrothed thirteen. Incidents of this nature were not a unique occurrence amongst the Stuart aristocracy, although some might wish it were otherwise. Sixty-five years later, the same predicament befell Wriothesley Russell, heir and grandson of the 1st Duke of Bedford, and his soon-to-be wife Elizabeth Howland. They formed the two junior halves of an advantageous match devised by the Russell and Howland dynasties in the 1690s, with Wriothesley being a teenage boy of fourteen and Elizabeth, possibly as young as twelve. On 23 May 1695, the pair were married at Streatham Manor House. The bridegroom and his grandfather rode in a coach pulled by six horses to the wedding venue, starting out from Bedford House in London and accompanied by at least eleven other carriages full of guests and attendants. The ceremony in which the two minors were united under God was conducted by the great churchman Gilbert Burnet, Bishop of Salisbury, and afterwards there was an opulent banquet. If those present that day had somehow allowed the juvenility of the bride and bridegroom to slip their minds, they would have been abruptly reminded of the fact when the newly-weds were found playing in a barn, with Elizabeth's fine bridal gown in tatters.[14]

The significance of aristocratic weddings in Stuart England was twofold; while fundamentally constituting an important religious rite in the lifecycle of an aristocrat, they also routinely marked the union of two distinguished families. In recognition of this, such occasions were often characterised by much stateliness and rich celebration. Weddings held at court in the reign of James I seemed particularly elaborate, with the monarch even giving the bride away at the nuptials of Sir John Villiers and Frances Coke, daughter of Sir Edward Coke, in September 1617. Frances was reputedly the picture of elegance that late summer day, garbed 'all in white with her hair hanging down behind, which did become her very well'. The church ceremony and accompanying feast took place at the magnificent Hampton Court Palace, boasting many of the greatest names in the country as guests.[15] A few years earlier, in 1613, John Chamberlain reflected on the ornate gifts presented at the court wedding of Robert Carr, 1st Earl of Somerset, and Frances Howard, daughter of the Earl of Suffolk, which included from one well-wisher 'a fire shovel, tongs and irons, creepers and all furniture of a chimney of silver', and from another 'a cradle of silver' in which to burn sea coal. 'The presents indeed were more in number and value,' he concluded, 'than ever I think were given to any subject in this land.' Chamberlain was less impressed by the wedding outfit chosen by his friend Sir Ralph Winwood, which consisted of a measly black costume 'without any kind of gold, silver, or embroidery'.[16]

Aristocratic weddings away from court could be just as showy. An acquaintance of Lady Abigail Harley of Herefordshire was married in 1682 in the following manner:

> There was a great dinner and a great deal of company. The bride seemed very well pleased and was mighty neat and fine. She has a very fine 'poynt coyfe' and cornet, cost £22, and as good shape and sleeves. A white satin petticoat laced with rich gold and silver, and another petticoat flowered rich with gold and silver. Her gown is black satin. Her grandmother has presented her with a large silver cup, her aunt Palmer with a teapot as large as I have seen, and her uncle Hunt the merchant, since her marrying, has given her a hundred guineas, a very fine pair of salvers and £20 towards plate. Her mother put £20 more to it, [so] that her table plate is very handsome.[17]

The most striking part of this account is the delightful description of the bride's costume, with its 'rich' floral design and abundance of gold and silver lace. In September 1661, in what was then Westmorland, the daughter of the baronet Sir John Lowther of Lowther Hall was married to a notable Yorkshireman with equal splendour. The cost of the wedding favours alone amounted to £120 (over £12,500 today), which were to be distributed amongst the many members of the local gentry expected to attend the event. John Beilby, the bridegroom, rode out of his home county of Yorkshire with no fewer than twenty horses towards his waiting bride, Barbara Lowther. On the return journey the wedding party were met by another eighty horses and their riders at Boroughbridge, and from there the entourage travelled on to an agreeable venue called 'the Grainge', where they were entertained 'with great freedom of music and feasting'.[18]

The future baronet John Verney and his first wife Elizabeth Palmer were effectively married twice in London in the spring of 1680. The first ceremony took place at Westminster Abbey, 'very privately in our old clothes', with only the bride's father, mother, brother, and an aunt in attendance. Save for the bridegroom himself, not a single member of the influential Verney family was present to see the couple officially become man and wife in the hallowed Henry VII Chapel. In keeping with the low-key nuptials that day, the wedding dinner played out quietly in a nondescript tavern on Queen Street called the Rummer. Just seven people, including John and Elizabeth, enjoyed a respectable feast here consisting of beer, wine, 'a dish of fish', two geese, four 'fatt chikens', two rabbits, eight artichokes, 'a dish of peese', oranges, a dish of strawberries, and a dish of cherries. A much grander ceremony was conducted several days later in nearby Chelsea, when the marriage was made public for the first time. On this occasion, Verney and his bride swapped their everyday clothes for suitably handsome wedding outfits and were joined in the church by 'all their neighbouring acquaintances of both the Chelseys'.[19]

While the weddings of Stuart aristocrats such as John Verney and Elizabeth Palmer embraced a mixture of simplicity and grandeur, others were entirely reserved affairs. Content with just the one ceremony, on 10 December 1622 the eventual baronet Hugh Cholmley married the daughter of Sir William Twysden, Elizabeth, with very little fuss at the now destroyed church on Milk Street in London. '[There were] few present at our marriage besides our parents and their families,' Cholmley recalled in his memoirs. The grandchild of Sir John Lowther, Mary, was destined for a similar wedding in July 1667. 'The marriage was solemnised,' Sir John wrote, 'but no public marriage ... only friends present.'[20]

Funerals

Something else a Stuart aristocrat was not likely to remember was his or her own funeral, the very last ceremony in the lifecycle. Like christenings, however, these solemn events had a considerable role to play in the seventeenth and early eighteenth centuries. Although retaining a fair amount of religious importance into the 1700s, one of the primary purposes of all aristocratic funerals in this period was to console and satisfy the grief-stricken living. Those obsequies organised by heralds could also symbolically represent the transfer of power and authority from one influential person to another, for example from a father to his heir. Indeed, the stately laying to rest of a duke or baronet might sometimes succeed in expressing what the physical absence of an individual could not.

The funerals of the aristocracy in Stuart England had the potential to be enormous spectacles, particularly if the deceased figure was a senior office-holder or had enjoyed an illustrious military career. The 3rd Earl of Essex, Robert Devereux, former Lord Chamberlain and a notable veteran of the English Civil War, fitted the bill in 1646. Dying from complications following a stroke, his was to be a heraldic funeral reminiscent of a monarch's in the autumn of that year, the event employing countless banners and escutcheons bearing Devereux's revered coat of arms. These adornments would have been organised prior to the obsequies by the College of Arms in London. An effigy of the deceased earl lay in state at Essex House in London during the planning stages of the ceremony, garbed in white boots, scarlet breeches, and a buff coat that the real man was supposed to have worn at the Battle of Edgehill in 1642. The likeness was removed from here and transported to Westminster Abbey in a majestic procession upon the sombre day of the funeral in mid-October. Many hundreds of soldiers guarded the processional route on both sides, while making up the long line of mourners were more men armed with pikes, muskets, and with black drums, pairs of servants, members of the nobility and gentry, and finally the wax impression itself, 'drawn in an open chariot of black velvet, with six horses covered with black velvet to the ground'. The cavernous interior of Westminster Abbey had been draped in black cloth to mark the occasion, with a hearse erected at the upper end consisting of 'a canopy on pillars about 12 feet high, gilt with gold, and hung with velvet, ornamented with the escocheons of arms of the Earl'.

Following a funeral sermon preached by the clergyman Richard Vines, white staves were broken and dropped into the grave by Essex's household officers, symbolising that their service to him was at an end. It is not clear if the physical body of Robert Devereux had been buried at an earlier date, or if it was interred at this point in the day's proceedings. Certainly the clothed effigy was present in the abbey, its glazed eyes staring unseeingly at the arched ceiling as the congregation listened intently to Vines' words. The funeral concluded with the sounding of trumpets and the tolling of the 'great bell' three times at the neighbouring edifice of St Margaret's, Westminster. Finally, 'one great piece of ordnance' was fired from the Lord Mayor's stone fort in Southwark, answered by a round of pistol shots that stretched from Westminster Abbey to Essex House in the Strand.[21]

The Earl of Essex's farewell, with its princely scale and legions of participants, sat alongside many other heraldic funerals in Stuart England. Gradually, however, the aristocracy began to move away from this type of ceremony in the seventeenth century, choosing instead to organise simpler and more private burials that mirrored both the modesty of Protestantism and a growing personal preference for intimacy. Aristocratic funerals held late at night or early in the morning became commonplace across the country as a result, with attendance always kept to a reasonable minimum. The funeral of Anne Howard, Dowager Countess of Arundel, was decidedly unornamented in 1630, the widow having stipulated before her death at the ripe old age of seventy-three that there should be 'no pomp nor ostentation by heraldry'. Following a quiet service held at Shifnal in Shropshire, the dowager's body was carried in her own coach down to

Arundel Castle in Sussex to be buried, wrapped in 'searclothes' and placed in a 'strong coffin'. Just fourteen of the noblewoman's servants accompanied the corpse on its final journey south, which took seven long days to complete. The sense of simplicity encircling this understated ritual was disturbed somewhat by the perilous state of the roads, 'in so much that almost all in the company did every day expect the breaking of the coach, and thought it a special providence that it held out to the end'.[22] The funeral of Elizabeth Cholmley, wife of the baronet Sir Hugh Cholmley of Yorkshire, occurred 'very early by day-light' in 1655. Her husband recollected of the event:

> Her funeral was very private... The body was carried out of town in a hearse with six horses all in mourning, attended with another coach and some horsemen that went next the body into Kent. My son Hugh came in time to wait on it; which was met on the way by her three brothers, Sir Roger, the Serjeant, and Francis Twisden, with their wives and children and retinue, and interred at the feet of her father, in the private choir belonging to that family.[23]

The aristocratic wife had been interred amongst her father's family at East Peckham in Kent, without fuss.

Nevertheless, even at the tail end of the Stuart period there were aristocrats who continued to look favourably upon sizeable, heraldic goodbyes. The funeral of Sir Dudley North included 'twelve peers' coaches' that rattled dolefully through London to the service at Covent Garden in January 1692, along with a sumptuous hearse, 'scutcheons', and 'flambeaux'. The house of his brother Roger North was hung with black cloth as a mark of respect for the deceased knight, the great room there 'from end to end ... put in mourning and lined down to the outward door', as well as being fitted with silver sconces and more escutcheons. Sir Dudley's coffin was similarly ornate, with its black velvet lining and gilt nails and handles, which before the burial lay dramatically in a withdrawing chamber populated by lit tapers, yet more silver sconces, and a crowd of sober mourners. Guests invited to this pre-ceremony gathering were given rings, scarves, hat bands, and gloves.[24]

Christmas, New Year, and Easter

Christmases were celebrated with great enthusiasm by the aristocracy in Stuart England. To ensure the success of the festival, preparations could be made many weeks in advance, for example tidying the mansion and stocking up with seasonal food and drink. The son of Sir Ralph Verney of Middle Claydon, Edmund Verney, was said to have bought 'more fruit and spice than half the porters in London can weigh out in a day' in the weeks leading up to Christmas in 1664. Prior consideration for the all-important festive diet could also be witnessed at the family seat of the Isham baronets of Lamport in December 1671, when on the twentieth day two oxen were killed in anticipation of the upcoming celebrations. Some years later in 1709, Nicholas Blundell of Crosby Hall wrote that he had 'readied [his] closet and cleansed it pretty thoroughly against Christmas' on 19 December, while five days later on Christmas Eve he appears to have systematically tidied the hall, decorated the building with escutcheons, and prepared 'paper bags to put Brass in'.[25]

Christmas Day itself involved a predictable combination of religious observance and secular ebullience. The aristocratic Mildmay family of Danbury Place in Essex went to church twice on 25 December 1640, but broke up the morning and evening services with jovial feasting and lively games. Lady Anne Clifford and her first husband Richard Sackville, 3rd Earl of Dorset, on the other hand, began Christmas Day with a sermon in the comfort of their own private chapel in 1617, enjoying afterwards a celebratory dinner and more generally a period of 'great housekeeping' at Dorset House in London.[26] The Christmas holiday as a whole predominantly revolved around such merriment and blitheness for the Stuart aristocracy, with music and dancing habitually added to the mix to lift the spirits even further. A few days before New Year in 1708, for instance, two fiddlers arrived at the gates of Crosby Hall in Lancashire to entertain the Blundell family and their various house guests. By the following evening the musicians had hit their stride, and after supper performed jocundly in the background when all and sundry leapt from their seats to '[dance] country dances'. The player hired to show off his skills at the Howard pile of Naworth Castle in historic Cumberland was unfortunately less well received in December 1648. When he went away at last and the time came to remunerate him, it was noted bluntly in the household accounts, 'paid the piper which could not play well'.[27]

Presents great and small might also be exchanged. Sir Walter Calverley of Esholt sent his acquaintance in Newcastle 'a dozen knives and a dozen forks' in December 1707, which were finished with silver handles. Food for the groaning festive table was probably the most common gift accepted and sent by the Stuart aristocracy, however. During the early years of the seventeenth century, Roger Manners, 5th Earl of Rutland, was the recipient of freshly killed game at Christmas from both officials and intimates, including 'moor-cocks', swans, partridges, turkeys, and even peacocks, the latter likely presented to the earl alive. Boiled and jellied meats were likewise frequently given and received. In December 1671, Sir Thomas Isham's father, Sir Justinian Isham, 'sent a brawn to Dr Outram wrapped up in some verses that he had made on Guido the Pig Killer'. A generation later in 1709, Nicholas Blundell's wife, Frances, likewise accepted 'a Rowl of Brawn' from a kinswoman on Christmas Day.[28]

Aside from its obvious religious connotations and somewhat materialistic feel, the aristocratic Christmas in Stuart England offered the chance for family and friends to come together and enjoy one another's company for a few days, sometimes after prolonged periods of separation. The esquire Nicholas Assheton of Downham in Lancashire spent Christmas with a cousin from nearby Whalley in 1617 and 1618, taking with him on each occasion his wife, his mother and father, and a handful of household servants. At Danbury Place in Essex, the cavernous house was purportedly filled to the rafters with friends and family of the Mildmays in December 1640, including a son who had been collected specially from Cambridge and 'the good and worthy Doctor Dorislaus', an acquaintance and resident of London. Sir Humphrey Mildmay, the head of the family, referred to his myriad guests that year as 'clowns' in his surviving journal, for he was also hosting 'Sir Henry Mildmay of Moulsham and his full company, who were all of them merry'.[29] Understandably, for some aristocrats the prospect of entertaining large numbers of raucous people over the festive season was a dire one. 'Now I hope all your troublesome time is over, but now mine is approaching, for Christmas brings abundance of troublesome guests,' Lady Isabella Wentworth wrote miserably from Twickenham to her son Baron Raby in December 1708. She seemed, in fact, to have quite a complex about it. 'I design to be as sneaking as I can,' the gentlewoman continued resolutely, 'and do no works of superfluity, only what just necessity forces.' She finished by assuring Thomas that her sole pleasure over the coming weeks of torture would be receiving letters from him.[30]

New Year, by this point mostly celebrated in late December and early January as opposed to March, represented for many noble and gentle families the much-anticipated crescendo of the Christmas season. New Year's Eve on 31 December was, as it continues to be in the twenty-first century, routinely structured around overindulgence. In 1681, the baronet and Yorkshireman Sir John Reresby 'ended the year in a more than ordinary debauch' in the depths of London with Theophilus Hastings, 7th Earl of Huntingdon, claiming sheepishly in a later memoir that it was 'neither my custom nor inclination much to do so'. The moderate baronet's New Year's Days throughout the decades, however, appeared just as unrestrained. A staggering 300 people feasted with him at Thrybergh in Yorkshire on 1 January 1676, while on New Year's Day 1685 even more dinner guests came to gorge at the same venue, 'so that whole sheep were roasted and served so up to feed them. For music I had five violins, besides bagpipes, drums and trumpet.'[31] At Danbury Place, the scene was much the same on the very first day of 1640. 'Many here and the hall full of idle company', Sir Humphrey Mildmay complained in a journal entry, his mood only improved by the welcome interlude of a peaceful supper that evening.[32]

It was traditional for the highest-ranking members of English society – apparently earls and above – to present a gift of £20 to the incumbent monarch at New Year. In January 1661, therefore, the 5th Earl of Bedford, William Russell of Woburn Abbey, duly handed over the said sum in gold coins in an 'embroidered silk and silver purse' to Charles II, via the Lord Chamberlain. The sovereign's household servants might also be rewarded at this time of year by aristocrats. The Earl of Rutland gave small amounts of money to a generous selection of James I's personal staff in January 1606, including, but not limited to, those working in the buttery, pantry, and spicery, as well as pages, grooms, 'the children of the chapel', and the 'hall waiters'. In return for this yearly show of goodwill to the royal faction, the Stuart ruler usually sent a present of 30 ounces of plate to every aristocratic benefactor. The twenty-year-old Thomas Howard, 14th Earl of Arundel, and his mother, the Dowager Countess of Arundel, both received their 'guilt plate' as planned in January 1606, with the Earl of Bedford likewise accepting his in January 1663, although on this occasion the nobleman decided to swap the customary offering with a goldsmith for two engraved candlesticks. William Russell clearly thought that the latter items would be of greater use to the family, or at the very least were more desirable, and one cannot but help agree with him.[33]

Following time-honoured convention, Roger Manners, 5th Earl of Rutland, also sent presents to his aristocratic contemporaries in the first few days of January 1611, on top of the usual £20 to James I. Amongst the dainty ornaments on offer were a scallop-shell basin and 'mermayde' ewer, made of silver and destined for the mighty Earl of Northampton, four gilt bowls and covers weighing around 24 ounces each, and a silver pepper box earmarked for the lord chancellor, Sir Thomas Egerton. Of course, not all New Year gifts presented by the Stuart aristocracy were so thoughtful and exquisite. Sir Daniel Fleming of Rydal Hall in Westmorland merely dropped two shillings and sixpence into the expectant hands of his sons and daughters on 1 January 1693, which, admittedly, was better than nothing; being a fair and considerate employer, he furthermore gave a shilling each to his servants. The Fleming youngsters fared slightly better in 1701. While the manservants and maids at Rydal still only received a shilling each on New Year's Day, the children of Sir Daniel were now valued highly enough by their father to be given five shillings apiece.[34] The practice of aristocratic gift exchange at New Year was fleetingly analysed by the Isle of Wight resident and knight, Sir John Oglander, in 1622, such was its apparent significance in Stuart England. He wrote of his local area:

> Sussex is the freest place in England for giving of New Year's gifts, and the Isle of Wight the basest. As it sheweth a thankful mind in the giver, so it is a charge and engagement to whom it is given, wherefore I like the custom well. If any man should think to engage me by his gifts, I would regive him twice as much again and thereby make myself a freeman.[35]

It is no surprise to learn that the ritual was more than just about kindness and affability, but that it could conceal underlying agendas that might benefit several parties.

Three or four months into the year came spring and Easter, which seems to have been humbler, more modest, and certainly a lot quieter than Christmas and New Year for the Stuart aristocracy. Church was an essential part of the festival, evidently, with Lady Anne Clifford reporting on Easter Day in April 1617 that 'my Lord [and] I and Tom Glenham and most of the folk received Communion from Mr Ran.' At the very end of the century in 1699, this religious component of Easter was as dominant as ever in England. One of the few preparations made by the baronet Sir John Verney this year involved the intended distribution of three-penny loaves to twelve of the poorest parishioners of Middle Claydon on Easter Sunday. To make certain that the dole was awarded to those most in need, on 30 March, Verney instructed a servant to send him a comprehensive list of the people 'that you think fit for this charity'. Although celebratory dinners and a touch of measured revelry might accompany trips to the family chapel or local parish church, it was domestic run-ins quite unrelated to the Christian festival that had the potential to provide the liveliest entertainment over the Easter period. Enter once again Lady Anne Clifford and her first husband, the free-spirited Richard Sackville, 3rd Earl of Dorset. Theirs was a famously tumultuous marriage that, not for the first time, had come undone dramatically on the sacred Friday before Easter Sunday in March 1619. 'Good Friday: After supper I fell in a great passion of weeping in my chamber,' the Countess of Dorset reflected in her diary, '[and] when my Lord came in I told him I found my mind so troubled as I held not myself fit to receive the Communion this Easter.' The Communion scheduled to take place on Easter Day at Knole in Kent was indeed postponed as a result of Lady Anne's woes, which were caused by disagreements over money. When Sackville visited his wife on the Sunday afternoon, he offered her an olive branch of sorts, 'protesting to me that he would be a very good husband to me and that I should receive no prejudice by releasing my thirds'.[36]

Birthdays

The passage of time in the lifecycle of a Stuart aristocrat (as for most people) was perhaps felt most keenly through the annual occurrence of a birthday. For some, such as the ageing baronet and politician Sir John Reresby, birthdays offered the chance for serious reflection and to be grateful to one's maker. Referring to the big day in April 1689, which ironically was to be his last birthday, Reresby wrote with touching ignorance: 'I humbly thanked God for preserving me through so many dangers till the 55th year of my age, and begged of Him to lead the remainder of my life better than I had hitherto done.'[37]

Older members of the aristocracy still celebrated birthdays, however. On the occasion of his eighty-eighth birthday in 1699, the knight and octogenarian Sir John Bramston had several of his relations over for dinner to rejoice 'for the continuance of my life and health', the gathering causing such a disturbance that 'our house was full of noise, dirt, and dust, and we were cooped up and scanted for room.' Bramston died the following February aged eighty-eight, and was buried in the chancel of Roxwell church in Essex.[38]

Younger individuals wasted no time in making the most of their birthdays, which resulted in substantial celebrations. The dashing James Bertie, 5th Baron Norreys, welcomed his twentieth year 'with great solemnity' in June 1672 at Adderbury in Oxfordshire, enjoying a round of merry bell-ringing in his honour and a 'great dinner' courtesy of Elizabeth Wilmot, Countess of Rochester. After supper Bertie and his guests loosened up even more and performed a dizzying sixteen dances. 'Because the weather was hot,' his sister explained in a letter, 'we danced some of them in the forecourt, some in the garden, and the rest in the Hall.' So, too, in June 1699, a 'great resort of gentlemen and neighbours' flocked to the esquire John Stanhope's new house at Horsforth in Yorkshire to wish him a happy birthday, with presents including ten bottles of white wine and 'two loaves of double refined sugar'.[39]

Drinking the health of aristocrats who had turned a year older was a popular tribute, the custom applying to both children and adults. On the evening of the fifth birthday of Richard Sackville and Lady Anne Clifford's daughter, Lady Margaret, in July 1619, the little girl's health was drunk throughout the house at Knole Park near Sevenoaks. Over sixty years later in 1681, it was instead the three young daughters of William, Lord Russell, who were excitedly drinking the health of their father on his birthday, having first devoured between them a 'red-deer pie' in celebration. Russell's wife, Lady Rachel Russell, told him as such in a letter, for he was absent from the family that day. Regrettably, the ill-famed politician's involvement in the Rye House Plot meant that he would soon disappear forever.[40]

2

CHILDREN AND CHILDHOOD

Aristocratic parents reacted particularly well to the birth of the first son and heir in Stuart England. Upon the successful delivery of the first son of William, Lord Russell, and his wife Rachel in November 1680, whose Christian name was to be Wriothesley in honour of his mother's family, such was the excitement that a messenger was immediately dispatched to Woburn Abbey to deliver the news to the delighted Russell dynasty. Gratitude was even extended to the bearer himself, who was to be 'duly rewarded' for his efforts in travelling to rural Bedfordshire so promptly. Daughters were welcomed by the Stuart aristocracy, too, although not always. Sir Simonds D'Ewes and his spouse Lady Anne Clopton, daughter of Sir William Clopton of Kentwell Hall in Suffolk, were overcome with happiness at the birth of their first child in April 1630, which turned out to be a baby girl. 'We were both so joyful of her own [his wife's] and her little one's doing well,' D'Ewes commented later, 'and in hope that we might have more as well males as females.' Sons did eventually come for the optimistic Sir Simonds and Lady Anne over the next few years – five of them in fact, and in relatively quick succession – but the harsh reality was that none of them would live long enough to continue their father's distinguished name.[1]

A service of thanksgiving was held on the staircase at Crosby Hall in Lancashire when a daughter was born there to Nicholas Blundell and his wife Frances in September 1704. While Blundell seemed perfectly content with the prospect of having a little girl to cherish and raise, his response would have been at odds with the reaction given by his Cavalier grandfather half a century earlier in the mid-1600s. The appearance of a daughter was a constant source of irritation to the esquire William Blundell, also of Crosby Hall, who desperately craved sons but was repeatedly given girls. Following the unsurprising birth of a female child in the early 1650s, he complained in typical fashion, 'My wife hath much disappointed my hopes in bringing forth a daughter,' adding that the newborn infant was 'not so welcome in this world as a son'. When Blundell's tenth daughter arrived in 1659, thankfully 'well delivered' on 30 March, the man had clearly reached his wits' end. 'The thing is called Bridget,' he wrote sourly to a son whom, seemingly against all the odds, he had managed to bring into the world just before the start of the Civil War. Blundell then reminded his adolescent offspring with no great enthusiasm that he had acquired three sisters in the short space of two-and-a-half years. 'You may well think,' the flustered father finished, 'that this is not the way to get rich.'[2]

The early years

Whether an aristocratic child was well received by its parents or otherwise, one thing more or less guaranteed in the Stuart period was that it would grow up living a life of relative privilege. This well-to-do existence commonly began with the appointment of a wet nurse to breastfeed the baby on behalf of the recovering mother, as was the arrangement after the birth of Christopher Guise, the first of the Guise baronets of Elmore Court in Gloucestershire, in February 1618. 'I was put to a woman in the town,' Sir Christopher reflected in later life, 'indifferently ancient and of a dry hot complexion and not very plentifully stored with riches, so that it was no wonder if there were neglects in my attendance.'[3] In the event that a wet nurse proved to be inadequate for the intimate task assigned to her, aristocratic mothers had no hesitation in seeking out a suitable replacement. One such parent was Mary Verney, wife of Sir Ralph Verney of Middle Claydon, who took the decision to change her son's wet nurse when the infant was just two months old in August 1647. The fretful mother set her sights on a local poor woman to take over from Ralph's first provider, the wife of a Raph Rodes; while the new candidate purportedly looked like a 'slatterne', she maintained that she would 'have a mighty care of' the baby, which Mary evidently believed. A wage of four shillings a week was agreed upon, in addition to 'two loads of wood' for Mrs Rodes and her deprived husband and children.[4]

Some aristocratic families in Stuart England looked closer to home when it came to the selection of an appropriate figure to breastfeed a newborn. Margaret Tufton, Countess of Thanet, the eldest daughter of Lady Anne Clifford and Richard Sackville, took it upon herself to breastfeed her first grandchild in 1654. When the noble grandmother eventually departed the house and left the infant in the care of its mother, Lady Margaret Coventry, it was Lady Coventry herself who assumed responsibility for the role and 'gave this child of hers sucke ... as her mother had done most of her children'.[5] A curious episode from early seventeenth-century Yorkshire saw the services of Sir Hugh Cholmley's wet nurse suspended so that his grandmother could feed the six-month-old 'from her own breast' for a period of twenty-four hours. In hindsight, this may have been a preferable set-up, for Cholmley recorded:

> She who was my nurse proved suddenly with child; but not revealing it, I was thereby so weakened, as I have heard my father say, when I was a year old, I had not strength to bear up my head, but which way soever my neck turned there it laid; but her being with child being discovered, I was put to another nurse.[6]

Fortunately, the second nurse was a much safer pair of hands, and in Sir Hugh's assured view helped to prevent his premature demise.

It was usual for an aristocratic infant to be delivered into the custody of a dry nurse or nursery maid once it had been successfully weaned. Nicholas Blundell's daughter, Mary, returned to Crosby Hall from her wet nurse at the age of ten months in July 1705, but just two days later she was sent off again 'to be dry-nursed by Ellen Harrison for some time'. By age three, Hugh Cholmley found himself living under the rule of a nursery maid in Yorkshire, whose main responsibilities were feeding the toddler at regular intervals and ensuring that he was kept out of harm's way at all times. We know, however, that on at least one occasion the woman failed spectacularly in her duty of care. 'At three years old,' Cholmley wrote, 'the maid which attended me let me tumble out of the great chamber window at Roxby, which (by God's providence) a servant waiting upon my grandfather at dinner espying, leaped to the window, and caught hold of my coat.' Nursery maids could come from a variety of backgrounds, and places. In the 1680s, there were three such servants employed at Bedford House in London to look after the children of William, Lord Russell, and his wife Rachel. Although two of the women were clearly locally sourced, their names 'Welsh Betty' and Elizabeth Fielder respectively, the third nursery maid was French and referred to only as 'Mademoiselle' by the family.[7]

Beyond the dominion of the nursery, aristocratic children's relationships with other household servants could be slightly more complicated, stemming in part from a parental desire to shield offspring from sinfulness and general bad behaviour. As a young girl in the 1620s and 1630s, Margaret Cavendish, Duchess of Newcastle, had restricted access to the servants in the employment of her mother, Elizabeth, the widow of the gentleman Sir Thomas Lucas of Essex. The great matriarch Elizabeth Lucas 'never suffered the vulgar serving-men to be in the nursery among the nursemaids', her daughter Margaret remembered years later, 'lest their rude love-making might do unseemly actions, or speak unhandsome words in the presence of her children'. On those rare occasions when the future duchess and her siblings did encounter the male servants of the house, Elizabeth strictly forbade rudeness in all its grotesque shades, along with any exhibitions of intimidating or 'domineering' behaviour.[8] Margaret Cavendish's recollection of the relationship she shared with her mother's servants continued in her autobiography:

> Neither were we suffered to have any familiarity with the vulgar servants, or conversation: yet caused us to demean ourselves with an humble civility towards them, as they with a dutiful respect to us. Not because they were servants were we so reserved; for many noble persons are forced to serve through necessity; but by reason the vulgar sort of servants are as ill-bred as meanly born, giving children ill examples and worse counsel.[9]

Lady Abigail Harley harboured similar anxieties over the harmful influence of uncouth servants on impressionable aristocratic children. In January 1671, she wrote to her husband, the Member of Parliament Sir Edward Harley, to suggest that their sons be sent off to boarding school with all haste because it was 'not possible to keep them from associating with servants and getting a strange clownish speech and behaviour'.[10] Lady Harley feared that the longer the boys were kept at home, the worse their imitations would get.

The measures of social separation put in place by parents such as Elizabeth Lucas and Lady Abigail Harley were designed to mould children into respectable and upstanding characters who would one day adopt positions of prominence in the ranks of the Stuart aristocracy. Disciplining offspring when required also aimed to achieve this. While some aristocratic mothers and fathers chose corporal punishment to aid the shaping of their youngsters into satisfactory adolescents and adults, others opted for less aggressive courses of action. The early seventeenth-century knight Sir Thomas Meautys informed his sister, Jane, Lady Cornwallis Bacon, in December 1632 that his young daughter 'hath been lapt in the skirts of her father's shirt, for she is beloved where she comes, and I love her very well, and so doth she me'. He added to this fuzzy sentiment, however, that 'sometimes I can whip her and love her too.'[11] The Duchess of Newcastle's mother, Elizabeth Lucas, had an altogether different approach to discipline. Margaret and her siblings were 'bred tenderly' by the Essex gentlewoman, 'for my mother naturally did strive, to please and delight her children, not to cross or torment them, terrifying them with threats, or lashing them with slavish whips.' She made use of reason as a tool of persuasion instead of menaces, and where Sir Thomas Meautys might have cast around for an implement with which to inflict pain on his daughter, Elizabeth preferred to teach her children all about 'the deformities of vice', thereby preparing them for their roles as both reputable aristocrats and good Christians.[12]

Being dressed appropriately from an early age was yet another way in which noble and gentle offspring were readied for their future positions at the forefront of society. It was a process that could almost be described as a rite of passage in elite circles. The five-year-old grandson of Dudley North, 4th Baron North, who would grow up to become 2nd Baron Guilford (but as a child was known simply as Frank), seemed to occupy a kind of stage in October 1679 when the family tailor came to measure him for his very first suit. The North clan had assembled specially in the village of Tostock in Suffolk to watch the excitable little boy don his new pair of breeches, from which the tailor would then be able to fashion the rest of the striking outfit. Frank's grandmother observed that 'Never had any bride that was to be dressed upon her wedding night more hands about her, some the legs and some the arms, that tailor buttoning and others putting on the sword, and so many lookers on that had I not had a finger amongst them I could not have seen him.'[13]

Little Frank appeared to appreciate the significance of the occasion as well. Once he had been kitted out, the young gentleman was said to have 'acted his part as well as any of them', confidently identifying himself as 'a gallant with very fine clothes and a sword' as he strutted about the house in his grown-up attire.[14]

The formal wardrobe tended to be introduced to aristocratic minors at about five or six years of age. The baronet and native of Yorkshire Sir Henry Slingsby sent his son Thomas a handsome pair of breeches and a new doublet from London in 1641, acknowledging in doing so that 'it was too soon for him to wear them being but 5 years old, but ... his mother had a desire to see him in them, how proper a man he would be.' The fashionable grandson of Sir Thomas Chicheley of Wimpole Hall in Cambridgeshire had already sported a succession of sophisticated suits by the age of six in 1674, with the latest addition to the collection incorporating a velvet coat, 'narrow pantaloons', stockings, buckled shoes, and a periwig. In the early seventeenth century, Lady Anne Clifford seemed determined to clothe her daughter suitably almost straight from the crib. At just two years old, Margaret, or 'the child' as Lady Anne liked to call her, was given her first whalebone bodice to wear, which was soon followed by the purchase of the infant's 'first coat that was laced ... being of red bays'.[15]

In spite of this marked concern for propriety, the children of the Stuart aristocracy were at times permitted to be just that: children. Dorothy Harley wrote cheerily to her brother, the future Sir Edward Harley, from Devon in 1658 to tell him that his young ones were thriving and were 'as merry and full of play as any of their age'. We also find two-year-old Wriothesley Russell, who would be married by the age of fourteen, driving his mother Lady Rachel Russell to despair at Stratton Park in Hampshire in September 1682 because he had gotten into the habit of banging everything in sight with his toy drumstick.

His grandfather William Russell, 5th Earl of Bedford, made a point of gifting toys and other 'fairings' to the boy and the rest of the Russell youngsters at regular intervals throughout the year, the seasoned man perhaps appreciating that their days as carefree children were numbered. Wriothesley's quite obviously were. The aristocratic Lamport brood of Isham in Northamptonshire, some miles away from the now demolished Stratton Park, partook in a whole range of frivolous activities during the second half of the seventeenth century. These included the docile pursuits of beekeeping in the garden, bowls on the lawn and, every once in a while, visiting local feasts and fairs, but also the slightly more energetic pastimes of throwing balls and, for the older children, wrestling.[16]

Education

A well-rounded education that surpassed anything that might conceivably be imagined for persons of lesser status was essential for the offspring of the Stuart nobility and gentry. Aristocratic boys in particular could expect to profit from extensive instruction over the seventeenth and early eighteenth centuries, which aimed to ensure, in theory at least, intelligent and multitalented individuals for the future who were distinctly set apart from their social inferiors. Academic subjects formed the foundation of male education in this 111-year period, just as they would continue to do in successive English epochs. Latin, Greek, other European languages such as French, Spanish, and Italian, classical studies, literature, writing, mathematics, and certain branches of science were all considered vital areas of study. The arts, too, enjoyed a place in the curriculum, with many boys learning to dance, sing, and play musical instruments. Some even learned to fence.

When discussing the study of classical texts in a letter dated June 1704, John Hervey, 1st Baron Hervey of Ickworth House in

Suffolk was remarkably specific as to the benefits. He advised his teenage son, Carr:

> Terence will make you master of purity in ye Latin style... Aesop and Phaedrus will teach you how to form your manners; Socrates and Epictetus will polish and perfect them. Tacitus inspires ye firmest politics; and Thucidides instructs you how to speak well in either House of Parliament. The art of reasoning well must be learned from Aristotle; that of writing from celebrated Tully. Plutarch will furnish various subjects for conversation; and Plato fill your mind with noble and sublime ideas.[17]

Many aristocratic parents were peculiarly insistent when it came to the study of Latin, the language of the Church, which resulted in boys often engaging with its complexities at a perplexingly early age. By the time he was four years old in 1640, for instance, the eldest son of Sir Henry Slingsby already knew the correct Latin for the main parts of the human body and most items of clothing. Looking back on his childhood in the 1600s and 1610s, the Suffolk knight Sir Simonds D'Ewes recalled in his autobiography that aged eleven he knew 'divers select Latin poets and other authors, was able to write themes, epistles, and dialogues', and could furthermore 'discourse a little in that tongue'.[18]

Aristocratic girls were taught Latin, too, although less frequently and on occasion with resistance. Lucy Hutchinson, daughter of Sir Allen Apsley and Lady Lucy St John, was 'so apt' at the language as a young lady in the 1620s that she reportedly 'outstripped [her] brothers that were at school'.[19] Indeed, the sheer brilliance of her talent led Lucy, the eventual wife of Colonel John Hutchinson, to make the first English translation of the Latin poem, *De Rerum Natura*, by Lucretius, in the 1650s. Throughout the autumn years of the seventeenth century, the defunct tongue so valued by the Stuart aristocracy continued to be studied enthusiastically by its female offspring, as well as its male. The future Duchess of Chandos, Cassandra Willoughby, memorised as a matter of course the Latin names for flowers, birds, and fish during her early education at Middleton Hall in Warwickshire in the 1670s, alongside her brothers Francis and Thomas.[20]

Displaying the endemic gender inequality existent in England at the time, however, there were certain aristocrats who strongly advised against allowing noble and gentle girls to engage with the Church's traditional means of communication. 'Let not your girle learne Latin, nor short hand,' Sir Ralph Verney counselled his life-long friend Dr William Denton, in a forthright letter dated 1650 concerning Verney's goddaughter Nancy. 'The difficulty of the first [Latin] may keepe her from that vice, for so I must esteeme it in a woman,' Sir Ralph continued, 'but the easiness of the other [shorthand] may be a prejudice to her; for the pride of taking sermon notes, hath made multitudes of women most unfortunate.' Nancy brazenly wrote back to her resolute godfather to dispute the controversial advice he had offered Dr Denton, but Verney's mind was not to be changed. In fact, the lord of Middle Claydon began his unapologetic response to the child with a genuine expression of surprise that she had hitherto 'been guilty of so much learning'.[21]

Dalliances with Latin aside, an aristocratic girl's formal education in this period tended to concentrate first and foremost on the arts and domestic skills, with reading, writing, and French sometimes added to the list. Ann, Lady Fanshawe, the daughter of Sir John Harrison of Balls Park in Hertfordshire, enjoyed a carefully crafted education that encompassed most of the above in the 1630s. Painstakingly overseen and implemented by her diligent mother, the young lady's studies included needlework, French, learning to play the lute and virginals, dancing, and singing, as well as, presumably, some form of written exercises in between. Ann conceded in adulthood that she had still managed to spend too much time as a child riding and running, noting wryly in her memoir, 'I was that which we graver people call a hoyting girl (meaning something like frolicsome or flighty).'[22] Margaret Cavendish, Duchess of Newcastle, benefited from a similarly structured education in the 1620s, which was again overseen by her concerned mother. Reading, writing, playing musical instruments, singing, dancing, and foreign languages were all featured on the plentiful curriculum drawn up by Elizabeth Lucas for her daughter, only in this case, limited importance was placed on them. Lucas' obvious passion for religion and morality ensured that, when it came down to it, she 'cared not so much for [her children's] dancing and fiddling, singing and prating of several languages, as that [they] should be bred virtuously, modestly, civilly, honourably, and on honest principles'.[23]

Most aristocratic children would be taught by at least one private tutor over the course of their education. While Sir John Reresby was forced to tolerate a single tutor at Thrybergh, Yorkshire, during the battle-weary 1640s, the more fortunate Lucy Hutchinson had eight different ones by the age of seven in the 1620s, who were charged with teaching Sir Allen Apsley's daughter, in regimental fashion, everything from foreign languages to needlework.[24] Tutors employed by the Stuart aristocracy were expected to have received exemplary educations themselves, with many boasting degrees from either Cambridge or Oxford. The man hired to instruct the offspring of William Russell, 5th Earl of Bedford, in the mid-seventeenth century was a typical Cambridge scholar called John Thornton. Having studied during the civil war, Thornton took up the post at Woburn Abbey in Bedfordshire a short time after graduating from Trinity College in 1646, receiving a respectable annual salary of £30 and acquiring his own room within the colossal building. Alongside the role of tutor to the earl's children, Thornton was also appointed William Russell's personal chaplain, a position that would have granted him unrivalled access to his master's innermost thoughts and feelings. Consequently, his relationship with the aristocratic Russell family developed quickly and in time became unbreakable. So trusted and valued was the Reverend John Thornton by his employers in the years to come that he even went on to educate the Earl of Bedford's fatherless grandchildren.[25]

Not all relationships between tutors and the ever-watchful aristocracy were so amicable. Having a child simply spend too much time with a particular educator was enough to cause friction in some families, as it did in March 1663, when Sir Heneage Finch got wind of a disturbing piece of information concerning his son's scholastic habits. The Member of Parliament for Oxford University and future Earl of Nottingham began a heated letter to fifteen-year-old Daniel Finch with ominous directness, proclaiming, 'you may discharge your dancing master when you please.' He continued: 'I think you did very ill to entertain him at all in the mornings; it was never your mother's meaning nor mine that you should lose an hour's study for him. My chief cares and desires for you are that you may prove a knowing and a virtuous man, that which the town calls a fine gentleman being to my understanding rather a libel than a commendation.'[26]

Here we catch a glimpse of the disdain felt by some aristocratic fathers when their sons pursued 'artistic' subjects at the expense of academic ones. The case of Edmund Verney and his tutor a decade earlier reveals that on occasion there could be active hostility between an aristocratic pupil and his or her instructor. Edmund, or 'Mun' as he was known to his father Sir Ralph Verney, found himself studying across the North Sea in the Low Countries in the 1650s, which was far enough removed from his family in England to behave exactly as he pleased. The Scottish intellect with him, Dr Robert Creighton, bemoaned the teenager's constant inability to get up at a reasonable time, and told Sir Ralph as such, writing in one letter that he 'loves his bed too well'. When Mun did eventually stir, he reportedly had a habit of lounging around until midday 'with his breast unbuttoned, his breeches unclasped [and] his stockings untied about his heels', which further aggravated his exasperated tutor. It was usually at 9:00am that Creighton attempted to ready the pupil for study, and Mun's lutist came at 11:30am, but 'all the afternoon it is a great chance if I see him till the next morning at 8.' Nonetheless, the Scotsman recognised a handful of redemptive qualities. He believed – perhaps naively – that for all Edmund's faults he was at the very least 'no tobacconist', 'no swearer', and no drinker.[27]

For many elite parents, the natural order of things included sending younger offspring off to a revered educational institution to be tutored. The very wealthiest and distinguished amongst the Stuart aristocracy had within their reach the famous establishments of Eton, Harrow, Winchester, and Westminster, four public schools that were growing in popularity towards the end of the seventeenth century.[28] As for every other aristocrat, a solid array of lesser public schools and grammar schools was available to choose from. While these may have lacked the unparalleled prestige radiating from the educational giants of Eton and Harrow, their academic credentials were seldom disputed. When detailing the moral characters and respectable upbringing of his two sons, Freeman and George Sondes, one of whom had barbarously killed the other at the family home of Lees Court in Kent in 1655, Sir George Sondes wrote of their education:

> As soon as they were of years convenient, I put them out to very good and careful schools, Brumly and Wye, where I was often myself with them, to see that their Masters educated them well, both for religion and learning, and was ever careful to have them accommodated with all other Masters, to learn from them such things as their ages were capable of.[29]

Indeed, the sheer quality of schools in Stuart England might cause those aristocratic pupils who had been home-tutored for a period of years before enrolling to feel as though they were lagging behind their peers. Sir John Reresby and his younger brother Edmund began schooling at Whitefriars in London as anxious, self-conscious teenagers in the late 1640s, where the former 'soon found the disadvantage of learning at home, many boys much younger than myself being much better scholars'. After six months, the pair moved on to another school near Enfield Chase, here learning languages, writing, and dancing.[30]

Memories of school days could be recalled fondly, apathetically, or with a certain level of disquiet, depending on the establishment attended and its respective ethos, and the predisposition of the attendee. Christopher Guise of Elmore Court was sent to be educated at a free school in Wotton-under-Edge aged about ten in the 1620s, and remembered later that the curriculum was 'profitable enough', but that the diet and other things were rather plain and uninspiring. Sir Edward Dering, on the other hand, seemed unable to forget even in adulthood the 'barbarous tyrant' with whom he had been confronted at a school in Heathfield in London in the early years of the reign of Charles I, at the impressionable age of just six. Of course, being a poorly behaved student was not likely to help matters much. The awesomely named headmaster of Sedbergh School in Westmorland, Posthumus Wharton, felt no hesitation in writing to Sir Daniel Fleming of Rydal Hall in 1689 to convey his concerns for Richard and Roger Fleming, Sir Daniel's eldest sons. Wharton wholeheartedly deemed it his duty to inform the antiquarian that both 'were a little inclined to drink, upon which score I have given them several sharp reproofs and told them how much I abhorred'.[31] One can only assume that Fleming's own reaction to his sons' misdeeds was just as humourless as the steely headmaster's.

Although boarding schools had also started to appear for aristocratic girls by the late 1600s, such as that opened by Josias Priest at Gorges House in Chelsea in 1680, one scholarly sphere a young Stuart lady would never be able to set foot in was higher education. The world-renowned universities of Cambridge and Oxford were for highborn men, and men alone. What distanced these two institutions from the rest of society was their costliness and inherent elitism. As a student at Cambridge in 1618, Sir Simonds D'Ewes recollected:

> Before my return back unto Cambridge, my tutor sending a bill of my expenses there, for my chamber study and other particulars, (of which a great part was to be repaid at my coming away) although

> no part of it could well have been prevented, yet my father was so far at first incensed with it, as I was at one time afraid I should have no more gone to Cambridge.[32]

Other aristocratic fathers in Stuart England could do very little but make peace with the extortionate costs of university living, viewing them as a necessary means to an end. In a letter dated 4 May 1651, William Fleming of Rydal Hall told his son Daniel, who was studying at The Queen's College in Oxford, 'I shall be loath to see you want anything fit for you: but with my utmost powers assist you in the pursuance of your accomplishment to make you a Man; [and] indeed a Gentleman.' University was highly valued by the aristocracy, being without question the most important part of a young man's education. It was with this in mind that a portion of John Wilmot, 2nd Earl of Rochester's funeral sermon in 1680 was dedicated to his time at Oxford. The preacher exclaimed to the congregation that Wadham College had 'laid a good foundation for learning and study' where Rochester was concerned, and more viscerally he insisted, 'There he first suck'd from the breasts of his Mother the University those perfections of wit, and eloquence, and poetry.'[33]

Following in the footsteps of their learned tutors, aristocratic boys were usually dispatched to either Oxford or Cambridge in their mid-teens. Over two or three years, the average student could expect to study logic and philosophy as core university subjects, with other disciplines such as history, languages, and mathematics making an appearance in the curriculum where time and inclination allowed. Sir Daniel Fleming told one of his many sons, George, that he should concentrate on logic, ethics, physics, metaphysics, and divinity while at Oxford University in the late 1680s, believing it to be a perfect combination of specialisms that guaranteed both a bright future for the boy and the continuation of his personal wellbeing. Letters sent from another of Sir Daniel's children, Henry, give a first-hand account of an undergraduate's academic exploits in the Stuart era. In December 1679, for instance, the studious young man reported proudly to his father that he had finished with logic and ethics and was making a start on geometry with his tutor. Five months later, there was a sudden need in the syllabus for a teetering pile of historical volumes and geographical tomes, which Daniel was expected to pay for, while by late summer logic and ethics appear to have been covered again, allowing the well-read Henry Fleming to move on to physics.[34]

Despite their gleaming reputations for learning and excellence, the Stuart aristocracy knew that Oxford and Cambridge were not impeccable environments. It was commonly acknowledged that both universities acted at least partially as breeding grounds for temptation and sin, corrupting even those adolescents who had hitherto led unblemished lives. Sir Simonds D'Ewes was greatly troubled by the things he saw as a Cambridge student at St John's College in the reign of James I. 'The main thing which made me even weary of the College,' he wrote retrospectively, 'was, that swearing, drinking, rioting, and hatred of all piety and virtue under false and adulterate nicknames, did abound there and generally in all the University.' The culture of drinking at Oxbridge was noticed by other aristocrats, too. 'The vice of Oxford scholars is their frequenting tippling houses,' Christopher Guise observed, admitting that he had once been a frequenter himself. Intimate relations with the other sex were also known to occur at university, with D'Ewes referring to 'the sin of lust ... practised by very boys', and Guise recalling that as an undergraduate he and his comrades 'followed and courted any whom we found to be "inbued" with the least beauty'.[35]

One alternative to university proposed in early Stuart England was an academy of learning, much like those seen in continental Europe. In 1635, Sir Francis Kynaston, a cultured knight from Shropshire, was granted a licence under the great seal to found such an institution at his Covent Garden residence, which he named the Musæum Minervæ. The academy would admit only the sons of aristocrats and aimed to rival Cambridge and Oxford with its extensive curriculum, offering classes not only in the mainstream disciplines of languages, mathematics, and philosophy, but also heraldry, husbandry, cosmography, navigation, optics, numismatics, fortification, and architecture. High-quality academics were to be hired to oversee and teach the ambitious programme, contributing skills in philosophy, music, astronomy, geometry, and languages. Astonishingly, it would take seven years for an attendee of Kynaston's Musæum Minervæ to complete the protracted course, after which he would be known forevermore as a Septennal, and presumably receive certain privileges for his pains.[36] The academy received financial support from the royal family and was even visited by Charles I's children, but ultimately it failed to take off in the grand fashion that its architect had envisioned. Although capturing the attention of Oxford and Cambridge, and perhaps even admitting some pupils through its doors, the ground-breaking Musæum Minervæ disappeared from the record entirely when Francis Kynaston died in 1642.

Love and loss

One day in 1608, Edward Herbert, soon-to-be 1st Baron Herbert of Cherbury, assembled his three children in front of his wife and asked her what she thought of them. 'Well,' was Mary's even reply.[36] The gentlewoman's straightforward, somewhat lacklustre response was no doubt echoed by a good many aristocratic parents up and down the country, suggesting that there was nothing very complicated about the relationships between elite mothers and fathers and their offspring in Stuart England.

In reality, however, feelings could vary enormously. At times, there was an air of unmistakable aloofness in the behaviour of Lady Anne Clifford and Richard Sackville towards their daughter Margaret in the early seventeenth century. Within her celebrated diaries, Clifford repeatedly refers to the little girl as merely 'the child', conjuring images of an inanimate object from which she had distanced herself, while there is written evidence that Sackville chose only to see his daughter at designated times of the day in the nursery, for example after supper. Yet Anne herself reveals that, on one particular occasion in May 1617, she had permitted Margaret to lie in the same bed as her all night long, which dispels rather abruptly any notion that she was a distant mother. Eighty years later in the 1690s, soon-to-be 1st Baron Hervey and his second wife, Lady Elizabeth Felton, pursued an actively affectionate relationship with their young children, whom they obviously adored. 'Don't let the sweet babes forget papa,' John Hervey wrote to Elizabeth in April 1697. The Suffolk-based couple had various pet names for their beloved youngsters, and as a rule always spoke warmly about them in letters, with Elizabeth calling one son 'my little boy' and both mother and father dubbing a favourite daughter 'sweet-face'. During a stay in London in 1698, Elizabeth informed her husband that little Jack 'was calling upon dear Papa', and 'would not be quiet in the morning till they carried him into your dressing-room', indicating that the love the Herveys showed for their children was reciprocated. Two days later, Lady Hervey wrote again to announce that Jack and Betty had decided to crawl into bed with her as she drank chocolate.[37]

Sir Simonds D'Ewes' and Lady Anne Clopton's tender feelings for their infant son were made painfully clear in May 1636 after the child died following a brief period of ill health. D'Ewes immediately sought comfort at a relative's house in Essex in the wake of the tragic passing, where he found 'condolements'. When Anne arrived at the same property from London that evening, she initially knew nothing. Simonds watched his wife enter the inner court of the mansion from the shadows of a dining room window, marvelling at how cheerful and confident she looked as she approached the building, but also pitying her immensely 'in respect of her near approaching lamentation'. She 'fell a-shaking' upon seeing the state of him, the man visibly grief-stricken and broken. 'Is the boy dead?' Anne demanded through 'an abundance of tears', barely able to ask the terrible question. There in the gloomy dining room, Simonds revealed the truth to his trembling wife, feeling such sorrow himself that he felt like crying afresh with her. His duties as a husband prevailed, however, and he was able to push aside his own torment to support Anne in her suffering, using 'the best arguments I had to mould and frame her to patience and moderation'.[38]

Childhood was an acutely dangerous time in Stuart England, with one in five infants expected to die before they had turned a year old between 1675 and 1700. The children of the aristocracy were not exempt from this sobering reality, as much as their parents hoped they might be, and so it was a fact of life that sickness and death surrounded them in their orderly nurseries. Diseases and ailments that were likely to cause problems early on included smallpox, measles, fevers, and skeletal disorders such as rickets. It is arguable that Sir Hugh Cholmley was both lucky and unlucky as a child in the first decade of the seventeenth century, for while he claimed to have suffered from 'the measles and small-pox thrice' before the age of ten, and was 'very subject to agues and sickness', he did miraculously manage to survive every sickness flung at him. All too often illness in aristocratic youngsters ended in the worst possible way. Sir Henry Slingsby's young nephew died just a short week after contracting measles in 1639, with the esquire noting knowingly that 'there's no danger of ye measles if they come well out, which they did not of this child.' An unidentified disorder similarly robbed Thomas Howard, 14th Earl of Arundel, of his son Charles in 1616, which began with the boy's seemingly inconsequential refusal to eat his breakfast one morning. The Dowager Countess of Arundel quickly became disturbed by her grandson's symptoms and wrote to tell Thomas that 'his wind [is] very short, and his pulse and heart worketh so extremely fast as I never knew the like... I assure sweetheart the poor child is exceeding evil.' In a short time Charles was taking his last breaths. 'He cast twice a little quantity of dark tawny colour,' the Dowager related on the day of the infant's death, stating that at noon the tawny substance was replaced by a hideous black bile. He was dead by 4:00pm that afternoon, having first endured a series of 'very sharp pains'.[39]

The wealth of the Stuart aristocracy meant that treatments could be obtained and advice purchased in the event that a child fell sick, although this was no guarantee of a successful cure. Doctors might be drafted in to prescribe medicines or even bleed the incapacitated boy or girl, as was the course of action taken in July 1690 when the son of Robert Harley, future Earl of Oxford, lay dangerously ill at Brampton Bryan Hall. Elizabeth, Robert's wife, recounted the scene:

> Yesterday Mr Wildish made him an issue in his arm. He thought it would be very troublesome to the child to have it in his neck. Uncle Harley was so kind as to be by when it was done. We all think it well made. He has very sad fits of coughing and is very black in the face and is almost strangled. Last night those that watched with him thought that he had sixteen strangling fits. I hope God will be gracious to us and spare him.[40]

Treatments designed to prevent an aristocratic child from becoming seriously unwell in the first place were sometimes sent by the aristocracy themselves to youngsters, being customarily superstitious in nature. In 1678, the Derbyshire-born Grace Manners, Viscountess of Chaworth, gave her godson a wolf's tooth to be worn around his neck and rubbed along his teeth, in the hope that it would allow his dentition to develop more easily and act as an 'antidotal against convulsions'.[41]

Conditions like rickets and other growth abnormalities were not usually life-threatening for aristocratic children in Stuart England, but they could require particularly intrusive remedies as part of the corrective process. In terms of the structural condition of the younger members of the family, the Verneys of Middle Claydon were dealt a noticeably bad hand in the seventeenth century. One of Sir Ralph Verney's sons, Jack, displayed crooked legs and a strangely pronounced stomach as a child, although no recorded treatment was thought necessary for him. Mun Verney, conversely, was diagnosed with a significant curvature of the spine in 1653, which necessitated the use of an iron harness to improve the boy's imperfect posture. The unforgiving harness was prescribed by a famed physician practising in Utrecht called Herr Skatt, and enclosed Mun's entire upper torso in iron, much like the breastplate and backplate of a suit of armour. Even though the underside of the peculiar garment was lined with soft leather for comfort and ease of movement, blood and signs of severe chafing were still to be found on the Verney minor's body whenever Skatt removed the device to change the linen shirt worn beneath. There appears to have been an eventual payoff, however. Six months after donning the harness for the first time, Mun's posture had by all accounts straightened considerably, with his governor in Holland confidently asserting, 'I may truly say the cure is almost perfected.'[42]

While Jack and Mun lived long enough to develop their respective growth disorders, many of the Stuart aristocracy's offspring did not. In fact, a baby dying during, directly after, or before the birth was a common occurrence in seventeenth- and early eighteenth-century England. The risk to the mother's life was considerable as well. Dame Mary Lowther, the wife of Sir John Lowther of Lowther Hall in Westmorland, was unable to shake the feeling that something catastrophic lurked around the corner when carrying her twelfth child in 1647. Her fears would sadly be realised, for one day she suffered 'a great breach' that severely weakened the northern gentlewoman. Although there was renewed optimism for the pregnancy following Mary's speedy recovery, the succeeding weeks saw two further breaches occur, at which point it became clear that a miscarriage was to blame. A merciless stream of blood flowed from Sir John's wife at Lowther Hall as a result of the trauma experienced, culminating in her own death three long days later.[43]

Religion

A sense of religious duty was instilled in aristocratic children from a young age in Stuart England, by both Catholic and increasingly

Protestant parents eager for their sons and daughters to lead model lives in the service of God. The children of the 5th Earl of Bedford were given Latin and English copies of the Bible from an early age in the mid-seventeenth century at Woburn, while at the beginning of the 1700s it is recorded that the offspring of Sir John Hervey regularly heard prayers from a French chaplain called John Pujolas.[44] When boys were old enough to begin receiving an education, it was often tutors who were tasked with monitoring and actively encouraging positive religious behaviours in their pupils. Sir Henry Slingsby of Yorkshire, the father of the Henry Slingsby we have already met, gave the tutor of his eldest son William precise instructions on the pious routines he wanted the young man to follow in the first years of the 1600s. God was to be thanked before and after the consumption of meat, either aloud or privately depending on the situation, Slingsby told Mr Snell, and the Sabbath was to be 'wholly spent in prayer and other good Christian and religious exercises'. In the same set of directions, Slingsby also advised that William 'temp his wine well with water' and 'take heed of fruits', particularly grapes, 'for they breed the bloody fluxes and are very dangerous for young persons.'[45]

The efforts taken by aristocratic mothers and fathers to make their children godly could produce different outcomes. As part of his written defence of his wayward sons, Freeman and George Sondes, in 1655, the 1st Earl of Feversham avowed that the older of the two 'never failed morning and evening, to betake himself to his private devotions', and that it would have been quite impossible for anybody to 'make him commit a known sin'. Sometimes an aristocratic child was so well indoctrinated in the beliefs of the church that it caused them to feel intensely fearful of the consequences of being irreligious. 'Robin last night waked in the night and prayed and was troubled and it was a good while before he went to sleep again,' Lady Abigail Harley wrote to her husband Sir Edward in 1670. She was referring to her young son Robert, who admitted to his mother the following day that he had begun contemplating sin when he had awoken suddenly in the small hours of the morning. 'He had heard of the sin against the Holy Ghost which was unpardonable,' Lady Harley continued in her letter, 'but did not know what sin it was and was afraid to ask lest he had committed it or the devil should tempt him to commit it.' She finished by disclosing, with an obvious tone of concern, that 'the poor child with tears told me he was afraid if he died he should go to hell.'[46]

3

STATELY PILES AND POSSESSIONS

> Surely it is, as they say, the greatest squadron [quadrangular building] by much in England; and of that exceeding height, and yet magnificent turrets above that height, a goodly front, and a brave prospect open to the meanest and most distant room, and that uniform proportion every way, generally, as would study a good architect to describe.[1]

This is how Sir George Chaworth excitedly described the mansion under construction for the Earl of Dunbar at Berwick-upon-Tweed in 1607. The houses of the Stuart aristocracy, as Chaworth intimates, were invariably impressive to behold and rarely lacking in grandeur. Aristocrats as a rule had at least one substantial house in the countryside to call their own, often referred to as the family seat because it was here that members spent a large amount of their time in either business or leisure. These edifices might be surrounded by private gardens, acres of parkland, swathes of land that were given over to farming, or a combination of all three, from which a substantial profit could occasionally be made. As well as possessing a prominent house in the provinces that would be known throughout the local area, it was also common for Stuart aristocrats to own a property in London. Such townhouses, ranging from the modest Leaden Porch Court in Holborn, the urban residence of the Newdigates, to the palatial Bedford House in Bloomsbury, the metropolitan stomping ground of the Russells, acted as convenient, comfortable bases for the aristocracy when country living was temporarily paused.

Whether situated in a bustling city or the verdant English countryside, one could always count on the houses of the Stuart aristocracy to be full of things. The many possessions owned by the upper echelon of English society that inhabited their interior spaces included fashionable and expensive furniture, paintings, ornate carpets, ornamental weaponry and other decorative items, clocks, silver valuables, and an array of practical objects that might be found in any reasonably equipped home. By the turn of the eighteenth century, there was an increasing number of foreign imports to be discovered in England's mansions, too. A Japanese cabinet, black 'large glass' and table, screen, and chest, were amongst the personal possessions of Sir Francis Rolle and his wife Dame Priscilla in 1708, along with a large Indian quilt, all of which were deemed valuable enough to be included as bequests in the latter's will.[2]

Country houses

Aristocratic country houses in Stuart England fell under two broad categories: those residences that were constructed in earlier eras, and those that sprang up brand new between 1603 and 1714 (or thereabouts). At the commencement of the 1600s, there existed a mix of Tudor mansions and older medieval structures housing the elite, which might, over the course of the seventeenth century, be added to, slimmed down, or even demolished altogether. Berry Pomeroy Castle in Devon began life as a stone fortification in the late fifteenth century, being superseded in the 1560s by an attractive Elizabethan house built by Edward Lord Seymour, son of Lord Protector Somerset. The latter years of the 1500s saw the ambitious construction of an east range, which underwent extensive remodelling between 1600 and 1610, while in around 1600 a majestic north wing was added to the mansion in the interests of further magnificence, including a long gallery measuring 213 feet.[3] With renovations rumoured to cost upwards of £20,000, Berry Pomeroy Castle constituted the jewel in the Seymour family's crown in the early seventeenth century, despite the fact that building work on the property was never actually finished. 'The apartments within were very splendid,' an eighteenth-century commentator enthused, 'especially the dining room, which was adorn'd, besides paint, with statues and figures cut in alabaster, with admirable art and labour.' There were countless rooms to maintain, which caused the same commentator to remark that 'the number of the apartments of the whole may be collected hence, if report be true, that it was a good day's work for a servant but to open and shut the casements belonging to them.'[4] At the time these comments were made in 1701, however, the castle had all but fallen into ruin, retaining only faint glimmers of its former splendour.

The myriad country houses that were built entirely new in the early Stuart (the Jacobean) period tended to be symmetrical, neat, and orderly in appearance, much like their Elizabethan equivalents. This was a deliberate design choice on the part of aristocratic owners, who had started to crave rural seats that reflected the neatness and orderliness of the respectable people who lived in them. Often Jacobean mansions followed the popular E-, U-, or H-shaped layout, which consisted of two uniform wings appended to either side of a central building, made of brick or stone.[5] The windows of such properties, typically square, mullioned, and extremely large, could be capable of letting unprecedented amounts of light into galleries, apartments, and walkways between rooms. Naturally, not all country houses erected around this time conformed to the characteristics listed above. Longford Castle in Wiltshire, the project of the courtier Sir Thomas Gorges and finished just before the accession of King James I in 1603, was built to an abnormal triangular design that comprised three walls and 'three great round towers' at each of its corners. In September 1603, the English lawyer Roger Wilbraham described the edifice as 'a fair new house of stone', noting that the trio of towers contained the 'fairest chambers'. 'All his windows are but two lights with a transom,' Wilbraham continued, 'and yet being set thick and uniform show well and fair.'[6] By around 1680, the purpose and nature of some of Longford's grand rooms had almost certainly changed, although the basic triangular shape of the building remained unaltered. Still the towers accommodated the three best bedrooms of the castle, named My Lord's Chamber, The Queen's Chamber, and The Marble Chamber, and with these there was a music room, matted gallery, dining room, drawing room, dressing room, terrace walk, and cedar closet for the proprietors and their guests to enjoy.

One rural dwelling that certainly did have all the features of a typical Jacobean mansion was Audley End House in Essex, with its U formation, symmetrical wings, rows of immense windows, and gargantuan scale that was unlike anything seen before in the country. Constructed between about 1605 and 1614, Audley End was the fantastical dream of Thomas Howard, 1st Earl of Suffolk, who envisioned that the enormous residence would be used to host James I and Queen Anna of Denmark when they embarked on royal progresses in the area. State apartments for the couple were incorporated into the first floor of the inner court, which had been designed by Howard himself, his uncle, Henry Howard, 1st Earl of Northampton, and a Flemish mason called Bernard Janssen. Flemish and French architectural styles subtly influenced the overall look of the house and can still be observed today in the pleasing design of the two porches that stand at the front of the vast Essex building. The Earl of Suffolk had been firmly focused on the needs of King James, Queen Anna, and their Anglo-Scottish heirs when bringing Audley End House together in the early seventeenth century, but it is probable that he lived here for at least some of the time before his death in 1626. By the mid-1600s, the stone marvel, already an outdated relic of a bygone age, was dividing opinion amongst those who were privileged enough to explore its rooms. The famous diarist John Evelyn was mostly impressed with what he saw when he visited the house in September 1654.

> It is a mixed fabric, betwixt antique and modern, but observable for its being completely finished, and without comparison is one of the stateliest palaces in the kingdom... It consists of two courts, the first very large, winged with cloisters. The front has a double entrance; the hall is fair, but somewhat too small for so august a pile. The kitchen is very large, as are the cellars arched with stone, very neat and well disposed; these offices are joined by a wing out of the way very handsomely. The gallery is the most cheerful, and I think one of the best in England; a fair dining-room, and the rest of the lodgings answerable, with a pretty chapel... For the rest, it is a perfectly uniform structure, and shows without like a diadem, by the decorations of the cupolas and other ornaments on the pavilions; instead of rails and balusters, there is a border of capital letters.[7]

Fellow diarist Samuel Pepys thought differently in October 1667. While he found the gallery 'good' and the cellars even better during his own visit, 'where we went down and drank of much good liquor', the rest of Audley End House proved something of a disappointment to him. The ceilings, for a start, were not as 'well wrought' and handsome as the Londoner remembered, and Pepys was so disapproving of the main staircase that he described it in his diary as 'exceeding poor'.[8]

The construction of country houses was largely suspended during the English Civil War, with aristocratic properties more likely to be pulled down than erected in those years, but by the Restoration period building projects had started up again. Grand rural residences of the 1660s and after were often built smaller than they had been in the days of James I, sometimes missing the symmetrical wings that gave Jacobean mansions their trademark H or U shape. What they lacked in size, however, they made up for in displays of Renaissance architecture. Around 1663, William, Lord Alington, enlisted the services of one of the greatest English architects of the age, Sir Roger Pratt, to design a fashionable country hall for him to live in at Horseheath in Cambridgeshire. It was to be of red brick and Ketton stone, and furthermore divided into eleven identical bays, with the central three bays jutting out slightly for effect and enhanced by a decorated pediment bearing the Alington coat of arms. The roof was to be steep, slated, and crowned with a leaded platform encircled by a stone balustrade, on top of which would be positioned eight chimneys and a cupola holding a copper ball. This ball was a family trophy of sorts, having been recovered from the Siege of Boulogne in 1544.

Inside Horseheath Hall, the family and their esteemed visitors would be greeted initially by an entrance hall and surrounding gallery that measured forty-eight by forty feet, enclosed on the left by a great staircase and chapel. The latter continued to be added to English country houses throughout the seventeenth century, although it was becoming increasingly common for existing domestic chapels to be employed for secular activities. At the bottom end of the entrance hall was to be the parlour, used either for eating or relaxing in, and to the right of the front doors the great back staircase. On the first floor a 'great' parlour, the more likely candidate for a dining space, and withdrawing room, where diners could retire to after meals, were in all probability planned. Below these rooms, running from one end of the hall to the other, was to be inserted a basement passage for servants.[9] Always willing to offer an opinion on the latest aristocratic abodes to be developed outside of London, in July 1670 John Evelyn paid a visit to the completed Horseheath Hall and judged it a house 'of great cost ... seated in a park, with a sweet prospect and stately avenue; but water still defective; the house has also its infirmities'.[10] What these infirmities were, Evelyn did not say.

Towards the end of the seventeenth century, the Baroque architectural style, already popular in continental Europe and especially in Italy, came to significantly influence the look of aristocratic new-builds in provincial England. English Baroque vigorously embraced ornate detail and extravagant features, readily observable today in the stately form of Dyrham Park in Gloucestershire. Built in stages between 1692 and 1704 for the powerful diplomat William Blathwayt, widower of the wealthy descendant of Sir George Wynter of Dyrham, Mary Wynter, the mansion was a sight to behold upon its completion. The east front in particular revelled in its intricacy, with its designer, William Talman, taking ideas liberally from a book by Peter Paul Rubens entitled *Palazzi di Genova*.[11] Close to forty decorated windows lined this portion of the house, their many panes of glass acting as a shimmering pedestal for the proud stone eagle and four vases that sat atop the flat roof, which also boasted a stone balustrade. The continental feel of the architecture, in fact, appeared to have an impact on the choice of building materials used. While the stone for the main structure was sourced locally, Blathwayt saw to it that supplies of high-quality timber for the floors, staircases, and doors came from as far away as the West Indies and North America.[12] Unfortunately, it seems that the widowed diplomat did not always have an easy relationship with the craftsmen who were employed to realise his grand Baroque vision. On one occasion in 1701, perhaps after a particularly trying day at Dyrham, he is known to have remarked waspishly, 'these people want stirring up roundly and not to be overfed with money.'[13]

In 1687, work began on the best surviving example of a Baroque country mansion in England: Chatsworth House. The Derbyshire seat was then owned by William Cavendish, 4th Earl of Devonshire, who retired to the estate for an extended period in the reign of James II, after running into political and financial trouble in London. Initially, Cavendish planned only to reconstruct the south front of the existing house in his exile. Having developed a taste for the building process, however, he went on to pull down and replace the other three sections of the property, too: the east, west, and north fronts. 'He first projected the new glorious pile at Chatsworth, as if his mind rose upon the depression of his fortunes,' the preacher announced at the nobleman's funeral:

> For he now contracted with workmen to pull down the south side of that good old seat, and to rebuild it in a plan he gave to them, for a front to his gardens, so fair and august, that it look'd like a model only of what might be done in after ages. When he had finish'd this part, he meant to go no farther ... he undertook the east side of the quadrangle, and rais'd it entirely new, in conformity to the south, and seem'd then content to say, that he had gone half way through, and would leave the rest for his heir. In this resolution he stop'd about seven years, and then reassum'd courage, and began to lay the foundations for two other sides to complete the noble square; and these last, as far as uniformity admits, do exceed the others by a west front of most excellent strength and elegance, and a capitol on the north side that is of singular ornament and service.[14]

The north front was completed just before the Duke of Devonshire's death in 1707 (he was given the title in 1694), meaning that William Cavendish was able to see Chatsworth House in its finished form, standing both proudly and imposingly in the heart of the rugged Peak District. The sculptor Samuel Watson made significant contributions to the northern segment of the structure, which included carvings of six Corinthian capitals, forty-five medallions and roses, and six lion's heads, in all costing around £54 to produce. William Talman, on the other hand, seems to have taken charge of the preliminary reconstructions of the south façade and east wing, which is why the seat bears some resemblance to Dyrham Park in Gloucestershire. Chatsworth, though, was widely held to be more impressive. For his input, Talman was paid the eye-watering sum of £13,000, in today's money equating to a fee of about £1.4 million.

The interior of Chatsworth House did not disappoint. By the early 1700s, it had a painted hall, intended to be one of the first things visitors saw upon entering the property, a long gallery, a state apartment for accommodating royalty, a dining room, several drawing rooms, and no fewer than ten state-of-the-art water closets. These closets and their fixtures, assemblages of cedar, brass, and alabaster, reflected the gradual development of technologies within English stately homes. The house also possessed a highly decorated chapel for private devotion, featuring the painstaking work of the Italian painter Antonio Verrio, as well as that of the French artist Louis Laguerre. The room was considered worthy of mention in Cavendish's funeral sermon in 1707:

> The area is black and white marble, laid in the most agreeable manner, not embarrass'd with any seats, but made convenient with chairs plac'd along the walls, and cushions for the use of strangers and servants. The walls are wainscoted with cedar and cypress in large panels, and carved works between them, about the height of eighteen foot: and then the remainder of the walls, and the whole roof, adorn'd with exquisite painting of the miracles of our saviour etc. The gallery at one end for the chief of the family, is very neat and suitable, supported by two black marble pillars, not jointed, fifteen inches diameter, twelve foot and a half high. The altar-piece is an admirable frame of white marble and alabaster, supported by two pillars of black marble, adorned with lively statues on the top of each of 'em, representing religion and virtue, and with a dove and glory very curiously cut in stone; and over it, in an oval black frame, a picture of St Thomas convinc'd of his infidelity by our saviour, said to be the finest piece that was ever done by Verrio's hand.[15]

This was a sacred space that clearly left an impression, to such a degree that it even encouraged the author of the sermon to declare that Chatsworth House 'seems to be art insulting nature'.[16]

London townhouses

'The new front towards the gardens is tolerable, were it not drowned by a too massy and clumsy pair of stairs of stone, without any neat invention,' John Evelyn wrote in June 1658, referring to the exterior of Northumberland House in Charing Cross.[17] At this time, close to the demise of Cromwell and the rebirth of the Stuart monarchy, the property was owned by Algernon Percy, 10th Earl of Northumberland, who may not have entirely appreciated his friend's comments. It is safe to say, however, that most other people would not have felt the same way as Evelyn did. Their frequent opulence and vastness, especially when contrasted with the compact streets of England's capital, meant that the London townhouses of the aristocracy were much more likely to command respect than evoke apathy in Stuart England. Such edifices maintained a constant presence in the city throughout the period, with many of them casting long shadows over the surrounding tangle of lesser houses and churches, both in a literal and figurative sense. As the eighteenth century arrived, designs were more ambitious and formidable than ever, leading to the emergence of exquisite mansions like William Winde's Buckingham House in Westminster, the urban seat of John Sheffield, 1st Duke of Buckingham and Normanby.

Algernon Percy's Northumberland House was completed in approximately 1605 for Henry Howard, 1st Earl of Northampton, the wealthy aristocrat who would go on to contribute to the construction of Audley End House in Essex. Initially referred to as Northampton House in honour of its first owner, the brick property consisted of three sections that formed a typical Jacobean U shape, with the central block of the building – or the bottom of the U – sitting alongside the busy Strand. This left the other side of the house that faced the Thames open, which constituted the ideal setting for a large garden that sloped lazily down to the water's edge. The men responsible for the edifice included Bernard Janssen, surveyor, and the carver Gerard Christmas, whose skills were used to create Northampton House's incredible frontispiece.[18] Christmas's involvement in the project was made known to passers-by for some time afterwards through an etching of his initials over the structure's stone gateway, which was demolished in the mid-eighteenth century to accommodate a new front. Beyond this original gateway and through the front doors of Henry Howard's London home, a world of luxury awaited. In 1614, Northampton House enjoyed a great chamber, dining chamber, withdrawing chamber, little study, bedchamber, 'pallet' chamber, little gallery, long gallery, great withdrawing chamber, bigger great chamber, parlour, long wardrobe, higher library, low wardrobe, lower library, kitchen, and gentlemen's chambers, along with plenty of other rooms that have been omitted here.[19] It was, truly, a palace in all but name, much like the numerous other aristocratic mansions that were situated on the banks of the Thames in Jacobean England.

To the north of the prodigy houses that lined the Strand, Thomas Wriothesley, 4th Earl of Southampton, commenced work on an aristocratic square in the mid-seventeenth century. It was hoped that the undertaking would bring the earl and his extended family great prestige, as well as providing a suitable abode in London that reflected the very latest in architectural fashions. The square's construction might also give the likes of Northumberland House a run for their money. Located in modern-day Bloomsbury, Southampton Square – as it was then known – would be completely taken up on one side by Wriothesley's new townhouse, which, once finished, was carved up into three parts and spread over as many floors. The first storey of the central segment contained eighteen rooms in total, including two great drawing rooms, three smaller drawing rooms, a dining room, private dressing rooms and bedrooms for the earl and countess, a cedar chapel, and a great hall that could be accessed directly via the main entrance. On the ground floor a lesser entrance hall was tucked away behind the sweeping front steps, where one could almost always find a seated porter, while on the second floor there were a further twenty-four rooms to explore. These functioned either as personal spaces for members of the earl's own family or living quarters for senior servants. Although there is no doubt that Southampton House looked every inch a sumptuous pile following its completion, the diarist John Evelyn was still underwhelmed when he came across the London landmark in February 1665. 'Dined at my Lord Treasurer's, the Earl of Southampton, in Bloomsbury, where he was building a noble square, or piazza, a little town,' he opened neutrally. Next, however, the man wrote, 'His own house stands too low, some noble rooms, a pretty cedar chapel, a naked garden to the north, but good air.'[20] Clearly, there was just no pleasing some people. Southampton House and its pretty square had come into the possession of the Dukes of Bedford by 1700, through the noteworthy marriage of Rachel Wriothesley, daughter of the 4th Earl of Southampton, to William, Lord Russell. The townhouse's adopted name in the eighteenth century, therefore, was Bedford House.

Later townhouses in Stuart London began gradually to combine grandiosity with the classical or Palladian architectural style that would dominate aristocratic buildings in Georgian England. Berkeley House in Piccadilly was constructed for John Berkeley, 1st Baron Berkeley, between 1665 and 1673, and incorporated several Palladian features. Most notably, it had stone pilasters that supported an entablature and 'pitched' pediment, beneath which was carved the delicate figure of Britannia, but there were also two circular galleries 'elevated on columns of the Corinthian order'. John Evelyn thought that the Piccadilly property was 'very well built' when he visited in 1672, although he added that it had 'many noble rooms, but they are not very convenient'. The diarist reckoned that Berkeley House had probably cost somewhere in the region of £30,000 to build.[21]

Thirty years later, in 1703, a similar townhouse of awe-inspiring proportions emerged majestically in the Westminster area, ordered by John Sheffield, 1st Duke of Buckingham, and designed by the English architect William Winde. This was Buckingham House. Like Berkeley House in Piccadilly, John Sheffield's new mansion comprised a central block that was connected to two lesser structures via a pair of arching galleries, which in turn were held up by a series of pillars. These smaller buildings were imposing classical edifices in their own right, even if the southern block only housed lodgings for servants, and the northern block the kitchens and laundry rooms. 'The fronts … are elevated on pillars of the Tuscan, Dorick, and Ionick orders, thereby constituting piazzas,' Edward Hatton observed in his valuable work, *A New View of London*, published in two octavo volumes in 1708. Of the main house, he noted that the walls of the mansion were 'very fine rubb'd and gag'd, adorned with 2 ranges of pilasters, of the Corinthian and Tuscan orders, on the latter (which are uppermost) is an Acroteria of figures standing erect and fronting the court, they appear as big as the life and look noble.'[22] Hatton, in fact, had nothing but praise for the predecessor of Buckingham Palace. Summing up his feelings, he wrote, 'in short the whole structure is spacious, commodious, rich and beautiful in its building.'[23]

Not all London townhouses owned by the Stuart aristocracy were quite as spacious, rich, or commodious as Buckingham House. Sir Richard Newdigate of Arbury Hall in Warwickshire (not to be confused with his son, Sir Richard Newdigate, 2nd Baronet) secured himself a modest dwelling in Holborn known as 'The Leaden Porch' during the seventeenth century, which was likely timber-framed and of moderate size, but obviously satisfied the man's needs and those of his immediate family. In the early 1700s, we find Sir Walter and Dame Johanna St John occupying another relatively low-key townhouse across the Thames in Battersea, which included several chambers, closets, a dining room, and a 'gilt leather' room.[24] The couple also owned a stately house at Lydiard Tregoze in Wiltshire, courtesy of Sir Walter, who had inherited the country pile and a baronetcy on the death of his nephew, Sir John St John, in 1657.

Back over the grey waters of the Thames once more, the Member of Parliament and courtier Sir Thomas Coke purchased a fair house in the new development of St James' Place in the 1690s, which could never hope to match Bedford House in Bloomsbury or Berkeley House in Piccadilly, but was still a fine establishment in most people's eyes. The exact building was No. 11, St James' Place, described by a relative of Coke's in December 1697 as 'really a very pretty house … two rooms on each floor, which is six in all, wainscoted from top to bottom'. This relative had been helping Thomas in his fervent endeavours to buy a London property, and accordingly she continued in her letter, 'I am confident you will soon find the ease of having a house to yourself, though but a little one.' The limited size of No. 11 prompted the Member of Parliament to also acquire No. 12 next door in February 1699, then standing empty, and by the middle of the year work had commenced to join the two townhouses together. It marked a significant improvement in living standards for Coke, who was also the fortunate owner of Melbourne Hall in Derbyshire; the enlarged property, according to the talented plasterer Edward Goudge, would have a hall, a dining room, and two sets of stairs, 'with back stairs quite through the houses'.[25]

The structural alterations Sir Thomas Coke made in St James' Place highlight the plethora of problems a Stuart aristocrat could run into when building in the capital. Upon first buying No. 11 in the late 1690s, one of Coke's primary acts had been to expand the house by constructing 'clossetts' in the garden. The garden in question, unfortunately, was overlooked by several others in St James' Place, meaning that his plans provoked outrage from neighbours who felt their privacy was in danger of being invaded. 'One Mrs Stroud is the most concerned,' a family member advised Thomas in July 1698. He went on to divulge that she had threatened to build a wall that was 'twenty-five or thirty foot high' if the works went ahead as planned, 'which will quite spoil that little prospect, which you have, and very much darken your rooms'.[26] The real troublemakers, however, turned out to be the irate residents living at No. 16, whose own garden directly backed onto that of No. 11. On 19 July, Edward Goudge wrote to Coke to convey his fears:

> At first Mr Stroud told me that they were the only persons disturbed, but since I hear nothing from anybody but Mr Charles Godolphin. I understand by the people I put into the house that all this disturbance is occasioned by his lady [Elizabeth Godolphin], who it seems cannot be satisfied till she sees your building down.

> Their builder came to tell me they would pull down our building on Monday. On Sunday I went and laughed at him for his news. He told me seriously that he had seen their lease, and they had so many foot of ground as reached the inside of our wall. To prevent a law suit I have contented myself with the loss of about five inches, and taken the timber off the wall and set it wholly on our own ground.[27]

Charles and Elizabeth Godolphin continued to vehemently resist the building project for several months. 'Madam Godolphin is still as troublesome as she can be, saying she hath not done with you,' Goudge reported to Thomas on 24 August, although by this point it had been made doubly sure that the 'closetts' did not encroach on the Godolphins' property.[28]

Hostilities reached an aggressive climax towards the end of the month. One day, while a workman was nailing some boards to the side of the structure that faced No. 16's garden, Charles Godolphin appeared at the perimeter with a 'pistol ready cocked' and declared that he would shoot anybody who dared to set foot on his land. The same thing happened again a few days later, as detailed in a letter written by Goudge:

> Since there were no thoughts of making a scaffold on Mr Godolphin's ground to plaster that end, I ordered it to be weather boarded; which when the carpenters were going about to do by standing within our own building and putting their heads between the quarters to nail the boards, Mr Godolphin came out with a pistol and swore he would shoot that man through the head that should offer but to swing his hand over his ground to drive a nail, whereupon the carpenters being scared from their work, I ordered it to be bricked up between the quarters, which is done.[29]

In early September, the Godolphins began exacting their revenge on Thomas Coke and his workforce through the erection of a tall fence between the two gardens, the sight of which caused Mrs Godolphin to laugh hysterically.

One issue with which Charles Rich, 4th Earl of Warwick, had to deal during renovations to Warwick House in Holborn was unsatisfactory labourers. This, needless to say, was not a problem unique to London, as William Blathwayt of Dyrham Park would cantankerously confirm in the early eighteenth century. Mary Rich, the Earl of Warwick's long-suffering wife, watched on in horror as her husband shouted and cursed at his urban builders in August 1667, who had let Charles down by failing to carry out their tasks properly. The whole affair put the countess off Warwick House entirely, and later she could be found in a private room begging God 'to forgive my poor husband his swearing, and to give him patience that the house might be perfumed with prayers, and not profaned by oaths'.[30]

Interior design

Often the staircase was the focal point of aristocratic houses in Stuart England. Sweeping out of view in lofty entrance halls across the country, these structures dictated the geography of buildings in many cases and were designed to leave guests breathless with admiration for the families who owned them. Most mansion staircases were made from timber in the seventeenth century, including those found at Berkeley House in Piccadilly and Great Fulford House in Devon, once the country home of Colonel Sir Francis Fulford. The former was merely described by Evelyn as being 'of cedar' in 1672, while the latter was praised in 1701 as 'a piece of great cost as well as cunning, being diversified with sundry pieces of party-coloured timber, very artificially inlaid, which leads you up to a noble dining-room'.[31]

As the Baroque and Palladian styles started to turn heads in the aristocratic world, it was not unusual to come across great staircases fashioned from stone instead of wood. At Buckingham House in Westminster, the central block's great staircase consisted of 'entire slabs' of stone in the early 1700s, adorned with two marble statues of Cain and Abel at the bottom. Be they timber or otherwise, what almost all aristocratic staircases shared in common in the Stuart period was their decorative element. Posts ornamented with the crests of Sir Henry Slingsby's friends and family featured on the staircase at Red House in North Yorkshire in 1638, save for one in particular that was located near the mansion's painted chamber. This last, incongruous post bore a 'blackamore cast in lead', sculpted by the Dutchman Andrew Karne, which held a candlestick in each hand and was used by the inhabitants of the house to light the stairs at night. Perhaps more conventionally, the staircase at Horseheath Hall in Cambridgeshire was finished with moulded banisters and rails in the 1660s, under the vigilant eyes of both William, Lord Alington, and the famed architect Sir Roger Pratt.[32]

The interior walls of Stuart mansions tended to be either fully covered in wood panelling or wainscoted, whereby panelling came up to a certain height. Henry and Rachel Bourchier, the Earl and Countess of Bath, had wainscoted walls in both the great chamber and the drawing room of their London townhouse, which they paid just over £1 to have coloured in 1643. So, too, the 14th Earl of Arundel, Thomas Howard, chose wainscoting at his newly acquired property in Greenwich in 1615, which was 'half a yard deep' and fitted with gilt leather. When Celia Fiennes visited Wilton House in Wiltshire at the end of the century, which was and continues to be the family seat of the Earls of Pembroke, she found that the wainscoting in the drawing room was 'painted with ye whole History of the Acadia romance', and that another room had a variety of sporting scenes depicted on the walls and ceiling.[33]

The aesthetic appeal of interior walls clearly mattered to the Stuart aristocracy, hence Sir Henry Slingsby's desire that 'ye lodging chamber above ye new parlour' be painted in 'colours suitable to those hangings I have bought to hang it with all' at Red House in 1638. To that end, the esquire was keen for the chimney piece in the room to be coloured blue and silver. The integral presence of fireplaces in early modern homes presented an additional design challenge, with many of the finest examples made from marble, like the 'curiously engraven' construction found in the dining room at Berry Pomeroy Castle in the early seventeenth century. The fireplaces at Dyrham Park in Gloucestershire were also marble-based, the veined material having been imported specially from France, as were the chimney pieces in a London property that Lady Wentworth had lovingly picked out for her son, the 3rd Baron Raby, in 1708. Writing to him in Berlin, the gentlewoman advised that the townhouse available in St James' Square had 'three large rooms forward and two little ones backward, closets and marble chimney pieces, and hearths to all the best rooms, and iron backs to the chimneys'. Celia Fiennes was quite taken with a black marble fireplace situated in an unidentified chamber of Wilton House in the late seventeenth century, swearing in her travel diary that it was possible to see Salisbury Cathedral reflected in it.[34]

Aristocratic floors increasingly came in the form of striking grids of marble slabs in Stuart England, although timber flooring could still be found in many stately halls, drawing rooms, and bedrooms. A portion of the interior of Gloucestershire's Dyrham Park, for example, was laid with cedar floorboards when it was constructed for Blathwayt at the turn of the eighteenth century. At Kiveton Hall near Rotherham, built for the Duke of Leeds in 1698 and demolished in 1812, one chamber off the great hall was 'paved with marble' and 'sometimes used for an Eating Room'; this was according to Cassandra Willoughby, future Duchess of Chandos, who visited the house in 1710 and appeared very pleased with what she saw. While the hall at Buckingham House, some miles away in London, was only 'partly paved' with marble in the early 1700s, it was nevertheless 'adorned with pilasters, the intercolumns [being] noble painture in great variety'. Often, the black and white chequered pattern was preferred in the event that marble slabs were chosen by Stuart aristocrats to decorate their floors. Such was the case in Devon in the great hall of Great Fulford House, which contained flooring that was described quaintly in 1701 as 'chequer-ways'.[35]

Structural failure and bad housekeeping

A fierce and famous storm battered Belvoir Castle in Leicestershire in November 1703, ripping trees cleanly from their roots in the surrounding grounds and even toppling the brick wall that encircled the garden. Staying as guests of the castle's owners at this time were Lady Rachel Russell, her only son Wriothesley Russell, 2nd Duke of Bedford, and his young wife Elizabeth. While Lady Russell knew full well that the tempest raging outside Belvoir was capable of unprecedented levels of destruction, she seemed to believe that the building itself was strong enough to withstand the worst of the gales. When Wriothesley and Elizabeth entered the noblewoman's drawing room in a dishevelled state early one morning, however, Rachel likely began to have her doubts. The couple proceeded to report that the chimney stack above their quarters had completely blown over as a result of the violent winds, sending a vicious cloud of brick and soot shooting down the flue and into the chamber where they lay sleeping.[36]

Like every other structure throughout history, aristocratic houses in Stuart England were first and foremost at the mercy of the elements and could easily fail given the right set of circumstances. Belvoir Castle had been relatively lucky in the face of the Great Storm of 1703, but other properties, and indeed the people in them, were not so fortunate. Strong winds brought down seven chimney stacks at the Yorkshire seat of the baronet Sir Edward Osborne in 1638, causing the roof to collapse to devastating effect onto the rooms below. Osborne's young son had been studying French with a tutor in what would turn out to be the primary impact zone, and the boy was killed. The Frenchman only survived because he had been standing near a window, so that the debris brushed past him. Sir Henry Slingsby's wife, Barbara, was so badly shaken by the incident that she immediately forced the esquire to pull down one of their own chimneys at nearby Red House, which he appears to have done willingly. Along with perilous English gales, water was another common reason for structural failure at aristocratic residences.

'The greatest flood' Mary Rich, Countess of Warwick, had ever seen led to both the drawing room and parlour of Leez Priory in Essex being overrun with water in September 1671. Likewise in November 1702, after a 'very stormy day' in Lancashire, Nicholas Blundell noted in his diary that it had 'rained into the dining room' at Crosby Hall, with a servant subsequently sent into the loft to see where the roof had been breached. Even townhouses in the capital might fall victim to a surfeit of rain on occasion. In December 1647, the household accounts of the Earl and Countess of Bath's London abode included a telling payment to a mason 'for stopping the pavement where the water came into the cellar'.[37]

Other imperfections with the houses of the Stuart aristocracy could be blamed on the owners themselves. Sir John Reresby had allowed his mansion at Thrybergh to become 'very ruinous to the south' by the 1660s, 'the timber being decayed as well as the outside, which was only laths and lime or rough cast, with which it was covered'. The situation appeared far worse in 1680 at the house of Thomas Barrington, son of the baronet Sir John Barrington of Barrington Hall in Essex, however. Thomas' new wife, the eligible Lady Anne Rich, was so distressed at the sheer squalor of her husband's dwelling that she ran away from the marital home at the earliest opportunity, 'to a fine place, where she should be very well pleased'. If dirtiness was not this young gentlewoman's thing, then she would have been none too pleased at being a guest at Crosby Hall in the early eighteenth century, around which time an infestation of rats was keeping the Blundell family very much on their toes. In December 1707, the beds and hangings were taken down in the parlour chamber by Nicholas Blundell himself in an attempt to catch some of the rodents that were running loose on his property. The disturbing problem still evidently hung over Crosby Hall in the New Year, for on 5 January 1708 Nicholas was to be found mixing 'spar for rats, some with oatmeal and some with butter'. Sir John Oglander seems to have been confronted with a similar predicament on the Isle of Wight in the 1600s. The diligent aristocrat had led a busy life that involved dabbling in politics, being caught up in war, and even becoming a Member of Parliament for Yarmouth, but this had not stopped him from finding the time to come up with a recipe for rat poison. The method was simple enough: arsenic and stibium were to be combined with brown toast, strong beer, and four spoonfuls of sack to make a paste, which when ready was to be laid about the house in oyster shells for rodents to come across.[38]

Some so-called imperfections of aristocratic mansions had an ethereal quality to them. Lady Cary Gardiner and her family, who were relations of the Verney baronets of Middle Claydon, spent a good while moving from townhouse to townhouse in London until they finally settled on a place that seemed satisfactory in 1678, located in Lincoln's Inn Fields. The only problem anybody could make out was of a potentially otherworldly nature. 'No spirits haunt it,' Lady Gardiner wrote defiantly in a letter intended to shut the conversation down, 'though some noises have been heard.' This was also the case at Crosby Hall in Lancashire, which experienced a spate of unexplained occurrences within its walls between 1706 and 1707. The first sign that something odd was going on came in October 1706, when knocking was heard at the kitchen door with no obvious cause. The incident was followed by another in February 1707, involving a group of maids, who witnessed 'knocking and laughing at the gates and windows' early one morning as they got up to begin the working day. Again, such an experience could not be explained. The knocking returned once more at Crosby, being heard 'three times between the hours of nine and eleven at night' that October. When a woman called Mary Howerd insisted in November that a disembodied voice had whispered in her ear 'pray for me' three times in a row, Nicholas Blundell felt that the time had at last come to act.[39] That same evening, therefore, a band of townspeople arrived from Great Crosby at his invitation to see the entity off through prayer.

Gardens

'There is no humane pleasure that hath so much of antiquity, and of the state of innocency in it, as the pleasure of a garden,' William Waller wrote in his *Divine Meditations* of 1680. Certainly, Stuart aristocrats took full advantage of the considerable open spaces that adjoined their country houses, with most creating picturesque gardens that demanded the attention of every visitor. Sir Ralph Winwood's garden at Ditton Park in Buckinghamshire was all the rage in 1617, with a dovehouse, a paved court, 'a spring or conduit of excellent water', several 'fair and large' ponds, an orchard, 'delicate arbors', and, in the words of John Chamberlain, 'as fair a brick wall as I have lightly seen'. Amongst the various landmarks found in the garden at Lyme Hall (later Lyme Park) in Cheshire, at roughly the same time, were a boathouse, a pigeon house, 'arbours', and 'quicksetts for the new poole'.[40]

As at Ditton Park, there was a pretty orchard in the windswept grounds of Naworth Castle in Cumberland in the 1610s, containing an enviable herd of deer that appeared to be the target of local poachers. This, at any rate, would explain why Lord William Howard, Naworth's proprietor in the early seventeenth century, sometimes paid a small fee to have the animals watched at night. Two orchards could similarly be admired at Nunwell House on the Isle of Wight in the 1630s, being the respectable handiwork of the horticultural enthusiast Sir John Oglander; what exactly might be grown in such spaces will be discussed in a later chapter. Alongside these orchards, Oglander had planted 100 elms and ashes, 'some chestnuts and serviceberries', and a huge amount and variety of flowers 'to see the sports of nature, how in every several species she showeth her workmanship'.[41]

Accounts of aristocratic gardens in early seventeenth-century England are few and far between, with a much greater number of descriptions surviving from the second half of the 1600s. Drawing inspiration from first French and then Dutch designs, outdoor spaces in the countryside tended to embrace precision and uniformity in this later period, with landscapes habitually including manicured hedges, elaborate water features, long avenues, gravel walkways, and statues.[42] The gardens at Wilton House in Wiltshire left Celia Fiennes in awe when she visited in the late seventeenth century. They were 'very fine with many gravel walks with grass squares set with fine brass and stone statues – fish ponds and basins with figures in ye middle spouting out water – dwarf trees of all sorts and a fine flower garden – much wall fruit. Ye river runs through ye garden that easily conveys by pipes water to all parts.'[43]

Her meticulous description of the grotto is also worth quoting:

> A grotto is at ye end of the garden just ye middle off ye house – it's garnished with many fine figures of ye goddesses, and about 2 yards off the door is several pipes in a line that with a "sluce" spouts water up to wet the strangers – in the middle room is a round table and a large pipe in the midst, on which they put a crown or gun or a branch, and so it spouts the water through ye carvings and points all round ye room at ye artist's pleasure to wet ye company – there are figures at each corner of ye room that can weep water on the beholders and by a straight pipe on ye table they force up ye water into ye hollow carving of ye roof like a crown or coronet to appearance but is hollow within to retain ye water forced into it in great quantities that disperses in ye hollow cavity over ye room and descends in a shower of rain all about ye room.[44]

Such grottoes, which were in essence artificial caves, had flourished in southern Europe during the Renaissance, often being positioned at the end of scenic walkways and housing fountains or waterworks. In Stuart England, many believed that an aristocratic garden was not complete without one. Robert Plot wrote in 1686 that a 'delicate' grotto was being designed within the grounds of the country mansion of the Astley baronets, Patshull Hall, 'which when finish't will add much to the perfection of this seat'.[45]

Garden waterworks had become particularly sophisticated by the late seventeenth century and were normally made possible through the installation of underground pipes. One hundred yards of lead piping was used in 1702 to bring water into the gardens of Melbourne Hall in Derbyshire, the country seat of Sir Thomas Coke. This system could also be employed to carry water to the grand buildings themselves. In 1664, Sir John Lowther noted that he had recently 'new laid most [of] the lead pipes from the high orchard wall unto the kitchen through' at Lowther Hall in Westmorland. Much earlier, in the 1630s, we likewise find Sir Hugh Cholmley laying underground pipes at Whitby, which aimed to supply the main house, the brew-house, and the washhouse with running water. While the theory behind the use of subterranean pipes was sound enough, occasionally the implementation of the system could run into trouble, leaving aristocrats somewhat befuddled and irritated. 'Since you are pleased to mention my gardens, I will tell you that I was never less pleased with them,' the Earl of Chesterfield, Philip Stanhope, wrote to Thomas Coke in June 1706. He went on to complain that the ponds he had been intending to use for his waterworks at Bretby Hall in Derbyshire had lost all their water. 'These things might be counted disasters to a person who sets up his rest in the country,' the earl scribbled despairingly, 'as much as greater matters to a person who is in the affairs and bustle of the world.'[46]

Even with their regimented layouts and fastidious touches, the country gardens of the English aristocracy continued to champion nature in late Stuart England. Flowers abounded and open, green spaces were welcomed. White violets, daffodils, tansy 'about a finger long', red apricot buds, apple blossoms, and hawthorn leaves 'as broad as a silver twopence' could all be glimpsed in the gardens at Crosby Hall in 1680, while at Wollaton Hall near Nottingham there existed a 'wilderness', a greenhouse, and a physic garden for growing medicinal plants in the 1690s. Tree-lined avenues, usually made up of elms or limes, were popular. Celia Fiennes remembered particularly the 'fine rows of trees running up ye avenue to ye house' when she wrote about her visit to Bretby Hall in the late seventeenth century. The stupendous

Blenheim Palace in Oxfordshire, the country pile of the Dukes of Marlborough, had two main avenues of trees extending to the north and east respectively in the early eighteenth century, which were up to four rows deep and consisted of a staggering 1,600 elms.[47] Although just outside the scope of this book, the tree-lined avenue designed by Charles Bridgeman for Wimpole Hall in Cambridgeshire in the 1720s deserves a mention, if only for its length. Remarkably, the feature arrowed away from the south side of the house for over two miles.

Due to a lack of space in the capital, it would have been quite unthinkable for the gardens of London townhouses to accommodate a two-mile avenue. Nonetheless, these plots were pleasant and enterprising creations in their own right, as is evidenced in contemporary descriptions of the urban gardens Thomas Howard, 14th Earl of Arundel, kept in the early seventeenth century, including that of Arundel House in the Strand. Here were exhibited the renowned Arundel marbles that had been collected by the earl over several years. In 1627, the ancient display was described by the Dutch artist Joachim von Sandrart while touring London with his master, Gerard van Honthorst:

> Foremost amongst the objects worthy to be seen, stood the beautiful garden of that most famous lover of art, the Earl of Arundel; resplendent with the finest ancient statues in marble, of Greek and Roman workmanship. Here were to be seen, firstly, the portrait of a Roman Consul, in long and graceful drapery, through which the form and proportion of the body could be readily perceived. Then there was a statue of Paris; and many others, some full-length, some busts only; with an almost innumerable quantity of heads and reliefs, all in marble and very rare.[48]

Arundel also had a property in Highgate, the nobleman periodically referring to the garden there. On one occasion in 1616, he wrote to his wife, Alethea, to tell her how much he envied the long hours she was able to spend in the place amongst the trees and shrubbery, adding that the new gardener was sure to help her make it 'somewhat handsomer'. We know that the grounds at the very least contained a smaller 'lanppry garden' and pond by October 1616. Decades later in the more excessive 1660s, Samuel Pepys paid a visit to Hackney to see Robert Greville, Lord Brooke, who owned a considerable house in the neighbourhood. Although his reaction to the building was lukewarm, the diarist was struck by the ornateness of the garden, which included a 'great variety' of exotic plants, several 'labarinths', and a 'pretty aviary'.[49]

Possessions

Despite the surveyor Edward Hatton lauding Buckingham House for its extensive and attractive structure, what impressed him most of all about the property was its 'finishing and furniture'. The Stuart aristocracy owned many fine pieces of furniture, from velvet couches lined with silver to eccentric beds painted gold, which were arranged scrupulously in mansions from Devon to Cumberland. In the long wardrobe at Northampton House in London in 1614, there was a 'fair' gold-framed chair, 'richly embossed' with copper, spread eagles, and a pattern of blue and white flowers; a silver-framed, white satin chair 'with a running work of crimson satin'; and a leather couch of silver and gold topped with velvet cushions. These were amongst the priceless possessions of Henry Howard, 1st Earl of Northampton, who died in this year and left a detailed inventory of his goods. In the great dining chamber of Thomas Savage, 1st Viscount Savage's country house in Cheshire, a selection of covered chairs and stools of tawny velvet were on display in the mid-1630s, being similarly noted in a probate inventory. Three decades later in 1663, one could find in the dining room of the Worcestershire esquire Henry Townshend no fewer than twenty-four Turkish chairs and a further eight seats lined with green cloth. The makers and maintainers of such exquisite pieces came from a range of backgrounds and disciplines. A French varnisher was paid accordingly by the future baron and earl, John Hervey, for his work on ten chairs, a couch, and two 'taboretts' (most likely upholstered stools) at Ickworth in Suffolk in 1689. Preferring to opt for cheaper craftspeople picked from the local area, the aristocratic Lowther family in Westmorland hired a 'skilful woman' and her two daughters to make their chairs in the 1660s, who seemed perfectly capable of constructing good quality items. The trio were employed for two years and produced 'all the setwork cushions, and the chairs and stools with the coats of arms; and couch chairs and window cushions; which were all wrought in the house by day'.[50]

Aristocratic tables might be made of wood, marble, or even glass, depending on the latest fashions and tastes. At Bretby Hall in the latter part of the seventeenth century, Celia Fiennes noticed a marble table standing all on its own in the middle of one room. A 'glass table and accompanying stands' were listed in an inventory taken at the baronet Sir John Pakington's Worcestershire property in 1689, which until then had been kept in the 'purple chamber' of the house. Dame Penelope Osborne of London included a simple cedar table as a bequest in her will of 1695. The gentlewoman's vibrant bed made much more of a statement, however, featuring lemon-coloured sarsenet, a lemon-coloured counterpane, and, one can only assume, four lemon-coloured pillows.[51] Rich fabrics and bright colours seemed to dominate the overall appearance of aristocratic beds in this period. Eleanor Wortley, Dowager Countess of Warwick, owned a 'crimson figured satin bed' that was 'trimmed with embroidered buttons and loops' in the late 1650s, at a time – conveniently – when Cromwell's austere rule was finally coming to an end in England. The widowed noblewoman also had in her possession a bed lined with satin, which included a counterpane 'trimmed with gold and silver fringe' and 'a rich gold and silver fringe about the vallins'. In the earliest decades of the Stuart epoch, bold, daring patterns appeared to be the fashion for bedroom furniture, as is clear from the 1614 inventory of the goods of the Earl of Northampton. There can have been few aristocratic beds in Jacobean London to rival that seen at Henry Howard's lodge in the royal park at Greenwich, with its gold-powdered main structure, powdered canopy and valance finished with blue stars and spangles, and quilt of 'popinjay-green sarcenet lined with blue calico, stitched with black silk'. The item in its entirety was valued at £40, roughly equating to £5,400 today. The eight 'pieces of beds of gold' that make an appearance in the famous 1609 inventory of the effects of John, 1st Baron Lumley, were individually thought to be worth somewhere in the region of £25, or £3,375 in today's money.[52]

Religion left a palpable mark on aristocratic furniture in Stuart England. The subject featured conspicuously in the designs of several tables found at Sir Richard Cholmley's Yorkshire mansion in the early 1600s, one of which included a depiction of Christ conquering hell, as it did in the pattern of a headboard located at one of Sir Francis Legh's properties in the 1640s, which showed a gold crucifix. It could also easily be picked out in the 'large and deep' tapestries hung ceremoniously at Northampton House in 1614. In the long gallery, seven of these pieces told the story of Christ through a series of woven images, while in the parlour another fabric described pictorially the biblical tale of Joseph. The 1609 Lumley inventory likewise noted twenty-one 'pieces of hangings' illustrating the heroic story of King Saul and David, along with six more hangings 'of a large ancient making' narrating the Greek myth of Jason and Medea.[53]

The content of aristocratic tapestries varied greatly and could go well beyond the themes of religion and classicism. Eleanor Wortley, Dowager Countess of Warwick, surrounded herself with compelling hangings in the late 1650s, with one set portraying each of the four seasons, another 'a design of flower-potts', and a third a handsome landscape scene complete with pillars, 'of 155¾ Flemish ells'. Elsewhere in her care were two 'suites' of hangings, one of 'blue wrought velvet, fringed with blue', and the other a work of 'crimson figured satin, with silk fringe and gilt nails', both of which could be found in the noblewoman's withdrawing rooms. To be discovered and admired on the floors in the countess's opulent bedrooms were two Chinese carpets finished 'with coloured silks and gold'. Be they for insulation or mere ornamentation, carpets such as these were invariably pleasing to behold in aristocratic houses. The Turkish style in particular was popular in the seventeenth century, with the Earl of Northampton keeping 'a long Turkie carpet of English work' in the dining chamber at Northampton House and another twelve 'small square Turky carpets' at his Greenwich lodge in the 1610s. There were also two large Persian carpets lying in the long wardrobe at Northampton House. The 1st Viscount Savage had filled the dining room at Rocksavage in Cheshire with twenty-four Turkish and nine Persian carpets by 1636, an incomprehensible number that may even have raised the eyebrows of the profligate Henry Howard, had he still been alive. The earl, however, would have been far less impressed with the quantity and quality of Henry Townshend's domestic carpets in the 1660s, which numbered only seven in the Worcestershire esquire's modest dining room and were largely made of 'Kidderminster stuffe'.[54]

Pictures fitted in ornate frames and of various sizes and subjects featured prominently. Referring to the many picture galleries contained in noble and gentle mansions in his lifetime, the seventeenth-century writer William Waller reflected, 'Here, without taking the pains to go abroad I can go abroad within doores, and in a small table see, a whole country, diversified with hills, and dales, with boscage, campagnes, cities, rivers, seas, all so perfectly represented.' Winking frames and their subjects could be glimpsed all over a Stuart aristocrat's home. In the early seventeenth century, Sir Richard Cholmley's dining parlour in Yorkshire was at one time decorated with both a 'picture of death upon canvas' and Man 'fighting against his mortal enemies', together with a portrait of James I on horseback. In the great parlour at Northwick Park in Worcestershire, in the early eighteenth century, the figures of Charles II, William III, Queen Mary, and the Duke of Gloucester silently watched the baronet Sir James Rushout and his family from their elevated positions on the walls. An inventory compiled in 1711 at Northwick Park allows more of Sir James Rushout's pictures to be known. These included one picture of a 'naked woman and a man', one 'small peece of an old man and woman', one landscape of 'a horse and figures', and one 'peece of a Dutch faire'. A combination of untold wealth and loyalty to the Tudor dynasty led to a comely portrait of Elizabeth I encrusted with rubies and diamonds being hung at Northampton House in the reign of her Scottish successor, James I. Here, too, were exhibited the resplendent likenesses of dukes, earls, duchesses, and countesses in the little gallery, with similar paintings, in addition to a selection of religious depictions, housed in the long gallery. The theme of piety continued in the long wardrobe, in the form of framed pictures of the Virgin Mary, the Three Magi, and Jesus being taken down from the cross.[55]

Over the course of the seventeenth century, it became distinctly fashionable for English aristocrats of every means to identify themselves as either amateur or serious art collectors. Twenty-three pictures of various provenances adorned the staircase alone at Westwood House in Worcestershire in 1689, the baronet Sir John Pakington's agreeable country seat. Such a figure pales into insignificance, however, when compared with the unbelievable art collection held by Thomas Howard, 14th Earl of Arundel, upon his death in Italy in October 1646. By this time, the well-travelled courtier and envoy had acquired hundreds of pieces of artwork from across the continent, including paintings by some of the most famous European artists of the day.[56] Works by Hans Holbein, Anthony van Dyck, Isaac Oliver, Paolo Fiammingo, Paolo Veronese, Michelangelo, and Raphael were all listed in an inventory drawn up in Amsterdam in 1655.

The busy schedule of Stuart aristocrats, both at and away from home, rendered timekeeping an essential part of everyday life. Pendulum clocks first appeared in English aristocratic houses in the second half of the seventeenth century, following the creative breakthrough in 1656 of the Dutch mathematician Christiaan Huygens. Sir Daniel Fleming noted the exact day his new pendulum clock and its accompanying case were set up at Rydal Hall in Westmorland in 1696, which he obviously considered to be an important moment in the life of the house. When Sir John Pakington died some years earlier in the late 1680s, a similar clock was already in place on the main staircase at Westwood House in Worcestershire, positioned somewhere amongst the twenty-three pictures that also occupied the wall space there. Pendulum clocks had become commonplace in England by the reign of Queen Anne, and indeed we can observe Dame Johanna St John freely giving away her own mechanical contraption in Battersea in her will, dated 1704. Despite this, decorative table clocks and watches that had existed before Huygen's groundbreaking invention continued to be valued and used by the Stuart aristocracy in the later years of our period, proving that reliability was not everything. The Duchess of Richmond swiftly notified *The London Gazette* when her gold watch went missing in the privy garden at Whitehall in November 1685. It reportedly had 'a shagreen case studded with gold studs', which hung from 'a little wire chain with three steel loops', the loops in turn holding 'a scale of gold enamelled, with an onyx cut in the figure of a man, and a tree behind him'.[57] According to the *Gazette*, a reward of three guineas was to be given to anybody who returned the item to the duchess's porter.

Weaponry that had either seen active service or was purely for display could be found in aristocratic properties at this time, usually in the armoury if a house was equipped with one. The adventurer Sir John Bolle kept a French pistol and a 'gilt sword and dagger' at Thorpe Hall in Lincolnshire at the turn of the seventeenth century, which were no doubt relics of his military exploits in Spain and Ireland. So, too, Sir Richard Cholmley's personal belongings included a suit of armour and a spear in Yorkshire in 1613, the armour comprising 'a helmet with earlapps, a gorgett, a breastplate with bases or tases, a backplate with shoulder pieces and arms'. The soldierly items stored in the armoury at Rocksavage in Cheshire appeared a little neglected when an inventory was taken there in the wake of the passing of Viscount Savage in the mid-1630s. Amongst the few articles present were 'some armours but out of fashion', several nondescript halberds, and a selection of 'other trifling lumber' that was not considered worthy of further description.[58]

There were plenty of other small objects in Stuart mansions, many of which were used as part of an aristocrat's habitual routines. One might come across ink bottles, brushes, a pair of tongs, a little trunk, a 'great broken seeing glass', an oak box with a lid, a little glass bottle, a stone pot for honey, and a pewter ewer and basin at Sir Richard Cholmley's northern seat in 1620. At Dame Alicia Greaves's house in Middlesex, a 'red pink coloured pincushion box embossed with silver' was in use by the gentlewoman in the 1680s; nearby at the abode of Dame Penelope Osborne in 1695, a 'black hood-box lined with pink coloured sarsenet' and a bible with silver clasps could be found.[59] Two chamber pots were received by the Earl and Countess of Bath at their urban property in March 1651, while in 1629 the esquire Arthur Coke's everyday possessions at Bramfield included a leather saddle for 'a great horse', which had been left in the hall, a 'box with beads on a string with a crucifix and a bull', candlesticks, a pair of scales, a pewter vinegar bottle, a case of knives kept in Elizabeth Coke's closet, a hawking bag, a bag of frankincense, six long towels stored in the parlour chamber closet, a black gilt box, and two badger skins.

Family silver that tended to be passed from one generation to the next was, with good reason, left alone in aristocratic houses for the most part, being kept locked in cupboards or strictly acting as ornamental pieces. Henry Howard, 1st Earl of Northampton's enviable collection in the heart of Jacobean London consisted of both silver and gilt treasures, for instance four gilt fruit dishes, fourteen gilt standing cups and covers, two gilt basins and matching ewers, four silver platters and six silver dishes. Sir John Pakington was similarly fortunate, holding at Westwood House in the 1680s two silver basins, four pairs of silver candlesticks, one silver cup and cover, eighteen silver spoons, sixteen silver forks, and twelve silver knives. The London will of Dame Penelope Osborne listed a wide and eclectic selection of silver articles that were in her possession in 1695: a 'great pair of silver candlesticks', a 'silver scallop drinking cup', an ash-coloured 'serpentine cup' with a 'flat silver cover' emblazoned with the Osborne coat of arms, a brown serpentine cup 'tipped with silver', and a 'silver scallop candlestick with a walnut stand to it'.[60] Much more curious than this, however, was Dame Johanna St John's valuable collection across the way in Battersea, which included, of all things, a silver chamber pot.

4

SERVANTS

The smooth running of aristocratic households in Stuart England would have been quite impossible without the assistance of dedicated teams of domestic staff. George Savile, 1st Marquess of Halifax, advised his daughter in 1688 that servants 'are the wheels of your family', which if 'stopped or moved wrong' could result in the catastrophic unravelling of 'the whole order of your house'. The future baronet Sir Henry Belasyse had fifty-one servants at Newburgh Priory in Yorkshire in 1609, the majority of whom were male. In 1633, Lord William Howard of Naworth Castle employed a grand total of seventy-eight servants, including a brewer, a cook, a smith, a coachman, a housekeeper in London, a butcher, a warrener, an upholsterer, a baker, a gardener, and a porter. Seven years later his staff had increased to eighty-three, to include fifty-nine male servants and twenty-four female. In the last four decades of the seventeenth century, the 5th Earl of Bedford's staff list remained consistently long, with £600 of the nobleman's income spent on wages in 1664. By the 1690s, this figure, already considerable, had risen to £700 annually as a result of the steady increase in the salaries of the earl's longest serving attendants. To remunerate his own servants, Sir Henry Slingsby of Red House parted with a similar sum of money each year in the

1630s, which he believed to be a significant expense. 'Our charge is much every year alone certainly,' he recorded in 1638, 'being well accommodated with good faithful diligent servants, so that at least I spend every year in housekeeping £500.'[1]

Servant hierarchies

At the top of the servant pyramid in most Stuart aristocratic households was the steward, who might expect a salary of £20 to £40 per year.[2] A steward's principal duties lay in the management of the rest of the indoor staff, though not always female servants, and the coordination of day-to-day activities around the house. He was often considered indispensable to his employers and could be well respected by them consequently, as in the case of Robert Spiller, steward to the Dowager Countess of Arundel, who died in 1615 after forty years of dedicated service. This man was of 'more than ordinary virtue and piety', according to a contemporary description, who expertly managed his mistress's estates and 'enabled her to overcome the burden of her debts' in the early seventeenth century. Sir Richard Cholmley's steward, William Leyfe, was noted to have 'kept court' at the esquire's properties of Brafferton and Brandsby in 1615, which clearly came with a fair amount of responsibility. At Lyme Hall in Cheshire, the steward to the privileged Legh family found himself in charge of various tasks in 1607 that one might class as essential, amongst them keeping the household accounts, paying staff wages when they were due, and riding to nearby market towns every once in a while to buy and sell goods on behalf of his master.[3] Successive stewards employed by the Leghs continued with these assignments throughout the 1600s.

Butlers at this time did not enjoy the unrivalled supremacy that would come to them in later epochs. They seemed more akin to the Victorian or Edwardian valet in Stuart England, being the servants responsible for shaving the master of the household on a daily basis and, latterly, dressing his wigs. 'As to a butler,' John Verney, 1st Viscount Fermanagh, wrote in January 1707, 'I would have a sightly fellow and one that has had the smallpox, and an honest man (for he is entrusted with store of plate) [who] can shave.' Sir John Chicheley's own opinion on the qualities that made a decent butler differed somewhat in the 1680s, for he believed that first and foremost the post-holder should be an able musician, preferably with the ability to play both the violin and the harpsichord.[4] Whether this particular domestic worker had an ear for music or not, what can be said with confidence is that he was oftentimes well paid for his efforts in attending the lord of the manor. The butler to William Wentworth, 2nd Earl of Strafford, had pocketed close to £900 from his employer upon his demise in 1669, a sum that was large enough to come to the attention of other members of the aristocracy and be commented upon, including by the Member of Parliament Sir John Reresby.

The role played by footmen was largely ceremonial in sixteenth-century England, their job being to walk or run alongside aristocratic family members when the latter embarked on journeys in coaches or on horseback. They might also deliver messages and carry gifts to relatives and friends of the people they served when required to do so. In the seventeenth century, this core function remained in many households. It was, for instance, one of Lady Anne Clifford's obedient footmen who first broke the news to his mistress of her mother's death in May 1616, having travelled direct from Brougham Castle in Westmorland with the information.[5] When the enigmatic knight 'Sir J S' made it known in May 1628 that he was looking for a new footman, one was found for him by an acquaintance in London who apparently fitted the bill because 'he hath a running head as well as running heels'. The acquaintance in question, James Howell, elaborated:

> There be some things in him that answer for his waggeries; he will come when you call him, go when you bid him, and shut the door after him; he is faithful and stout, and a lover of his master. He is a great enemy to all dogs, if they bark at him in his running, for I have seen him confront a huge mastiff, and knock him down. When you go a country journey, or have him run with you a-hunting, you must spirit him with liquor.[6]

Even in the second half of the century such male servants were frequently expected to use their proven stamina and speed to good effect. Those footmen who worked for the 5th Earl of Bedford at Woburn across the Restoration years spent much of their time accompanying the Russell family on trips around the country, or running messages and presents to neighbouring members of the aristocracy. Increasingly, however, they were also relied on as practical attendants within Woburn Abbey itself, particularly to wait at tables during grand dinner parties. This was a marked change in the purpose of footmen witnessed almost universally in the final decades of Stuart England, bringing with it a predictable need to increase numbers.[7] The 5th Earl of Bedford employed as many as twelve footmen in the 1660s, who were paid between £2 and £6 annually for their expanded duties in rural Bedfordshire and elsewhere, depending on each man's rank, ability, and general level of experience.[8] Pages were kept in reserve by the earl as well, but unlike their liveried counterparts, these young boys received no remuneration for work undertaken beyond basic bed and board.

Housekeepers who were invested with control over the female staff of a noble or gentle household were on the rise in England from the Restoration period onwards. Before this ascendancy, and occasionally after it, they could be found working for affluent bachelors or widowers in less influential roles. The politician Sir John Bramston of Skreens in Essex hired his eldest daughter Abigail for a housekeeper in the mid-seventeenth century, having lost his wife Alice prematurely in 1647. 'She began to be my housekeeper when she was very young; loved a liberal table whilst I continued at Skreens, but was never prodigal nor wasteful; when I removed to Greek Street, she proportioned my expense to my family,' Bramston reflected in his autobiography towards the end of his long life. Abigail's specific responsibilities included putting her father to bed at night, seeing him out of it again in the morning, and feeding him at regular intervals throughout the day. She died in London before Sir John in 1694, after which the aged widower 'took resolution to quit my house in Greek Street, and return to my house, Skreens, in Roxwell, in Essex, where my son, his wife and family, had resided all the time I was absent'. The growing number of female servants employed in the houses of the aristocracy can account for the increased authority of the housekeeper in the late 1600s. On top of her substantial needlework obligations, there were up to eight women at any one time in need of management by the housekeeper Ann Upton at Woburn Abbey, in the years leading up to 1700. For this she might have expected an annual wage of around £10, which was £10 short of the lowest salary received by her male equivalent, the steward.[9]

The women who would eventually report to the likes of Mrs Upton at Woburn consisted mainly of low-ranking maidservants, including laundry maids, chambermaids, lady's maids, and even dairy maids – or, as they were referred to at Naworth Castle in the 1640s, dairy 'wenches'. Nicholas Blundell Esq. kept a chambermaid at Crosby Hall in the early eighteenth century called Mary Barton, whom he described positively as 'a brisk mettled workwoman' and 'a neat cleanly lass'. Certainly, it was anticipated that maids entering service would be able to clean, sew, and wash as a bare minimum. Integrity and good manners, however, were also sought-after characteristics. When Blundell's relative, Winifred, picked out a suitable maidservant for her unnamed friend in 1666, she commended the candidate for 'her honest civil behaviour, having never heard her taxed with anything to the contrary by anyone, and few of that number are to be found... I never saw anyone make more good resolutions of doing well than she does.' The maids labouring in the various households of Lady Anne Clifford throughout her colourful life were required to act as intermittent companions and confidantes to their mistress, in addition to being proficient in washing, cleaning, sewing, and displays of civility. When Anne's first husband Richard Sackville fell gravely sick in March 1617, the countess spent an entire day walking the grounds at Knole in Kent with Judith Simpson, one of her laundry maids, 'carrying my Bible with me [and] thinking on my present fortunes and what troubles I have passed through'.[10]

Aristocratic kitchens were for the most part the domain of men in Stuart England. Overseeing the day-to-day running of this busy environment was usually the clerk of the kitchen, who had beneath him at least one male cook. The qualities looked for in a cook by the aristocracy varied considerably in the seventeenth century, with experience in the preparation of foreign cuisine seeming to be especially valued. In 1653, one of the first assignments given by Sir Ralph Verney to his new, inexperienced cook was learning how to bake French bread in 'the brass baking pans' kept at Middle Claydon; around the same time, the knight sent a 'very little footboy' off to Blois in France to master the art of French pastry-making.[11] Some years earlier in June 1630, James Howell wrote to a great lady to inform her that a worthy cook had been found for her kitchens, who could

> ... marinate fish, make jellies; he is excellent for a piquant sauce, and the 'Haugou'; besides, Madam, he is passing good for an 'Ollia': He will tell your ladyship, that the reverend matron the 'Olla podrida' hath intellectuals and senses; mutton, beef, and bacon, are to her as the will, understanding, and memory, are to the soul: cabbage, turnips, artichokes, potatoes, and dates, are her five senses, and pepper the common-sense; she must have marrow to keep life in her, and some birds to make her light; by all means she must go adorn'd with chains of sausages. He is also good at larding of meat after the mode of France.[12]

Not all aristocrats were so particular. Sir Henry Slingsby of Red House did not care much if a cook was creative with his trade in the 1630s, except 'when we have a meeting of friends, and then only to comply with ye fashions of ye times, to shew myself answerable to what is expected, and not out of any love unto excessive feasting'. What most Stuart aristocrats did acknowledge was the importance of the servant or servants who fed them. When Sir Ralph Verney's cook, 'honest' Michael Durant, died in 1671, he left a noticeable void in the lives of his employers. 'Such was his fame,' a family member observed, 'that no wedding breakfast, or funeral supper, or Christmas feast in the neighbourhood was felt to be adequate without his supervision.'[13]

To help them in their culinary exploits, the cooks employed by the aristocracy had a variety of implements at their disposal. In the mid-1630s in the well-equipped kitchens of the Staffordshire pile of Lettice Knollys, Countess of Essex and Leicester, there could be found a copper pan, a brass pan, three lesser pans, four dripping pans, five brass pots, two iron pots, two posnets, a pair of iron racks, three frying pans, two ladles, three pairs of pot hooks, a mortar and pestle made of brass, three 'beef forks', two mincing knives, one cleaver, one grater, four trays, one fire fork, a pair of tongs, and one colander.[14] Making use of such items, along with the cook or cooks, would be the essential but ultimately lowly kitchen support staff. At Woburn Abbey in the 1660s, the cook was apparently assisted by 'a heterogeneous collection of scullions and turnspits', who were paid as little as ten shillings a year for their hot and heavy work. Locals would be temporarily employed on those common occasions when extra support was required. In 1612, a 'poor woman' came briefly to Thornthwaite Hall in Cumberland, a hunting lodge acquired by Lord William Howard in the early seventeenth century, to help out in the kitchens there, receiving for her labour just a few pence. Ten years later, the nobleman hired another destitute female to work in the kitchens at neighbouring Naworth Castle, who was this time paid seven shillings for a six-week stint. It can be said with a fair degree of certainty that Howard was not a bad employer to his various kitchen hands, irrespective of their low-ranking status. One nameless 'kitchen boy' based at Naworth, for instance, was given his own knife and a brand-new pair of shoes to wear around the estate in 1614.[15]

While most readily associated with medieval and Tudor England, jesters or fools could still be found in seventeenth-century aristocratic households. One such was Alethea Howard, the Countess of Arundel's personal jester. She had him included in a painting of herself completed by Peter Paul Rubens in 1620, along with a dwarf called Robin. The wife of Sir John Oglander, Frances

More, appointed her own fool for the purposes of amusement in 1628, keeping him mainly on the Isle of Wight. 'He was a poor, lame, decrepit fellow, one Stockwell, a gunner's son,' Oglander recalled, 'but of a bold spirit and excellent wit. My wife, having compassion on him, took him into the house and made of him a kind of jester.' Even as late as the 1690s, references were being made to such comedic servants, although they were not always positive in nature. The Herveys of Ickworth House in Suffolk employed a fool of sorts named 'Welch Tom' in this final decade of the seventeenth century, who, however admirable his enthusiasm, seems to have gotten on the wrong side of Lady Hervey more than once. 'That monster Welch Tom... I hate him now more than ever for being so happy while I am so miserable,' the peeved gentlewoman wrote to her husband, John Hervey, in April 1698.[16]

Outside and away from the toil of the house laboured the aristocracy's garden staff. Weeding and other mundane tasks were reserved for casual workers, both male and female, leaving professional gardeners to tend to the plants. The role of a gardener could without question be tough, and it is no wonder when one considers the size and scale of many of the idyllic gardens the Stuart aristocracy created for their great properties. When Sir Henry Slingsby's chief gardener, Peter Clark, died in 1640 after fourteen years' exemplary service in Yorkshire, his master thought he knew what had ultimately caused his demise. 'He was for no curiosity in gardening, but exceeding laborious in grafting, setting, and sowing,' Slingsby wrote, 'which extreme labour shortened his days.' A gardener needed more than staying power and reasonable determination, however. One man was thought suitable for employment in Sir Ralph Verney's gardens at Claydon House in 1656 because he seemed to be the 'most eminent of any about, for neat houses, melons, asparagus and cauliflower, and all other ordinary things'. In keeping a tidy and plentiful garden, which constituted a highly visible segment of a Stuart aristocrat's overall estate, gardeners could gain the respect and even admiration of their employers. Other outdoor labourers might similarly earn approbation, with subsequent appreciation for their contributions being expressed in curious ways. The avid traveller and commentator Celia Fiennes was most surprised in the late seventeenth century to come across a memorial statue of an 'old weeder woman' in the cherry garden at Woburn Abbey, which was 'done so like and her clothes so well that at first I took it to be a real living body'.[17]

In an aristocratic house where being careful with money was the norm, one might find servants juggling several roles at once. There is no better example of this economical set-up than that in place at Crosby Hall in the early eighteenth century, the northern home of the esquire Nicholas Blundell and his family. In August 1702, the year of Queen Anne's accession, the sad death of William Arnold was commented on in the daily journal Blundell kept, who had been an employee at Crosby since childhood and had assumed the positions of groom, coachman, and butcher. Evidently, Nicholas believed such an arrangement worked well in his household, for when he hired a new groom in September, a man by the name of Henry Bilsbury, the servant was soon taking the coach out and butchering as part of his duties as well. Female staff could expect a similarly varied array of responsibilities on a day-to-day basis if they came to work for the thrifty Blundells. Ann Johnson, for instance, was officially the resident cook when she left Crosby Hall in December 1708, but according to Nicholas upon her departure, 'for some little time she has been employed in other work.'[18]

Going about their business alongside the assorted gardeners, weeders, maids, cooks, kitchen hands, butlers, housekeepers, and stewards of an aristocratic household in Stuart England were artisans and other individuals with specific skills outside the remit of standard domestic servants. Roger Manners, 5th Earl of Rutland, parted with forty shillings a year to keep a regular rat-catcher at Belvoir Castle in Leicestershire in the 1610s, while another £4 10 shillings was spent on a full-time cooper in the same period, 'for which he is to keep in good repair all vessels belonging to the brewhouse, buttery, and laundry'. Sir Richard and Dame Lucy Reynell of Forde House in Devon also considered it good practice to have experienced rat- and mole-catchers on hand in the early seventeenth century, together with carpenters, glaziers, chimney sweeps, masons, blacksmiths, and butchers, some of whom may have been employed by the couple part-time. If an aristocratic house had an armoury, then an armourer might call in from time to time to clean and service the contents. Henry Bourchier, 5th Earl of Bath, seems to have had a full-time armourer to 'cleanse' his collection of weapons and military artefacts in London in the 1640s, who was paid £6 for his services over two years.[19]

Foreign servants

The majority of servants working for the aristocracy in Stuart England were of course white and English, being sourced from the areas local to the country mansions and London townhouses. Sometimes, however, this was not the case. *The London Gazette* announced that a Welsh boy named Edward Evans had run away from the Sussex stables of Charles Seymour, 6th Duke of Somerset, in November 1687, describing him as a 'thin, lean' child who was approximately fifteen years old.[20] So, too, as we have already seen, there was both a Welsh and a French nursery maid employed at Bedford House in London in the 1680s. Of all the countries across mainland Europe, nationals from France were by far the most likely to be serving in an English aristocratic household. In 1613, a French boy known only as Lowry was included in Richard Sackville, 3rd of Earl of Dorset's extensive staff list, although his precise occupation was not revealed. Some sixteen years later in rural Yorkshire, the future baronet Sir Hugh Cholmley chose a Frenchwoman to 'wait on my little girl Betty' over the winter months, who died soon afterwards at Fyling Hall in Whitby under mysterious circumstances. When the parliamentarian Sir Edward Harley found himself without a gardener at Brampton Bryan in May 1688, he wrote to an intimate to divulge that 'there is a poor Frenchman that is very much recommended to me.'[21]

The London Gazette eagerly reported on another domestic deserter in 1677, from the house of the esquire Paul Nicol in Middlesex, but he was neither white nor Welsh. The offender, in fact, was described as 'a negro named Robert Moore, about 18 years of age, of middle stature, in livery of fawn-coloured cloth edged and lined with crimson bayes'.[22] Black servants were more common than might be anticipated in the exclusive households of the Stuart elite, often selected for their novelty factor and perceived exotic looks. The French boy Lowry was joined by at least two 'blackamoors' in the service of the 3rd Earl of Dorset in Jacobean England, one a laundry maid called Grace Robinson, the other a kitchen hand by the name of John Morockoe, which made for an unusually diverse array of staff members. As far as the surviving evidence tells us, black servants could expect to be treated just as well as their white peers. Sir John Reresby proudly stated that he had acquired a 'fine moor about sixteen years of age' during the Restoration era, who had originally come from Barbados and was given to him, almost like a Christmas present, by an obscure gentleman known as Mr Drax. The young servant died in 1676 as a result of an 'imposthume in his head', leading some to speculate darkly in London that Reresby had played a part in the Barbadian's unexpected passing. 'It was credibly reported there that I had caused him to suffer an operation, which had occasioned his death,' the baronet recollected in his memoirs. 'I laughed at it at the first, knowing it to be false, as a ridiculous story.' To settle the matter, Reresby arranged for a coroner and jury to examine the body before it was 'too much decayed', which brought back a resounding verdict that the unfortunate man had died 'by the hand of God'.[23]

Liveries

Whereas strict uniforms for all members of staff in the employment of the English aristocracy would arrive in later centuries, in Stuart England there was a singular concern for the physical appearance of servants who were most likely to be seen by other people. It was the footmen, pages, and postilions (of which more later), therefore, who required appropriate costumes during the seventeenth and early eighteenth centuries.[24] Each aristocratic household tended to have its own peculiar livery for attendants to wear while on duty, intended to be instantly recognisable to external parties and act as an emblem of the associated family. A close relation of Thomas Coke of Melbourne Hall in Derbyshire wrote to tell him in August 1696:

> Jack Gardiner was seen ushering two galloping ladies into a wood near Rochester, humble servants of his own I guess; for I believe if they had belonged to any of your company, they would have been so civil as to have provided them some better accommodation than only one servant, and that in your livery, which is so easily known at a distance too.[25]

The footmen in the service of the baronet and politician Sir William Whitmore wore 'green livery cloth suits lined with yellow [and] laced with gold and silver lace' in the later seventeenth century at the Whitmore seat of Apley Hall in Shropshire. Around the same period, the attendants waiting on Charles Seymour, 6th Duke of Somerset, including the Welsh page who would dramatically flee the nobleman's stables, sported a 'grey livery lined with yellow, with a black and yellow chain in the seams, long pockets, and pewter buttons'.[26] If a special occasion was on the horizon or an aristocrat was intending to go abroad for a while, servant outfits might be updated or replaced to ensure that they stood out in a crowd. Before crossing the Channel to visit France in July 1699, Sir Richard Newdigate of Arbury Hall in Warwickshire thought it best to first spend a large sum of money on new uniforms for his footmen, Jack Royl and Harry Haines, which comprised two 'stuff coats' and two pairs of breeches 'faced with black and strong black buttons'.[27]

So important was the overall look of footmen and pages to the Stuart aristocracy that they were even known to provide this class of servant with fashionable accessories and equipment for grooming and keeping clean. 'Tom the footboy', who worked at

Naworth Castle for the Howard family, was given a sword belt, a feather for a hat, boots, shoes, and stockings in 1653. This was nothing, however, compared to the relentless titivating the household pages were forced to endure at Woburn Abbey several decades later.[28] Some were given combs with which to keep their hair tidy, others were provided with hats and cases to put them in, and yet more had their hair regularly cut or even shaved off entirely to accommodate the increasingly popular periwig.

Servants misbehaving

Generally speaking, Stuart aristocrats were taught from an early age that servants should be treated decently and with respect by those who employed them. George Savile, 1st Marquess of Halifax, was a great advocate of this line of thinking, advising his daughter Elizabeth in 1688 that 'servants may be looked upon as humble friends ... returns of kindness and good usage are as much due to such of them as deserve it, as their service is due to us when we require it.' He went on to warn against 'a foolish haughtiness in the style of speaking' to one's staff and finished by telling Elizabeth not to be 'too hasty in giving your orders, nor too angry when they are not altogether observed'. Others echoed Savile's sentiments. At the funeral of John Wilmot, 2nd Earl of Rochester, in 1680, who had died from complications of venereal disease, the sermon included an emotional anecdote concerning the nobleman's final hours, and the warmth he had shown his servants even at death's door. 'How tender and concern'd was he for his servants about him in his extremities,' the preacher relayed, 'pitying their troubles in watching with him, and attending him, treating them with candor and kindness, as if they had been his intimates.' When the eldest daughter of the Duke of Newcastle, Lady Jane Cavendish, passed away eleven years earlier in 1669, her funeral sermon also praised the tender-hearted way she had treated her attendants in life, who all purportedly believed that she was 'the best of mistresses'.[29]

Relations between Stuart aristocrats and their employees could sour. The misbehaviour of servants might take many forms in this period, ranging from the trivial to the downright absurd and dangerous. Like the Welsh boy Edward Evans, domestics deciding to take off without prior warning was one such misdeed with which the aristocracy had to deal. A maid working for Sir Richard Newdigate did just this in the second half of the 1600s, although the gentleman was thankful that she 'stole nothing, only is, and was formerly, distracted'. *The London Gazette*, ever willing to assist its influential readership in their hour of need, included a section on a Scottish 'running' footman employed by Henry Howard, 7th Duke of Norfolk, in April 1689, who had disappeared from his master's house in the capital and taken with him three silver plates and an engraved candlestick. Servant thievery, of course, was another significant problem, with valuable goods stored in almost every corner of aristocratic properties. The temptation to pilfer was simply too great for many who had come from nothing. Edmund Verney complained in a letter written in the 1660s that his 'little boy', Thomas Warner, was guilty of 'more faults than this sheet will contain, picking pockets, opening boxes that were locked, picking locks, stealing, lying'.[30]

Servant drunkenness was all too common and seemed to appal the aristocracy perhaps more than any other wrongdoing. The inebriated antics of Sir Humphrey Mildmay's servants late in the reign of Charles I left the master of Danbury Place wholly exasperated. The serving men in question ruined a wedding feast on one occasion because of their wilful inability to control their alcohol consumption, even when the reputation of the family was at stake, and according to Mildmay it was usual to find them drunk and disorderly most other days.[31] A servant might be a capable worker around the house and perform reasonably well, but if alcohol misuse became an issue it could quickly tarnish their abilities in the eyes of their employers. Thus, Sir Richard Newdigate of Arbury Hall rated his cook William Wheeler 'good if less given to drink'. Newdigate would have found it rather more difficult to say the same of one man employed by the 1st Viscount Fermanagh and Elizabeth Verney at Claydon House in Buckinghamshire. Elizabeth was utterly bewildered by this particular servant's erratic behaviour. 'The keeper is such a dreadful fellow that for my part I can't imagine what the maids will do with him,' Elizabeth wrote to the viscount in December 1710. Here was another employee who enjoyed a tipple or ten, with Lady Fermanagh reporting in her letter that the keeper had recently spent three hours in the cellar drinking inordinate amounts of small beer. In an attempt to deny him any further access to Claydon's store of alcohol, Elizabeth had ordered the cook to lock the cellar door, but this appears to have made matters worse. As an act of revenge for his banishment, the keeper had proceeded to nail shut the doors leading to the larders and the cook's own chamber. 'Indeed you never saw so strange a fellow in your life,' the perplexed mistress finished.[32]

Violent or abusive servants, and violence between servants, was another problem. These intermittent instances had the capacity to cause such drama that they might become topics of aristocratic hearsay, as was the case in July 1673 when the soon-to-be baronet of Lamport, the teenage Thomas Isham, received intelligence of 'a wicked and nefarious crime' committed by a servant of Sir Edward Boughton in Warwickshire.[33] Isham noted that the felon in question was an unspecified groom of no great consequence, who had fallen out with Boughton's butler, Clerk, over which man should open the gate for his master when Sir Edward decided to take the air in his carriage one day. Clerk won the argument and took charge of the gate, but the heated encounter had him so incensed that he decided to report the groom to Boughton, who was reprimanded at once for his conduct. This move on the part of the butler, the groom concluded, was unforgivable. 'Clerk has told, and I will take my revenge on him,' he is said to have uttered chillingly. A while later, the quarrelling servants embarked on a riding expedition together in the Warwickshire countryside, possibly alone, during which the groom took his chance to strike back. Drawing a sword and facing his opponent, he stabbed Clerk and killed him instantly.

An equally vicious disagreement broke out between two of Sir Peter Legh's servants at Lyme Hall in Cheshire in 1611, the outcome of which was another violent death.[34] Remarkably, the figure charged with the murder was Legh's steward and most senior attendant, Edward Thorniley. The unhappy episode began in the kitchens at Lyme one unexceptional afternoon, when a fellow servant named Ratcliffe burst into the room unannounced and accused Thorniley of going through his things without his permission. The aggrieved man insisted that the steward follow him to his chamber, where he might see for himself the disarray he had caused. Once there, however, it became clear that Thorniley had been lured from the kitchens and his midday meal under false pretences. The real cause of Ratcliffe's ire was different. Drawing a weapon, he bellowed, 'This sword shall cut thy flesh and this rapier shall run thee through, for thou hast told thy master I have stolen twenty staves.' Thorniley denied ever doing such a thing, but even so he armed himself with 'a staffe about two yards and a quarter long with two blunt pikes in' when he set off from the house later that day to run an errand for Sir Peter. Ratcliffe made after him, as Thorniley suspected he would, and the pair engaged in combat, resulting in the slaying of the former by the latter.

The aristocracy's response to servant misbehaviour was probably viewed as unkind by some and totally fair by others. Sir Richard Newdigate took to fining his employees in the seventeenth century whenever they stepped out of line, an approach he evidently believed would help to prevent repeat offences. His cook, for example, was deprived of ten shillings after being discovered 'dead drunk' one day, while another servant at Arbury Hall was fined two shillings 'for pride and slighting'. Sacking the wrongdoer was an obvious option. A servant of Sir Humphrey Mildmay referred to colourfully as 'Saucy Ralph' found himself out on his ear in the late 1630s, for reasons that do not require a great deal of imagination; he was closely followed by two more members of Mildmay's staff, who were fired by their master on account of being 'drunkards and rascals'. Then there were the violent forms of discipline that no servant would have much fancied. The Verney family appeared particularly keen to exercise corporal punishment on their domestics, although it was certainly in regular use elsewhere in Stuart England. The 'little boy' caught stealing by Edmund Verney in the 1660s, for instance, was whipped for his delinquency. In 1699, Sir John Verney's 'footboy', Perry, managed to avoid the wrath of his employer after he disappeared for several hours one morning, but only because the aged man 'had not the strength to beat him'.[35]

Sometimes Stuart aristocrats behaved unkindly towards their servants for less understandable reasons. Often this manifested in unpleasant comments made behind an employee's back that focused on their inadequacies, however slight or impossible to change they might be. Edmund Verney was one such aristocrat who was inclined to speak disrespectfully about his servants over the course of his life, at one time describing a senior woman called Nurse Curzon as 'old, crazy and decayed', who 'hath more need to have one to look to her, than to look after others'. On another occasion he ridiculed the literacy of a footman in his employment, stating, 'It is as impossible to make the man a better scribe as to wash a blackamoor white.' The wife of the baron John Hervey, Lady Elizabeth, could be just as cutting about her own servants in the early eighteenth century. She branded the couple's London porter a 'stupid creature' for letting a guest into the house without her express permission, and when recounting to her husband how the family nurse had offered her a drink in the middle of the night to help her sleep, she remarked derisively, 'Poor soul, as if her slops could have been any comfort.'[36]

Kindness and loyalty

Some members of the Stuart aristocracy, conversely, were unusually caring towards their servants, going far beyond what was advocated by the 1st Marquess of Halifax in the 1680s. The moment Mary Rich, Countess of Warwick, learned that her husband's carter was dangerously unwell in April 1668, she provided him with every remedy she could think of to bring about his recovery. Discovering that the servant was no better in the morning, the countess then called upon the services of her own doctor and organised for the man to be publicly prayed for in church that day. Despite these various interventions, the faithful carter's death was declared inevitable, which encouraged Mary to instruct some of the remaining servants 'to make their peace with God, for fear they should be so suddenly taken away'. Even Sir Humphrey Mildmay, who sacked three of his employees in quick succession, had the capacity to be uncommonly good-natured given the right circumstances. In March 1640, he decided to keep on his Irish footman, Tegg, after it was revealed that the servant was expecting a child out of wedlock with a woman called Margett, and furthermore paid him six months' wages to 'receive his bastard'.[37]

One of the most generous things an aristocrat could do for a servant was to leave a sum of money for them in their will. The baronet Sir William Cowper's uncle, also William Cowper, ensured that each staff member in his employment was well provided for in London in 1697. A bequest of £10 was to go to the person 'that waits on me in my chamber', the 'gentlewoman who is my housekeeper at the day of my death' was to receive £50 and 'all my points and laces whatsoever and all sorts of my wearing linen whatsoever', and the footman and cook were to be given £5 each.[38]

More generous still, however, and a testament to the perceived value of those who worked in service in Stuart England, was when a master put himself in harm's way to protect or even rescue a stricken servant. The Anglo-Welsh Edward Herbert, eventually 1st Baron Herbert of Cherbury, risked his own life in 1614 to save an attendant who had been caught in a fast-moving current near Usk, Monmouthshire, a short distance from Herbert's seat of Montgomery Castle. The servant's name was Richard Griffiths. 'Dick Griffiths is drowning!' some other servants were said to have yelled as their friend was violently swept down the river and out of sight. At this cry for help, Edward Herbert moved quickly and decisively. 'I put my spurs to my horse, and coming up to the place, where I saw him as high as his middle in water, leapt into the river a little below him. Swimming up to him, I bore him up with one of my hands, and brought him unto the middle of the river, where (through God's great providence) was a bank of sand.'[39]

In return for being exemplary employers, the Stuart aristocracy could hope for industrious employees who were genuinely interested in making the lives of the families they served easier. They could also hope for servant loyalty and long-lasting relationships with their staff. An attendant of Nicholas Blundell, Walter Thelwall, completed thirty-five years with his master before deciding to move on to other things in March 1709. Longer still was the tenure of Sir Daniel Fleming's servant, John Banckes, who had originally been in the employment of the knight's father, William, and had therefore racked up fifty-three years with the Fleming family when he died following a short illness in November 1688. It was not unknown for servants to continue visiting their aristocratic betters even after periods of employment had come to an end. Lady Anne Clifford repeatedly welcomed former staff to her northern properties during the later seventeenth century. 'My old servant' Elizabeth Gillmore travelled up to York in a hired coach in 1668 to pay the noblewoman an informal visit, where she was met by two footmen who escorted her to Brougham Castle in Westmorland. Two years later, one Mr William Edge 'who had been formerly my domestic servant' arrived at another of Lady Anne's houses, Appleby Castle, to show off his new wife to his ex-mistress, where they stayed 'for 7 nights together in the Baron's Chamber'.[40]

Servant leisure

Servants were entitled to free time at the discretion of their aristocratic employers, with strict guidelines often in place to curb social activities and keep the focus of employment on quality service. The devout Catholic Anne Howard, Dowager Countess of Arundel, regularly allowed her staff time off in the early 1600s, provided a number of different rules were adhered to: 'She was very well content that they should all have convenient sport and recreation, yet with this proviso, that it were in due time and place. Sitting up by night she would by no means permit; nor that any public sport should be made on Sundays or other Holy Days at the times of the Protestants' service, not to give them offence.'[41]

Other Stuart aristocrats were slightly breezier in their outlook. Fellow Catholic Nicholas Blundell, esquire of Crosby, seemed not to give too much thought to when or under what circumstances his domestic help should be granted leisure time. In September 1706 he noted in his diary that one evening he had freely authorised 'many of the workfolks and most of the servants … to be merry at Great Crosby'.[42] In October 1710 he permitted three servants to go off to Liverpool from Crosby Hall 'on their own business'.

A leisure activity involving servants in Stuart England, although one that they might not have always chosen to participate in, was footman racing. Aristocrats themselves tended to organise such events, the aim invariably being to place bets on the two candidates taking part. On 30 July 1663, the London diarist Samuel Pepys reported that 'the town talk this day is of nothing but the great foot-race run this day on Banstead Downes, between Lee, the Duke of Richmond's footman, and a tyler, a famous runner.' The outcome of the race, which saw the former emerge victorious, was a disappointment to Charles II and his brother James, Duke of York, both of whom had placed large bets on Lee's opponent. A similar contest was held half a century earlier in April 1618, between a footman 'belonging lately' to Lucy Russell, Countess of Bedford, and a nameless 'Irish youth' in the service of the Howard family.[43] This time the route stretched from St Albans in Hertfordshire down to Clerkenwell in London, with close to twenty-five miles for the runners to cover. According to John Chamberlain, Lucy Russell's ex-footman won the race, which earned the future Duke of Buckingham, George Villiers, in excess of £3,000.

5

ATTIRE AND APPEARANCE

Lady Elizabeth Bennet, wife of the civil lawyer Sir John Bennet, found herself under attack in The Hague in 1617. Strutting about the crowded streets and public spaces of the Dutch settlement in her 'huge vardugals' (hooped structures, also called farthingales, kept beneath skirts to shape them), it was not long before the English gentlewoman became an object of ridicule to the many 'boys and wenches' who crossed paths with her and spotted the elaborate clothes she was wearing.[1] Chants of 'whore!' purportedly followed Elizabeth wherever she went in the city, and even when travelling discreetly the lawyer's wife could not escape the constant jeers, for her skirts were so enormous and unwieldy that it was impossible to fully tuck them inside a carriage.

The taunts of social inferiors, however insulting, would probably have mattered little to this fashionable woman. It was the opinions of her social equals, of the English and indeed wider European aristocracy, that counted when it came to clothing and general appearance. If they were satisfied with her wardrobe choices, then Lady Bennet would be satisfied, too, regardless of the common abuse she received in the street. The dress code and overall image of the Stuart aristocracy changed noticeably over the course of the seventeenth and early eighteenth centuries, perhaps more so than any other aspect of their lives. An aristocrat living in 1714 would have looked vastly different to one residing in England some 111 years earlier at the end of Elizabeth I's reign, from the hair right the way down to the shoes. So revolutionised was the style by 1665 that one commentator communicated his complete inability to identify the genders of aristocratic figures who inhabited court. 'I shall tell you that one cannot possibly know a woman from a man, unless one hath the eyes of a lynx who can see through a wall, for by the face and garb they are like men.' The rise of the male periwig in the mid-seventeenth century constituted one of the more conspicuous shifts in fashion, but there were other striking amendments to appearance embraced by elite men and women alike, including the adoption of face paint and beauty spots. Unsurprisingly, in the midst of these changes calls for caution and moderation arose. Counselling his daughter in 1688, the 1st Marquess of Halifax stated flatly, 'A woman is not to be proud of her fine gown; nor when she hath less wit than her neighbours, to comfort herself that she hath more lace.'[2]

Basic dress

The clothes worn by English aristocratic men at the start of the Stuart era were of course akin to the fashions of the late 1500s. Thus, a typical male outfit in the early reign of James I consisted of a jerkin, doublet, upper hose or breeches, nether hose or stockings, and sometimes a cloak.[3] The jerkin was a sleeveless garment usually donned for warmth over a doublet and cut to the waist, with buttons running up the front to allow the wearer to cool down if necessary. As with most articles of clothing in this period, it might be embellished for effect, like the jerkin of Sir Henry Beaumont of Coleorton in Leicestershire, left as a bequest in the will of his widow Dame Elizabeth in 1608, which was made of velvet and finished with gold buttons.[4] The doublet worn beneath the jerkin tended to be snugger than its counterpart and had sleeves that were either separately fastened or permanently attached to the main garment, the whole once again concluding at the waist. Sir William Fitzwilliam of Milton Hall in Cambridgeshire requested for himself a brown canvas doublet 'trimmed with blue silk and silver lace' in 1605, while listed in the extensive inventory of Henry Howard, Earl of Northampton, in 1614 were a white satin doublet 'raced with flowers and silver buttons' and a 'silk grogeron' equivalent 'laced all over with a white satin lace cut and ravelled between'. Below the jerkin and doublet could typically be found a pair of breeches or upper hose, which covered the top portion of the legs and might come out slightly at the waist. These extended down to the thighs and no further. Before he died in 1614, the Earl of Northampton had acquired a smart pair of 'black satin paned' hose that were 'raced and cut, laced with satin lace and embroidered between'. The nether hose or stockings more or less completed the early seventeenth-century look by covering the remaining part of the legs. Sir Richard Cholmley of Yorkshire recorded purchasing a pair of 'sea-green' silk stockings at a cost of thirty shillings in 1620, along with another pair of stockings that were 'willow-coloured', which, he amusingly noted, 'fit myself but fit my wife better'. A billowing garment that was likely to have comfortably fit most members of the aristocracy was the cloak. A successor to the sixteenth-century gown and used, like the jerkin, to keep warm in cold weather, this item might be viewed as an early form of overcoat. It, too, could be richly decorated to reflect the status of its wearer. The plush wardrobe of Roger Manners, 5th Earl of Rutland, included in 1612 a hooded cloak trimmed with fur and made serviceable by 'six pairs of silver clasps', three other cloth cloaks 'lined with silk or velvet', and a white riding cloak.[5]

Through the Jacobean years and into the disastrous rule of Charles I, the outfits of elite men developed steadily. The iconic Elizabethan ruff, sported by both males and females, had all but disappeared by the mid-seventeenth century, to be replaced by bands or collars that fell across the shoulders instead of standing upright around the neck. Hose, on the other hand, became looser and grew in length and volume, sometimes even making their way past the knee. By the Restoration period, breeches were enormous. Accompanying such articles of clothing were, oddly enough, shorter doublets that left a noticeable gap between the upper and lower garments.

It was in the later seventeenth century, however, that male clothing altered unrecognisably. Elegant vests or waistcoats took the place of doublets, breeches were slimmed down to a more manageable size, and both jerkins and cloaks were ousted by the long, close-fitting coat. This 'three-piece' suit would last well beyond the reign of Queen Anne, dominating the appearance of aristocratic men for generations to come. The landowner Sir Edmund Warneford of Warneford Place in Wiltshire, who died breaking his neck on a hunt, left a 'coloured cloth coat and waistcoat' in his will dated 1700, together with six of his 'worst' shirts, some old stockings, and a new 'stuff suit of clothes'. A decade later, Wriothesley Russell, 2nd Duke of Bedford, was the lucky owner of a sumptuous array of expensive coats kept at Bedford House in London, including two 'of pearl colour and yellow flowered silk', both furbelowed to ensure the extremities were not damaged, two of 'grey mohair', also furbelowed, and two more of black-and-white striped silk.[6]

Aristocratic women of the early Stuart period, like their husbands, continued to dress in clothes that had become fashionable in the last decades of the sixteenth century. The standard outfit worn by females comprised a bodice encasing the torso, a large skirt, and a gown that went over the top of both. The bodice was commonly reinforced with whalebone, such as that presented to the Countess of Dorset's infant daughter in 1617, and worked to pull in the stomach and shape the upper body in a way that was deemed flattering and modish. Sleeves were sometimes stylistically flared and, as with men's doublets, they might not always be sewn on to the main garment. Although full bodices were only really seen by the wearer herself and the attendants who dressed her, some were still carefully adorned. Probably acquired during the reign of James I, the esquire Arthur Coke's wife, Elizabeth, had in her possession two such items at Bramfield in Suffolk in the 1620s. While one bodice was 'laid with a spangled gold lace', the other was 'cut upon' blue and red taffeta and 'laid with a silver spangled lace'.[7]

The skirt was without doubt the most intriguing feature of the early Stuart costume. Characterised by its unmistakable farthingale shape, which was achieved through a hoop structure beneath the fabric, this garment stretched away from the waist before flowing vertically to the floor. Such a peculiar form can help to explain, at least partially, why Lady Elizabeth Bennett was given a hard time by the locals in The Hague in 1617. There is an argument to be made that skirts were in fact synonymous with 'petticoats' in early seventeenth-century England.[8] By the time Dame Ursula Sames of Dorset drew her last breath in the 1630s, she had accumulated an impressive number of them, including one of satin 'laced up to the middle with gold and silver bone lace', another of 'silver velvet' that came from Bristol, and a yellow petticoat that she 'wore every day'. A V-shaped piece called a stomacher might be positioned over the bodice for ornamentation or to hide gaps, with the outfit then completed by the gown. This latter garment was frequently made of either silk, velvet, or taffeta, and could be highly rich in appearance. In the 1610s, Lady Anne Clifford tried on a 'sea water green' satin gown that had been sent specially to her by a tailor in London, which was deemed 'fit for me to wear with open ruffs after the French fashion'.[9]

As with aristocratic men, women's fashion inevitably changed over time. Dorothy Randolph wrote to Jane, Lady Cornwallis Bacon, in 1632 to give her an update on the latest in elite clothing in England:

> I have sent you some patterns of stuff such as is worn by many, but not much [lace?] upon those wrought stuffs; but the newest fashion is plain satin, of what colour one will, embroidered all over with alcomedes [jewels and stones] but it is not like to hold past summer. They wear white satin waistcoats, plain, raised, printed, and some embroidered with lace, more than any one thing, and white holland ones much.[10]

Waistcoats, sleeved and worn with skirts or petticoats, grew in popularity over the Jacobean period, as is evident from the references Lady Anne Clifford makes to them in her diaries: amongst her personal collection in 1617, for example, were a white specimen and another of yellow taffeta. These appeared to be worn in place of bodices and were still mentioned by the aristocracy in the 1660s, the esquire William Blundell of Crosby Hall buying for his daughter, Mary, a 'sky-coloured silk mohair' waistcoat in London in 1665. Farthingale-shaped skirts had practically vanished by the succession of Charles I in 1625, together with female ruffs of almost every variety. By the 1670s, such Elizabethan hangovers, including the whalebone bodice (or waistcoat) and skirt combination, were a thing of the past.

The mantua came to England from continental Europe in this decade, which did away with the obvious constraints of multiple garments and instead comprised a looser, complete dress that would find favour with aristocratic women well into the eighteenth century.[11] Cut from a single piece of material, often silk, it had sleeves, pleated shoulders, and a bustle-shaped exterior below the waist. Mantuas were meant to be seen and admired by society. In 1676, Lady Chaworth, formerly Grace Manners, wrote a letter to her brother Lord Roos to inform him of the preparations being made for Catherine of Braganza's birthday in the capital. One female courtier, she relayed, was planning to wear a mantua of 'ermine upon velvet embroidered with gold and lined with cloth of gold', which was expected to cost £300 to put together. Even for the aristocracy this was an expensive purchase, the price so appalling the woman's love interest, Sir Carr Scrope, that he was forced to re-evaluate whether or not he really wanted to marry her.

Curiously enough, elite women's fashion came full circle in 1709 with the unexpected introduction of the hoop petticoat, which strongly resembled the farthingale of the early seventeenth century. Shaped like a cupola and formed of as many as eight whalebone or cane hoops taped together, this piece made a colossal statement, and would not have looked out of place next to Lady Bennett's 'vardugals' in Holland in the 1610s.[12]

The so-called intimate clothes of the Stuart aristocracy were surprisingly basic. As a general rule, men wore long shirts beneath their outer garments, sometimes linen drawers, too, while women donned chemises or 'smocks' only to protect their modesty. The male shirt was usually made of holland and tended to be adorned with lace at the neck and wrists; the same could be said for the female chemise. Plain shirts with a larger neck opening and again finished with decorative lace were worn in bed by aristocratic men, unless a house was in mourning, in which case all garments had to be black.[13] Sir Ralph Verney obtained six nightcaps 'marked V in black silk', two black taffeta 'night-clothes', and a black comb and brush following the death of his first wife in 1650. Elite males sported fetching nightcaps throughout the Stuart period, including Roger Manners, 5th Earl of Rutland, who in 1611 had 'two wrought night caps, one of gold and silver, the other with black silk'. In 1700, Sir Daniel Fleming owned several nightcaps made of holland. For aristocratic women, the broad picture is somewhat hazier, although it is probable that by 1700 many of their best night garments featured silk. A female relative of Catherine Manners, Duchess of Rutland, mentioned a set of 'grey night clothes' she had recently bought for herself in a letter dated 1682, costing £5 5 shillings in total.[14]

Aristocratic shoes were commonly fashioned from leather that was often imported from southern Europe. Sir Richard Cholmley of Yorkshire owned a pair of 'black Spanish shoes' in 1620, his wife a pair of 'Spanish leather shoes' five years earlier in 1615. When Lady Brilliana Harley wrote to her son Edward Harley at Oxford in 1639, the matriarch of Brampton Bryan Castle made plain the fashions of the day when she added seriously, 'I hope you now wear Spanish leather shoes'.[15] Footwear evolved over the seventeenth century along with most other items of aristocratic clothing, adopting a taller heel after the 1660s and gradually featuring buckles instead of laces. The exact type of shoe an aristocrat donned might depend on what time of year it was or the activity in which he or she was partaking. Sir Richard Cholmley, for instance, had winter boots and shoes to navigate the icy Yorkshire roads around his country seat in the 1610s. High boots or 'jack boots', meanwhile, were worn exclusively by the elite for riding and hunting in the later 1600s, and could be seen on the feet of Sir Thomas Cave of Stanford Hall when he hunted in the mid-1710s.[16] Aside from cloaks, gowns, coats, and the like, for extra warmth an aristocratic man or woman might wear muffs or gloves. Gloves functioned as social statements, too, as observed in the two pairs produced for the Earl and Countess of Rutland in 1608, which were of stag's leather and elegantly fringed with watchet and silver.

Generating all these different garments called for the skill of a decent tailor or seamstress. Tailors often travelled to Lady Anne Clifford at Knole in the Jacobean period to take measurements for new outfits, which would then be made up in London and sent down to Kent upon completion for her to try on. 'My Lord St John's tailor came to me hither to take measure of me and to make me a new gown,' the countess wrote in her diary in 1617. A surviving tailor's bill received by Sir Richard Cholmley in 1620 is revealing, as well as extensive. Turkish grogram for a doublet and hose was priced at seven shillings a yard, to be added to the thirty-three shillings charged separately for 'making and trimming' the garments; a black cloak with velvet 'lining and seaming', on the other hand, would set the gentleman back just two shillings, with an extra two shillings to be paid for the inclusion of silk and buttons. Five years earlier, twenty-five shillings had been paid to Henry Fothergyll, another tailor, for a gown of Flemish serge for Margaret Cholmley, Richard's wife.[17]

Seamstresses could be hired to make dresses for aristocratic women, and they could even become part of the household staff if they worked for the right family. In December 1671, a girl – 'well-dressed enough' – turned up on a whim at Lamport Hall in Northamptonshire to offer her services to the lady of the house, Margaret Isham, claiming that she 'could make all kinds of female dresses'. Whether or not she was taken on is unknown. On rare occasions, Stuart aristocrats might have a go at making clothes themselves, especially if money was in short supply or employing a professional was thought unnecessary. The esquire Nicholas Blundell noted on 2 November 1703 that he had set up at Crosby Hall 'a tent for my wife to work a petticoat in as I think', the 'tent' being a frame on which to stretch material.[18]

Outside the remit of the tailor or seamstress, but essential to the appearance of a comely aristocrat, were items of jewellery. The Dowager Countess of Arundel's Catholic faith prevented her from wearing anything of the sort in the early seventeenth century: 'As for other ornaments she never used any; only upon great feasts and principal Holy Days in honour of the solemnity she used to wear about her neck, either a cross of gold, in which a particle of the holy cross was inserted ... or else a plain pair of beads.'[19]

This was atypical. A contemporary of the dowager's, the Earl of Northampton, kept at Northampton House in London an array of precious pieces to wear, including 'a long jewel with a large ruby in the top', 'a pendant pearl', and 'a blue sapphire in [the] form of a half moon hanging in a chain of seven diamonds'. Dame Alicia Greaves, a fellow citizen of the capital, likewise left in her will dated 1684 a necklace consisting of forty-four pearls, a stomacher set with diamonds, a diamond locket, some 'white sapphire rose pendants', and 'my white sapphire buckles for shoes'. Dame Elizabeth Stampe of Springfield Hall in Chelmsford carried around a diamond ring that supposedly contained the hair of Mary II of England in the early eighteenth century. Items of jewellery linked to distinguished figures were, in fact, regularly seen amongst the Stuart aristocracy. Sir Edward Cleere of Blickling in Norfolk, for instance, had in his possession at the turn of the seventeenth century a 'great chain of gold' that had been presented to his father by none other than Charles V, Holy Roman Emperor.[20]

Lockets or rings filled with human hair, like Dame Elizabeth's diamond ring, were also common pieces, holding sentimental as opposed to decorative value in many cases. Dame Anne Seymour of Berry Pomeroy Castle owned two rings containing the hair of her Portman relations in 1695, which she considered significant enough to leave as bequests in her will. So, too, a few years earlier, Dame Diana Warburton, widow of Sir George Warburton of Arley Hall in Cheshire, included in her last will and testament a locket carrying a sample of her late daughter's hair, to be delivered to her grandson Edmund Trafford when the end came.

Various accessories worked with rings and other pieces of jewellery to complete the aristocratic look. The future earl John Hervey purchased for himself a cane with a silver head to walk about with in Suffolk and London in the 1690s, being a relatively rare object before the Restoration period. Much earlier, in May 1618, Mary, Countess of Bath's desire for another fashionable accessory is easy to discern. 'If you please to get me a black fan bought, I will leave troubling of your Ladyship,' the noblewoman wrote in a desperate letter to Jane, Lady Cornwallis Bacon.[21]

Hats, hair, and periwigs

Flamboyant hats of various incarnations were expected to be worn by aristocratic men throughout the waking day. The male hat in the early 1600s was typically made of beaverskin and included a wide, distinctive brim, with a hatband and ostrich feathers added for decoration. Arthur Coke, the third son of Sir Edward Coke, Lord Chief Justice, kept a 'black beaver hat' with interchangeable bands at Bramfield in the 1620s; one was a 'goldsmith's work of stars and half moons', the other three a mixture of silver and gold. As well as boasting 'a white beaver hat with [an] embroidered band' in 1612, Roger Manners, 5th Earl of Rutland, also owned a Monmouth cap, a knitted, circular item of headgear worn predominantly by soldiers and sailors. Having the brim of a hat cocked slightly became fashionable late in the century, before the famous tricorn design took over in England around 1700. Hats were to be removed by aristocratic men only in certain situations, such as when they came into contact with an individual of superior rank or a family elder. Women took to beaver hats at the height of their popularity as well, if they covered their heads at all, including the wife of Lord William Howard, formerly Elizabeth Dacre, who had several black specimens made for her during the reign of James I.[22]

The fashion for aristocratic men was to wear their hair short in the first decade of the seventeenth century. In the concluding years of the Jacobean period, however, longer styles were preferred, often coming down as far as the shoulders and sometimes incorporating a left-sided lovelock. This look survived the English Civil War and continued through the Interregnum, until hair was shortened again to accommodate the French peruke, or periwig, which arrived with King Charles II from the continent in 1660. Such wigs constituted a significant departure from anything seen before in Stuart England. In their early form they comprised an abundance of curls falling in waves from a centre parting, being either of horse or human hair. This style morphed into a less convincing and ultimately showier arrangement partway through the reign of Charles II, with tight ringlets now spilling down the shoulders and back and framing the chest like a pair of thick curtains.[23] The periwig had grown upwards as well as outwards by the arrival of the eighteenth century, culminating in two high peaks at the top of the head that, to modern eyes at least, lend a very strange look.

There seemed to be wigs for every occasion in the second half of the seventeenth century, as is evident in a list compiled by Sir Richard Newdigate in the 1690s. The esquire had three perukes for use in London alone, together with two for wearing 'abroad in winter', two for 'summer abroad', and a further two for summer and winter 'at home in the house'.[24] In 1677, William Blundell of Crosby Hall was especially particular about the types of wigs he required for daily use, which included one to be worn on a horse:

> I desire to have the hair to be of the lightest brown without any appearance of red. The periwig must be very large in compass by reason of the size of my head, but I would not have it long... Upon

> these terms I should be glad to be fitted (besides the former) with a very short riding wig for summer for the lowest price, and the hair may be considerably darker than the former mentioned above.[25]

Some months later, the Lancashire esquire highlighted one of the more practical purposes of a periwig in a letter to his sister-in-law, Margaret Haggerston. 'I must likewise put it in your choice either to buy me a peruke or to suffer me to expose this old bald pate of mine to cold and scorn,' he wrote dryly. Wigs were not cheap. William Russell, 5th Earl of Bedford, paid £20 for one periwig in 1672, on top of £34 for three others of various kinds.[26]

The locks of aristocratic women were worn high and neatly at the beginning of the Stuart epoch, climbing tightly over a pad fitted to the top of the head and finishing in a chignon at the back. Long curls arranged at the sides of the face followed in the middle of the seventeenth century, with a bun remaining at the rear that might be ornamented with pearls or strips of ribbon.[27] After the return of the king in 1660, a fringe featuring short curls, sometimes called 'cruches', began to be sported in elite circles, accompanied by a profusion of different ribbons that caught the attention of Lady Mary Bertie in 1670:

> [At court] they wear their gowns as I wrote to you before, but I think the fashions of their ribbons and hair alters according to everybody's fancy, for some wear all small ribbons, others broad ribbons, others broad and small mixed and all 'frowzes' of their own hair.[28]

Hairstyles crept upwards again in the reign of Queen Anne, mirroring the re-emergence of hooped skirts that had not been seen since the Jacobean farthingale, although side curls continued to be widely observed.

In certain extreme cases, aristocratic women of the Stuart period chose to completely disregard the hair formations that were deemed socially acceptable by the majority. As Jane, Lady Cornwallis Bacon, reported, Frances Stewart made a promise to herself in the event that she outlived her husband, Ludovic Stewart, 2nd Duke of Lennox, one of the most powerful men of the Jacobean age. When the duke did indeed die before her in 1624, she set about fulfilling that promise. 'Her hair, in discharge of a vow she had formerly made, she cut off close by the roots that afternoon,' Lady Jane wrote, 'and told us of some other vows of retiredness she had made ... which I hope she will as punctually perform.'[29]

The need for hair to be regularly cut became especially pressing with the introduction of the male periwig in the 1660s, although, naturally, periodic trims had always been required by the Stuart aristocracy. Many aristocrats employed professional barbers to cut their hair, such as Henry Bourchier, 5th Earl of Bath, who took on the barber Richard Wickett in 1642 and agreed to pay him an annual salary of £4, in addition to supplying him with 'some old clothes'. In the absence of a professional, a servant with the necessary skills might be called on to perform the task instead. A servant of Lady Anne Clifford's, George Goodgion, assumed the role of hairdresser for his mistress in her later years, on one occasion in the 1670s 'clipping off all the hairs of my head' at Appleby Castle. At Rydal Hall, it was Sir Daniel Fleming's butler, Roger Fleming, who saw to the knight's head of hair in the reign of William III, being paid six pence each time his master's locks were crying out for a clip. When neither a barber nor a skilled attendant was available, unqualified servants or members of the immediate family might offer their services, particularly if the weather was hot. On 4 August 1708, seemingly because of the summer heat, Nicholas Blundell's wife and her maid, Mary Howerd, took it upon themselves to give the esquire a much-needed trim at Crosby Hall in Lancashire.[30]

From the death of Elizabeth I in 1603 to the Commonwealth years of the 1650s, moustaches were popularly worn by elite men, some curled at the ends, others flat and slanting downwards, with beards gradually restricted to the chin and resembling small tufts.[31] However, facial hair of any description had disappeared entirely by the early eighteenth century, when a clean-shaven face was considered best suited to the periwig look. For sculpting the moustache worn widely in pre-Restoration England, there were 'beard' irons or curling irons; for daily shaving throughout the Stuart period, razors, scissors, and shaving basins were used, plus orange flower water with which to freshen the skin. The act of shaving, as has already been mentioned, tended to fall to an aristocrat's butler, and might be one of the first tasks of the day.

Cosmetics

'I now observed how the women began to paint themselves, formerly a most ignominious thing, and used only by prostitutes,' John Evelyn wrote in his diary in 1654. The painting of the face was a fashion choice that spread quickly through the ranks of English aristocratic females at this time, the makeup being an instant indicator of status and prestige. As revealed by the informed courtier Henry Savile, though, such a pursuit of visual perfection could come at a cost. 'My Lady Henrietta Wentworth is dead,' he announced in a letter dated 1686, 'having sacrificed her life to her beauty, by painting so beyond all measure that the mercury got into her nerves and killed her.'[32] In response to the perceived dangers of face paint, advertisements began to appear in elite publications offering alternative products that were apparently safer to use. *The Spectator* included the following notice in the 1710s:

> The famous Bavarian Red Liquor: Which gives such a delightful blushing colour to the cheeks of those that are white or pale, that it is not to be distinguished from a natural fine complexion, nor perceived to be artificial by the nearest friend. Is nothing of paint, or in the least hurtful, but good in many cases to be taken inwardly. It renders the face delightfully handsome and beautiful; is not subject to be rubb'd off like paint, therefore cannot be discovered by the nearest friend. It is certainly the best beautifier in the world.[33]

Little black spots, or patches, accompanied painted faces in the later seventeenth century, with Dame Alicia Greaves owning a 'patch box' at her London property in the 1680s. These curious adornments were mocked by some for their tendency to move about the skin at random, including a contributor to *The Spectator* in 1711:

> The women look like angels, and would be more beautiful than the sun, were it not for little black spots that are apt to break out in their faces, and sometimes rise in very odd figures. I have observed that those little blemishes wear off very soon; but when they disappear in one part of the face, they are very apt to break out in another, insomuch that I have seen a spot upon the forehead in the afternoon, which was upon the chin in the morning.[34]

A touch of derision from time to time was certainly understandable. One 'maiden lady of a good fortune' spoke in March 1712 of 'shifting a patch for half an hour before I could determine it', eventually settling on a position 'above my left eyebrow'.[35]

Aristocratic men dabbled in cosmetics, too, which blurred the line between the male and female wardrobes and baffled moderate commentators. '[It is] a strange effeminate age when men strive to imitate women in their apparel, viz. long periwigs, patches in their faces, painting, short wide breeches like petticoats, muffs, and their clothes highly scented, bedecked with ribbons of all colours,' Anthony Wood noted in the 1660s, surrounded by highborn men and women in Oxford.[36]

Cleanliness

Good hygiene played an important role in the overall image of Stuart aristocrats. Soap and wash balls were bought in large quantities throughout the period to keep clothing and the elite body clean, being so valued by Henry Bourchier, 5th Earl of Bath, in 1648 that he kept his own supply of wash balls locked in a box. Sir Edward Wise of Sydenham House in Devon similarly left nothing to chance in October 1659 when he purchased an impressive thirty-six pounds of both white and Castile soap. At Lyme Hall in the early seventeenth century, meanwhile, soap was made on the premises by a dedicated 'sope man', which ensured that the commodity was always available for the Legh family to use. To clean aristocratic teeth, rubbing cloths, toothpicks, and latterly 'utilitarian' powders were applied to the inside of the mouth each day, no doubt with varying degrees of success. By 1712, an 'abundance of nobility and gentry' in England were allegedly using a 'delightful chymical liquor' advertised in *The Spectator* to maintain all aspects of oral hygiene, which 'in a moment' made 'the most nauseous breath smell delicately fine and charming', turned 'the blackest and most foul teeth perfectly white', and miraculously cured scurvy in the gums.[37]

For a pleasant odour, sweet bags filled with scented herbs were placed amongst aristocratic clothing and linen. Similar embroidered items were even worn around the waist in the reign of James I, although it is probable that their function in these instances lay principally in warding off exterior smells or carrying valuable objects. No fewer than fourteen sweet bags were found in one chamber at Drayton Manor in Staffordshire following the death of Lettice Knollys, Countess of Essex and Leicester, in 1634, with another sizeable collection unearthed at Northampton House in London in 1614. The latter hoard belonged to the late Henry Howard, 1st Earl of Northampton, and as was typical with his possessions, they were exquisitely decorated. One sweet bag was 'embroidered with embossed mosswork, having two sea nymphs upon dolphins and other figures of fowles, edged about with lace of silver and gold, lined with carnation', another 'embroidered with pelicans, butterflies, and flowers and lined with carnation satin', estimated to be worth over £2.[38] Sometimes perfumes were sprinkled directly onto garments, as opposed to being stored in little bags. Loose rose powder sweetened the wardrobe of Rachel Bourchier, Countess of Bath, in the 1640s, while in the later seventeenth century the 5th Earl of Bedford's entire dressing room at Woburn was covered in a fine layer of aromatic powder, including the dressing table. Should the aristocracy feel the need to make rooms themselves smell fragrant, perfuming pans that boiled sweet water could be used to good effect, such as that kept in Elizabeth Coke's closet at Brook Hall in Suffolk in the 1620s.[39]

Portraits and self-regard

Having one's picture painted was a must for an aristocrat in Stuart England, as is clear from the vast numbers of portraits that have survived from the period. The wife of Thomas Wentworth, 1st Earl of Strafford, formerly Anne Johnson of Bradenham in Buckinghamshire, seemed satisfied with the individual portraits produced of the couple in March 1712, writing to her husband that the artist had 'mended them both extremely and has made yours a good deal taller and the robes are well of them both'. Several months earlier in November 1711, however, the noblewoman had been less than impressed. 'I went last week to see our pictures,' she informed Thomas at the time, 'and I like them worse than ever I did, for he has made a dwarf of you and a giant of me, and he has not touched the dressing of them since you went.' Dissatisfaction and even unbridled anger were common responses to portraits when they did not meet the expectations of their subjects. In the spring of 1640, the baronet Sir Hugh Cholmley commissioned pictures of himself and his wife that, as far as he was concerned, 'resembled us both, yet both to our disadvantage, especially hers'.[40]

Eleanor Wortley, then Countess of Sussex, lost all composure in the same year when she set eyes on a new portrait of herself for the first time. Even the manner of its delivery was a disappointment to the noblewoman, who thanked a member of the Verney family for sending the 'likeness' to her, but nonetheless complained that 'the frame is a little hurt, the gilt being rubbed off.' This was nothing compared to the contempt she reserved for the portrait itself. 'The picture is very ill favoured,' she noted hotly, '[and] makes me quite out of love with myself, the face is so big and so fat that it pleases me not at all.' She went on to liken the said visage to 'one of the winds puffing'. The portrait had been the work of the celebrated court painter Sir Anthony van Dyck, but this made no difference to the displeased Eleanor, who intended to have the Flemish artist significantly alter the picture when she was next in London to better represent her features. 'Though I be ill favoured I think [the portrait] makes me worse than I am.'[41]

While aware of their defects and able to show modesty when required, most Stuart aristocrats considered themselves physically attractive on the whole. Self-declarations of beauty, heavily encouraged by the competitive element of court culture, were particularly rife in London during the reign of Queen Anne. 'Lord Bathurst was here this morning to show us his person before he went to court,' Anne, Lady Strafford, reported in February 1713. 'His clothes were both extremely fine and very handsome,' she continued, 'and he like one you know very well pleased with his own person.'[42] Here she may have been referring to the recipient of the letter, her husband Thomas Wentworth, who obviously thought a lot of himself, too. A week or so later the subject of self-admiration came up once again in a letter written by Lady Strafford to the earl, where she went back on herself: 'If you are ever jealous of anybody it must be Lord Berkeley, for I have heard in several places where he has said no man in the world was so happy in a wife as you. You know I am like you and have no vanity at all, so to be sure I don't believe what he says.'[43]

Lady Strafford certainly had a funny way of showing her total lack of vanity. Even earlier that year she had decided to be 'vain in my turn' by enthusiastically informing Thomas that the French ambassador and 'several other foreigners' had named her 'the handsomest woman' at court. As justification for such a revelation, she wrote to her husband, 'You have so often told me of your beauty that I was resolved to return it as soon as I had any opportunity.' The previous year, Anne had disputed with 'Sis Betty' over which of the two women was more attractive. The jury was still out when Thomas was told about the altercation, with Lady Strafford explaining, 'We both argue [on] behalf of our own persons. Forget I am that insipid thing your wife, and be an impartial judge.'[44]

When judging the attractiveness of other people, however, aristocrats could be extraordinarily harsh. Remarks might be especially cutting if a sworn enemy's appearance was assessed. Sir Simonds D'Ewes of Suffolk seemed positively gleeful in 1631 upon the passing of his great foe, the Lord Chief Justice Sir Nicholas Hyde, writing later in his autobiography that 'never was any man's death more generally rejoiced at.' An attack on his countenance followed. According to D'Ewes, Hyde had been 'of a yellowish complexion like tallow, and of a mean aspect, altogether unbeseeming a place of that eminence [lord chief justice]'. D'Ewes further commented that the man 'rode in his circuits many times on horseback in a whitish blue cloak, more like unto a clothier or to a woolman than a Lord Chief Justice'.

Aristocrats might even evaluate the appearance of their own family members unfavourably, although malice was rarely intended in these instances. Sir John Lowther of Lowther Hall in Westmorland thought that his daughter-in-law had 'grown very gross and corpulent in body' of late in 1662, but he conceded that in general she was 'a good handsome yellow-haired woman'. On his daughter Abigail's looks in the later seventeenth century, the politician Sir John Bramston also had mixed opinions. 'She was of a moderate stature, and well shaped; handsome, but not a beauty; her complexion sanguine, which inclined to choller.'[45] Margaret Cavendish, Duchess of Newcastle, had only praise for her family's physical qualities when she revisited them in an autobiographical work of the late 1600s, including those of her mother: 'Her beauty was beyond the ruin of time, for she had a well-favoured loveliness in her face, a pleasing sweetness in her countenance, and a well-tempered complexion, as neither too red nor too pale, even to her dying hour…'[46]

The duchess was even more complimentary about her siblings. None of them were 'crooked' or 'deformed' as children, she wrote, 'neither were they dwarfish, or of a giant-like stature, but every ways proportionable; likewise well-featured, clear complexions, brown hairs (but some lighter than others), sound teeth, sweet breaths, plain speeches, [and] tunable voices.'[47]

6

DIET AND DINING

> His custom was to dine at six or seven at night, and his meal lasted till seven or eight in the morning. Sometimes he drank; sometimes he heard his music; sometimes discoursed; sometimes took tobacco, and sometimes ate; whilst the company did what they pleased. They might do the same, or rise, go or come, sit down or sleep. The meat and bottles continued all the night before them.[1]

So lived the nobleman Charles Paulet, 6th Marquess of Winchester. While Paulet's personal attitude to dining, food, and drink in the late 1680s may have been extreme, the underlying reference to dietary extravagance made in this contemporary observation was not. The aristocracy kept their bellies constantly full and their lips perpetually wet in the Stuart period, often eating and drinking under conditions that would have left the average Englishman lost for words. 'We live very pleasantly here, [and] eat and drink very plentifully, finely and neatly,' Lady Isabella Wentworth wrote to her son, the 3rd Baron Raby, in April 1705. Most other aristocrats of the period could report the same, even Margaret Cavendish, Duchess of Newcastle, who claimed to live off a basic diet of boiled chicken and water. Such was the excessiveness of aristocratic dining that, as with attire, moderation might sometimes be urged. 'It is sumptuous fare, that is the soul's snare,' the poet Richard Brathwaite wrote in *The English Gentleman* in 1641, which acted as an informal rulebook for elite males to follow. 'Neither is it fare, but delight in fare, not simply the meat, but the desire or liquorish appetite, which produceth those odious effects... So then, temper your desires, that neither too much restraint may enfeeble them, nor excess surcharge them.'[2]

Food

Meat, both red and white, was eaten in large quantities by the Stuart aristocracy. The larders of Sir Richard and Dame Lucy Reynell at Forde House were plentifully stocked with a side of mutton, a joint of 'roast' beef, rabbits, a cock, and a partridge in January 1628, which was expected to last the Devon couple just one week. Partridge was likewise brought to Naworth Castle in Cumberland for Lord William Howard and his family to dine on in May 1621, along with five calf's heads, twenty-four calf's feet, fifty chickens, a lamb, a kid, and a pig, to be eaten over seven days. During the Interregnum years, when moderation in all things was encouraged by Cromwell and his puritanical followers, the supply of meat at Woburn Abbey in Bedfordshire was greater than ever. A week's worth of flesh for the majestic Russell family in March 1655 included 380 pounds of beef, a breast of veal, 'a side and a neck' and a breast of mutton, 168 pounds of 'pork', 'two gammons of bacon' weighing sixteen pounds, an unspecified number of sheep's feet, five tame and five wild pigeons, three pullets, and seven chickens. There was also a neat's tongue – taken from a cow – and 'a cock for broth'. Almost every part of an animal, from the head to the feet, was considered fit for consumption by elite diners and their economical kitchen staff. It was in this spirit, therefore, that the household of Sir Edward Wise in Devon acquired five tongues, six udders, and six marrow bones in September 1659 for culinary use.[3]

Red meat and poultry were often locally sourced, originating either from the parkland surrounding a country house or a nearby butcher's shop of good repute. Roger Manners, 5th Earl of Rutland, reared and slaughtered lambs for their meat in the rambling grounds of Belvoir Castle in 1611, with wild rabbits also found and caught here for the nobleman's table. So, too, in the middle years of the seventeenth century, a noteworthy proportion of William Russell, 5th Earl of Bedford's store of venison, rabbit, and pork came from the extensive lands bordering Woburn Abbey. Sometimes an aristocrat had a direct hand in the acquisition of the meat he or she consumed. In September 1617, the esquire Nicholas Assheton of Downham in Lancashire recorded how he had accompanied a hunting party to nearby Totridge Fell and then, immediately afterwards, tucked into the carcass of the stag that had been killed in the day's sport. 'The keeper's two hounds cast off: brave sport: killed him in the fence,' Assheton wrote, before noting, 'Broke him up [the stag]: ate the chine and the liver.'[4] For the politician Sir Edward Wise, the procurement of meat for the dining table at Sydenham House required a little less exertion in 1659. Pork, mutton, veal, lamb, and beef were all to be bought from a decent butcher based at Tavistock that year.

Served alongside meat in most aristocratic households was an abundance of fresh fish and shellfish, notably salmon, herring, trout, flounder, cod, and oysters. Nicholas Blundell enjoyed pickled oysters at Crosby Hall in December 1709. During January and February 1649, the Howard family of Naworth Castle had a large selection of fish for their table, including three cod, eighty-one codling, eighty-seven fluke, forty sparling, five salmon, eight hundred herring, and unspecified amounts of trout and eel.[5] Earlier in Naworth's history, in the reign of James I, saltwater fish were sourced principally from the North Sea and carried to the Cumberland estate via Newcastle or Morpeth, although some varieties made their way up from the capital. Freshwater fish, conversely, came from lakes and rivers that were local to the castle. If a country mansion in Stuart England had grounds containing at least one body of water, which was common for aristocratic estates, freshwater fish might be bred in these. The 5th Earl of Rutland's healthy supply of carp, bream, and tench came from ponds the nobleman personally owned in the early 1610s, which were all overseen by an employee of the Manners family called Robert Bingham.

Dairy products, including milk itself, were a common addition to the aristocratic diet. The baronet Sir John Brownlow and his intimates used up to sixty quarts of milk every week while residing in London in the early 1690s, with a further £2 8 shillings spent on the family's weekly supply of butter. From time to time, cream, purchased in pints and costing six pence each, also featured in the Brownlows' food bill. Butter and cheese were bought on a regular basis for the privileged inhabitants of Naworth Castle in the early seventeenth century, the latter being so favoured by Lord William Howard and his extended family that on one occasion in 1640, shortly before the nobleman's death at the end of the year, a stupendous thirty-six slabs of cheese were obtained from nearby Farlam Hall. More impressive still, however, were the two 'horse loads' of butter and cheese reportedly carted from Thornthwaite Hall, Lord Howard's hunting lodge, to Greystoke Castle near Penrith at around the same time.[6]

With dairy products came other basic foodstuffs for the aristocratic larder, such as eggs and various types of grain. At Naworth, now owned by William Howard's great-grandson Charles, one month's worth of grain included ten bushels of rye, thirty-five bushels of malt, six bushels of oats, and three 'pecks' of wheat in 1649. Should affairs be well run and estates big enough in scale to accommodate arable farming, crops could be homegrown. The grain arriving at Woburn Abbey increasingly originated from lands owned by the 5th Earl of Bedford at Thorney Abbey in Cambridgeshire after 1660, where an overhaul of management had led to greater productivity and the welcome erection of a new granary in 1673.[7]

All manner of fruits and vegetables graced the great tables of the aristocracy in Stuart England, with the variety of produce only increasing as the seventeenth century progressed. In July 1663, at the height of summer, there were raspberries, strawberries, pears, white and red plums, peaches, apricots, cherries, lemons, oranges, and gooseberries for the Russell family to eat at Woburn Abbey. Much of this fruit would have come from the mansion's gardens, which were described by Celia Fiennes at the close of the century:

> There are three large gardens, fine gravel walks and full of fruit. I ate a great quantity of ye Red Coralina gooseberry... In the square, just by the dining room window is all sorts of pots of flowers and curious greens, fine orange, citrus and lemon trees and mirtles... On the side of this you pass under an arch into a cherry garden.[8]

Fruit trees and other fruit-bearing plants were a typical feature of most aristocratic gardens by this time, and certainly at Horseheath Hall in Cambridgeshire they filled the immediate landscape. Here one could find growing in the Restoration era ten varieties of plum, five varieties of grape, twelve varieties of peach, five varieties of apricot, and three varieties of fig, all of which were probably arranged in orchards. In the 1630s, Sir John Oglander of Nunwell House on the Isle of Wight noted that he had planted two orchards there 'with my own hands', seeming to need no gardener to assist him. Both were in time brimming with bright, tempting fruit, the lower 'pippins, pearmains, puttes, hornies, and other good apples and all sorts of good pears', the upper 'apricocks, mellecatoons [melons] and figs'.[9]

Fruit picked from noble and gentle gardens could taste very good indeed, despite the temperamental nature of the English climate. In August 1706, Elizabeth Coke wrote to her brother, the courtier Thomas Coke, with some encouraging news from the family seat of Melbourne Hall in Derbyshire:

> We are all in danger by the temptation of your fruit, which we have in much greater abundance than we can dispense with ourselves; and therefore I have disposed of some to those of your neighbours that have no walls of their own. Some peaches of the same trees that you

despised last year are excellent. Nectarines are also very excellently good this year; and there has been a few figs in great perfection.[10]

Sir John Oglander advised would-be gardeners, if planting an orchard ever took their fancy, to 'set your crabs and pear-stocks in their places, where you mean they shall ever remain, three years before you graft them.' He continued that it was important to surround newly planted fruit trees with a thick wall of debris so that the trunks were adequately protected from the cold. 'Pigeon dung or lime, with good earth or ashes, are good.' Of course, in many aristocratic gardens across England the methods of preservation were much simpler. 'I have pretty well beat off the jays and crows and magpies from the gardens, but there is a great many blackbirds and "threeshes" that come to the cherries and other fruit, of which I have killed a great many,' Sir John Verney's gamekeeper informed his master from Middle Claydon in July 1700.[11]

With regard to vegetables, one might come across any of garden peas, onions, garlic, carrots, turnips, radishes, artichokes, cucumbers, spinach, celery, and beetroot in the house of a Stuart aristocrat. Very often these were grown in the surrounding gardens, like fruit. In October 1695, one of Sir Daniel Fleming's daughters, Alice, weighed a cabbage that had sprung up in the 'low garden' at Rydal Hall in Westmorland, which came in at a hefty thirty-two pounds. The vegetable patch here was no doubt full to bursting at various points throughout the year, for in July 1688 records show two shillings and six pence being paid by Sir Daniel for 250 cabbage plants alone. Sir Richard and Dame Lucy Reynell grew cabbages in their gardens at Forde House in Devon, too, along with carrots, turnips, onions, parsnips, and radishes. Right at the beginning of the period in 1611, Sir William Fitzwilliam likewise boasted carrots, onions, and cabbages in the sprawling gardens of his Cambridgeshire pile of Milton Hall, together with cucumbers, artichokes, and endives.[12]

As we have seen, festivals and celebrations provided the perfect opportunity for the English aristocracy to be even more indulgent with their food. Over Christmas 1668, the Newdigates of Arbury

Hall in Warwickshire kept an enormous store of red and white meat in their larders, to the extent that one wonders how they were able to eat their way through it all. A note compiled at the time of 'what hath been spent in the twelve days' by the family included two 'beefes', six 'muttons', six 'veales', three pigs, and one hundred rabbits. Added to this substantial list was an unusual amount and variety of poultry: eighteen turkeys, fifty geese, sixteen ducks, forty-two capons, two pullets, three chickens, and a swan. Expensive spices and other luxury ingredients might be introduced to the diet at Christmas to give food additional flavour, as they were at Forde House in December 1628. Sir Richard and Dame Lucy Reynell went all out this year when they bought in for the festivities a pound of nutmeg, half a pound of mace, half a pound of dry cloves, half a pound of cinnamon, seventeen pounds of currants, thirty-six pounds of sugar, a pound of ginger, and two pounds of 'the best case pepper'.[13]

Mentioned briefly in the household accounts of Sir Edward Wise of Sydenham House around Christmas 1656 were one woodcock pie, another of turkey, and five 'minced' pies. These largely savoury creations of crumbling, hot water crust pastry and cooked flesh were popular with the aristocracy throughout the year, with fillings dependent on the occasion and the palate of the eater. Sir Ralph Verney's cook, according to the future baronet himself, was more interested in making hare pies for his master than learning to read and write at Middle Claydon in the 1650s, being 'wild to get a gun' to shoot the creatures. Venison pies were regarded as extra special and might be sent as gifts to neighbours and friends. 'If your man had brought me your letter but one day sooner I might have delivered him two or three pies of a stag, for yesterday morning early I sent from this house seventeen red deer pies towards London,' the 8th Earl of Shrewsbury, Edward Talbot, wrote to Sir Richard Beaumont in October 1609. Talbot had been hunting at Sheffield Lodge and was prepared to rectify such an injustice. 'You shall not fail to have two,' he added, 'and those to be of the first fat hind that shall be brought me.'[14]

The perils of transporting meat over long distances were acknowledged by Sir John Verney's diligent gamekeeper in July

1700, who, having dispatched a couple of rabbits down to London for the gentleman to enjoy, was glad to hear 'they did not stink... I was afraid they would, the weather was so hot.' Aside from venison pies and the like, there were countless other savoury dishes endorsed by the Stuart aristocracy, some of which were dreamt up by the aristocrats themselves. Lady Elizabeth Legh of Lyme Hall believed her potted venison to be second to none in the 1680s, which when made correctly was sliced, seasoned with salt and pepper, and blanketed in butter. The inventive Sir John Oglander, meanwhile, swore by his calf's feet fritters in the early years of the seventeenth century, the batter consisting of 'a little sack, mead, or any other wine or strong beer', cream, egg yolk, and flour.[15]

Those aristocrats with a sweet tooth were catered for. Fruit tarts, puddings, cakes, and 'puffs' were all baked for the Brownlow family of Belton House during an extended stay in Hammersmith in the early 1690s, incorporating cherries, currants, damsons, apricots, apples, and oranges. A few years earlier in July 1688, Robert Harley, in writing to his father Sir Edward Harley at Brampton Bryan, saw fit to mention a 'naughty chesscake' that had recently made a close relative ill. Strangely enough, it was likewise reported in May 1684 that one Lady Hutten had been left 'indisposed' after helping herself to an early version of ice cream, although the real cause of the gentlewoman's suffering turned out to be a fatal case of smallpox. Lady Elizabeth Legh received a recipe for bread pudding in the 1680s, of which she seems to have approved. In it went small amounts of lemon and orange peel, 'plump' currants, and saffron to give the dish added colour. 'These puddings take up a deal of marrow, and sometimes when I could not get enough, I have been forced to take some beef kidney suet,' the creator of the recipe noted in her letter.[16]

Dining

In 1621, Sir Richard Cholmley of Yorkshire commented one day that he had eaten 'neither breakfast, dinner, [nor] supper'. By making a note of his apparent hunger, the esquire had unwittingly provided a useful outline of the different meals typically taken by the aristocracy in the 1620s. Breakfast, in fact, declined in popularity over the course of the seventeenth century, before making a triumphant return in the early 1700s. The traveller Celia Fiennes was treated to 'cold things and sweetmeats all served in plate' for breakfast by Lady Katherine Lowther at Lowther Hall late in the 1600s, although the hostess herself did not partake because 'it was so early in the morning'.[17] Supper was an evening meal and appears to have been enjoyed by the aristocracy throughout the Stuart period. Two chickens costing just over a shilling each kept Sir John Brownlow and his family happy in the evening during the early 1690s, while in March 1711 the 1st Baron Hervey and his son were content with mutton at Newmarket one night, having first inspected some horses.

A much heavier dinner came before supper in the households of elite men and women, being served initially around noon and then later in the day as the eighteenth century edged closer. In 1689, William Russell, 5th Earl of Bedford, paid for a sumptuous two-course dinner at a Cambridgeshire inn called the Red Lion, which began in style with a large pike flanked by 'all sorts of fish', two geese, a dish of capons and sausages, eight chickens, eight cauliflowers, and a dish of 'mince pies', amongst other things. The second course featured pheasants, partridges, pigeons, and pickled eels, and was rounded off with a selection of tempting tarts and a dish of fresh fruit.[18] If eating dinner at home during the early Stuart period, aristocrats as a rule tended to dine in the great chamber, normally located on the first floor of the house. This left servants to take their meals in the equally, and somewhat ironically, grand setting of the hall. By the outbreak of civil war in 1642, aristocratic dining had all but moved away from the great chamber and could instead be observed in parlours or 'dining' chambers. Following this development was the permanent addition of 'dining rooms' to mansions in the final years of the seventeenth century, with withdrawing rooms often built next door for aristocrats to retire in. Servant dining had disappeared from halls entirely by this stage, being relocated to designated spaces in other parts of the house.[19]

Dinner constituted a dizzying experience in many noble and gentle abodes. At St Giles House in Dorset, the country seat of Anthony Ashley Cooper, 1st Earl of Shaftesbury, the dining room was a hive of activity in July 1675. Pages, footmen, a coachman, the butler, the clerk of the kitchen, and even a falconer had all been ordered to bring up the first course of a large dinner, with some of them forbidden from leaving the room until the earl and his third wife, formerly Lady Margaret Spencer, had finished eating. While the clerk of the kitchen dashed about the place ensuring that all was in order, the first course was cleared away by many of the same individuals who had presented the food, and then systematically replaced with a second course and a helping of fruit. At the end of the feast, one of Cooper's footmen was given the unenviable task of taking the mountains of dirty plates down to the scullery to be washed, having been supplied with a few boys to help him. Meanwhile, the 'usher of the hall' and the under butler were made responsible for the removal of the oyster shells and 'cleaning the room after them'.[20]

In terms of the look of the dining table, there was much to be admired. The 5th Earl of Rutland kept spoons emblazoned with peacocks, pewter dishes and platters stamped with the family coat of arms, drinking vessels made of Venetian glass, silver dishes, and glass fruit dishes for use at Belvoir Castle in the early seventeenth century. Lord William Howard of Naworth Castle had forks fancily engraved with his own coat of arms in the 1620s, together with silver candlesticks, silver spoons, silver flagons, and a 'silver fork for carving'. Whether any of these items were regarded as ornamental only, or even as family valuables that were to remain locked away, is not known. In preparing for the knight Sir John Stanhope's much anticipated visit in August 1609, Sir Peter Legh of Lyme Hall in Cheshire hired 'two garnishes of pewter' for his table, and also procured the services of a harpist, whose role presumably would be to play in the corner of the room as the aristocrats ate and drank. Such was Sir Peter's fondness for music that a piper appears to have been permanently employed at Lyme for his entertainment.[21] A spot of background music and other agreeable entertainments were key to the success of an aristocratic dinner, with Dorothy Spencer, Countess of Sunderland, outdoing herself in October 1672 when hosting John Evelyn at her family's London property. 'She made me stay [to] dinner at Leicester House,' Evelyn wrote in his diary,

> ...and afterwards sent for Richardson, the famous fire-eater. He devoured brimstone on glowing coals before us, chewing and swallowing them; he melted a beer-glass and ate it quite up; then taking a live coal on his tongue, he put on it a raw oyster, the coal was blown on with bellows till it flamed and sparkled in his mouth, and so remained till the oyster gaped and was quite boiled. Then, he melted pitch and wax with sulphur, which he drank down, as it flamed; I saw it flaming in his mouth, a good while; he also took up a thick piece of iron, such as laundresses use to put in their smoothing boxes, when it was fiery hot, held it between his teeth, then in his hand, and threw it about like a stone ... then, he stood on a small pot; and bending his body, took a glowing iron with his mouth from between his feet, without touching the pot, or ground, with his hands.[22]

It is doubtful whether a harpist or piper could ever hope to compete with such a display, which clearly left the diarist awestruck.

Guests often made a dinner shine in the vainglorious world of the Stuart aristocracy, although naturally aristocrats ate on their own too. Lady Anne Clifford entertained relatives, friends, and neighbours regularly throughout her long life, from national stars at court to members of the very poor. Francis Manners, 6th Earl of Rutland, and his daughter Lady Katherine Manners were honoured dinner guests at Knole in July 1619, for example, followed in the December by Sir Ralph Boswell, who 'dined here and played and sung to me in the afternoon'. Years later, when Lady Anne was an old woman in her eighties, the callers kept coming. The postmaster of Penrith was invited to dine at Brougham Castle in January 1676, as were many others that month, the official taking his meal in the painted room before having a private audience with the noblewoman in her chamber. A local parson and two tenant farmers, plus their close families, had the same experience two months later. On each occasion, Anne very likely did not eat with her guests, but dinner guests of hers they were. The esquire Nicholas Blundell and his wife went to dine at Aigburth Hall in June 1708, accompanied by some noteworthy friends, but often it was the Catholic couple themselves who did the hosting. Just two days after Aigburth, for instance, it was noted in Blundell's diary that 'Lady Anderton, Mr Blund and his wife and Mr Charles Harington dined here with ye rest of my guests.' Some four years later, the Blundells entertained at Crosby Hall a watchmaker from Ormskirk named Mr Taylor, who presented Frances Blundell with 'a pair of silver clasps for her necklaces'.[23]

Manners and decorum counted in any aristocratic dinner setting, being particularly important to those figures with a strong sense of morality. In the later seventeenth century, inappropriate chatter and swearing at the table greatly disturbed the pious Mary Rich, Countess of Warwick; it was unfortunate, then, that she was married to a man who seemed to enjoy engaging in both during mealtimes. 'I had, both at dinner, and till evening, a great deal of vain company, which were a trouble to me,' the countess wrote in February 1667, 'for, blessed be God! I did not lift up my soul to vanity; but their discourse was a trouble, and no kind of pleasure to me.'[24] In March, she despaired again:

> My brother Hatton dined with us that day, and swore dreadfully, and talked so very ill that I thought nothing out of hell could have done: I was troubled to hear it, and did all I could to keep him from it; but not being able to do it, I did show my dislike at it, and was, by God's mercy, enabled to own religion, and to speak good of it before him. After dinner, I got away from that wicked company;

> my soul being much grieved to hear my poor husband swear so much.[25]

During August of the same year, however, Mary was pleasantly surprised by the behaviour of 'Sir H S' at Durdans in Epsom. Before dining with him there, she had been somewhat concerned about the knight's apparent penchant for swearing, but, as she mentioned in her diary afterwards, 'it pleased God to restrain him.'[26]

Aristocratic dining was never a completely smooth and pleasant affair, however much noblewomen like the Countess of Warwick might wish it to be so. Following a dinner hosted by Lady Frances Withypoll in 1613, Sir Nathaniel Bacon of Culford Hall in Suffolk informed his wife in a letter that he had gone to bed feeling out of sorts. 'A distemper came upon me, so as I slept little till the morning,' he wrote agitatedly. The landowner and respected painter believed he knew the reason behind his sudden discomfort, adding, 'I could not impute it unto anything but [that] diet and ale of hers, which she commended unto me, and which I verily believe caused it.' In May 1618, Mary Bourchier, Countess of Bath, thanked Jane, Lady Cornwallis Bacon, for an edible present she had received from her, mentioning that 'no meat in the world could have been so welcome.'[27] This, the countess explained, was saying something, for the previous night she had fallen dreadfully ill after eating an undercooked chicken.

While upset stomachs experienced in the wake of meals might put a slight damper on the overall dining experience, mishaps occurring directly at the table were likely to be much more impactful. Over dinner at Langton Hall near Malton in 1660, the mansion of Sir Thomas Norcliffe, a fight broke out between Sir John Reresby and a young gentleman who was to be married to one of Norcliffe's daughters, ending with the former throwing a glass of wine in the latter's face. A duel was scheduled for the following day to settle the dispute but was later called off. In November 1671, meanwhile, one Mr Right caused quite the commotion during an intimate dinner at Lamport Hall in Northamptonshire. 'At dinner [he] asked for beer, which he did not see brought to him,' Thomas Isham jotted in his journal.[28] When the man, clearly drunk, then took off his hat to speak to the lady of the house, Margaret Isham, he knocked over the drink in front of him and covered the rest of the guests in ale.

Beverages

No aristocratic table in Stuart England would have been complete without the warming presence of alcohol. Wine, beer, ale, cider, and, latterly, distilled spirits and punch were a common sight within and indeed away from the dining room. For their prodigious supplies of red and white wine aristocrats looked abroad, favouring sack from Spain and the Canary Islands, Rhenish wine from Germany, and claret (Bordeaux wine) from France. The 5th Earl of Rutland purchased his claret from Boston in Lincolnshire in the early seventeenth century, thirty-two miles away from Belvoir Castle, while his provision of sack and Rhenish wine was predominantly sourced from London. The expensive habit of drinking champagne kept the Russell family smiling at Woburn Abbey in the Restoration period, with one hogshead of the stuff costing £13 in June 1669; the following year this figure had risen to £15. Because all wines were comparatively costly and fashionable to drink, English aristocrats might be picky about the type they required for a given occasion. 'I desire some good wine. You know what I like, neither hot, sharp, nor sweet. Some Canary, requisite for friends. If you could find a right sort of white wine, neither eager nor stummed it would do well,' Sir Edward Harley wrote to his son in July 1684. The idea of an aristocrat being deprived of a sufficient store of this exclusive beverage was too much for some to stomach. 'I can't bear the thoughts of your being quite without wine,' Elizabeth Hervey wrote dramatically to her husband in April 1709, 'that

I shall send you but a dozen bottles by the waggon tomorrow, which will be at Newmarket on Friday; there is six of Annadea and six of claret.'[29]

Beer and ale were often home-brewed at country estates, and essentially constituted the Stuart equivalent of modern-day water, with seventeen hogsheads of the former and another three of the latter set aside for the Christmas season alone at Arbury Hall in 1668. Sometimes, these brewed beverages were drunk as part of breakfast, other times as part of supper. In April 1705, Lady Wentworth informed her son that she was drinking 'strong ale' with every meal at Twickenham, complaining in the same letter that the beer also provided was so bitter 'that none can drink it'.[30] Cider was enjoyed by the Stuart aristocracy, too, being particularly popular in the south-west of the country. Many aristocrats were eager to grow the apples required for this drink themselves, including the prominent 1st Earl of Shaftesbury, who in 1671 bought 100 cider apple trees from a gentleman in Gloucestershire. 'The names of the cider apples,' the earl announced, 'are the Redstreake, the Black Apple, the Streake Must, the Sour Pippin, the Bramsbury Crab, the Foxwhelp, [and] the Grouting.' Towards the end of the seventeenth century, distilled spirits, at times referred to broadly as 'aquavitae', emerged in large quantities in aristocratic households. Sir Daniel Fleming sent for thirteen quarts of brandy in November 1689 for use at Rydal Hall, while in December 1708 Nicholas Blundell even had a go at making 'Aqua Coelestis' himself, a drink incorporating brandy, crab apples, lemons, and sugar. Punch came to be widely consumed alongside spirits, and was purportedly drunk hot following a hunt near Lyme Hall in the 1680s, with 'ye fox's foot stewed in it'.[31]

Aristocrats could be guilty of having one too many beverages on occasion, just like their insubordinate servants. In 1629, Sir John Oglander preached the following:

> Of all vices, hate drunkenness. It not only wasteth thine estate, maketh thee incapable of any business or employment

> in the Commonwealth or in thy own estate, ridiculous to all men, hurts thy body and hated of thy friends, but also metamorphoses the estate, that God gave thee, from man to beast and, without repentance, damneth both body and soul into hell-fire.[32]

Lady Strafford pleaded with her husband, Thomas Wentworth, not to touch alcohol in a letter dated 1712. 'I beg of you for my sake as well as your own that you won't drink, for though you don't presently find the effects of it you see by the Duke of Beaufort what ill consequences come after it,' she wrote. It would appear that some aristocrats instinctively knew their limits when drinking a substantial amount of alcohol, while others definitely did not. Sir John Reresby cordially invited Henry Cavendish, 2nd Duke of Newcastle, to dine with him in York in October 1688, at which meeting the duke drank wine 'so plentifully that he grew so kind as to kiss me and to call me his mistress'. In March 1635, however, Sir Humphrey Mildmay of Danbury Place had dinner at a friend's house and ended up being sick as a result of his alcohol consumption. This was not an unusual occurrence for the Essex man; on another occasion, Mildmay wrote in his diary, 'I fooled and abused my health all day and came home drunk and sick to bed.'[33]

The local alehouse, although insalubrious and filled with shady individuals of inferior rank, could be a temptation for men like Sir Humphrey, with its plentiful store of good beer and rowdy, animated atmosphere. 'To the ale[house] all', the esquire Nicholas Assheton scribbled in his diary in Lancashire in July 1617, obviously with great enthusiasm. 'When I laid me down,' he continued in the same entry, 'I was sick with drink.' Sir Ralph Verney was horrified to learn in 1656 that his son, Edmund, had earned himself some nicknames as a regular at the bar of the Eagle and Child near the Old Bailey in London, including 'Theodore Berry' and, perhaps more tellingly, 'Brewer'.[34]

There were a growing number of alternatives to alcohol in Stuart England, though this by no means affected its enormous popularity.

Coffee houses began to appear in English cities in the early 1650s, leading to the beverage's adoption as a fashionable, aristocratic refreshment around two decades later in the reign of Charles II.[35] Lady Wentworth and her daughter-in-law Lady Strafford were regularly drinking coffee in London in the early eighteenth century, often in the afternoons. Referring to the beverage as the 'Turkish drink' while travelling in Italy as a middle-aged man, Sir Ralph Verney seems to have drunk coffee for medicinal purposes in the 1680s, hoping that it 'would carry him through his fatigues'. Knowledge of the price alone would surely have been enough to pull the Buckinghamshire lord of the manor out of his intermittent spells of tiredness. A pound of coffee cost on average six shillings in England in 1692, having risen by two shillings in as many years. It is no wonder, then, that Nicholas Blundell was left enraged when he was forced to pick a stomach-churning sixty-nine stones out of a packet of coffee sent up from London in December 1709, which ought to have been of good quality. With the rise of this hot beverage came an inevitable explosion in related paraphernalia, from silver and 'Prescot ware' coffee pots to 'coffee mills', which the aristocratic Roger North desired to be 'screwed fast to a table board, rather than to have it the ordinary way, so that a post must be set up on purpose for it'.[36]

Tea arrived in England to tempt the taste buds of the Stuart aristocracy at about the same time as coffee, in the mid-seventeenth century. Now a staple of the English diet, this Chinese import was at first drunk sparingly by aristocrats because of the phenomenal cost, being initially sold in the capital for £3 10 shillings per pound.[37] As the price gradually fell, however, consumption rates soared. Like coffee, Lady Wentworth and Lady Strafford frequently drank tea in the afternoons in the early 1700s, with Thomas Wentworth sometimes sending new and interesting blends from the continent for them to try. Accessories might again be invested in for this familiar ritual, including tea tables and tea kettles.

One item found in the early eighteenth-century will of Dame Johanna St John was functionally described as 'the cup I drink my chocolate in'. Drinking chocolate, in fact, was more expensive than coffee, and found its way into the diet of the Stuart aristocracy in the later 1600s. Advertised as a beverage of West Indian origin, the time of day at which chocolate was enjoyed appeared to vary. In March 1712, a 'maiden lady of a good fortune' wrote to *The Spectator* to tell the world that she recently 'drank two dishes of chocolate in bed, and fell asleep after 'em'. Conversely, when filling in her husband on the latest news in London in November 1711, Lady Strafford noted that some irresponsible acquaintances had been drinking chocolate 'from morning till night'.[38]

Tobacco

Tobacco was first introduced to England some time in the sixteenth century. By the early 1600s, we find it being carried regularly from London to Lyme Hall in Cheshire, to be inhaled by Sir Peter Legh, as well as pipes being routinely sent to Belvoir Castle in Leicestershire for the Manners family to use. Only the very best tobacco would do for Francis Manners, 6th Earl of Rutland in 1613. Smoking was seemingly used by the inhabitants of Belvoir to project wealth and status, as was the case with so many other aspects of their lives. John Manners, 8th Earl of Rutland, for instance, had his tobacco box completely revamped in June 1669, 'adding in weight and goodness of gold four ounces sterling', which was done solely to compete with the 4th Earl of Exeter's superior model.[39]

In general, aristocrats bought into the idea that smoking was a pleasant, sociable, and actively healthy way to spend one's time. It was not, however, for everybody, with some finding the habit a rather disagreeable element of daily life. 'It is hard to sit amongst tobacco takers and not carry away the smell, though one smokes not,' Robert Harley, future Earl of Oxford, complained to his father in 1693. Sir Ralph Verney emphatically banned his servants from using tobacco at Claydon House in Buckinghamshire in the seventeenth century, 'for it not only stinks up my house, but is an ill example to the rest of my family'. Amazingly, a member of the Legh family of Lyme Hall was advised to smoke in moderation in the reign of James I because of the potentially negative impact of tobacco on the body. 'I would not have you take too much to do yourself harm, for they say it doth many men harm, they never live so long as they were wont to do,' an acquaintance warned.[40]

7

ANIMALS AND AMUSEMENTS

Aristocrats craved leisure time as much as any other member of society in Stuart England. Happily for them, their lofty positions on the social ladder allowed them unique levels of freedom and choice in this sphere, which went far beyond anything a lowly labourer or humble maid could hope to experience when not working. Loosely speaking, aristocratic leisure time might be split between keeping and maintaining domestic animals on the one hand, such as dogs and horses, and engaging in recreational activities on the other, for example outdoor sports and indoor games. There was a fair degree of overlap between the two, and in any case aristocrats themselves would hardly have gone to the bother of categorising what they got up to in their spare moments. While recreational activities were often characterised by grandiosity and even frivolity, the pious climate in England under the Stuart monarchy meant that overly immoral or immodest activities were infrequently seen amongst the elite. Nevertheless, this kind of behaviour was not unheard of, as is evidenced in a letter sent from a disapproving Robert Harley to his father Sir Edward in September 1677. 'Mr Martin will give you particulars of the beastly prank of my Lord Rochester and my Lord Lovelace and ten other men, which they committed on that Sabbath day [when they] were at Estington, which was their running along Woodstock Park naked,' the future earl wrote reproachfully.[1]

Domestic animals

Dogs of various breeds scampered around the feet of aristocrats throughout the seventeenth and early eighteenth centuries. Alethea Howard, Countess of Arundel, in an attractive work by the Flemish artist Peter Paul Rubens, was painted caressing the head of a large white hound in 1620; Dame Johanna St John, similarly, felt compelled to include her Cavalier King Charles Spaniel in her own portrait completed decades later by Godfrey Kneller. That the aristocracy often behaved affectionately towards their canine companions is incontrovertible. Lady Rachel Russell took great care to keep her husband's dog out of harm's way in 1681, writing to William, Lord Russell: 'But your new dog, I hope you will think of, for what to do with him I know not: I have a mind to have him led along with the waggon; for then he will be safe going through towns, and Betty Forster [maid] may take care of him at nights.'[2]

For a more categorical example, though, we turn to the relationship shared between Lady Isabella Wentworth and her little dog, Fubs. This companion was treated more like a human than an animal in the early eighteenth century, with Lady Wentworth informing her son by letter in April 1705 that the creature had been to church and behaved very well, even though she was known to bite strangers. The aristocrat quite lost her mind whenever Fubs went missing in Twickenham. 'If a dog happens to be shot, then I am out of my wits till I see her,' she wrote in another letter. When the cherished pet did eventually die in November 1708, it was an episode of great sadness and drama. 'I shall never love anything of that kind a quarter so well again,' Lady Wentworth observed, her hand no doubt trembling as she put pen to paper. The manner of Fubs' death had by all accounts been decidedly unpleasant, although at the very end the dog appears to have stabilised enough to nestle in Isabella's arms without struggling. By this time, perhaps mercifully, she had completely lost the ability to nip anybody who approached her. The animal was eventually buried in the garden at Twickenham and given a headstone to ensure that nobody forgot her. Another of Lady Wentworth's dogs, Pearl, seems to have been regularly dressed in a nightgown in April 1712, which amused the gentlewoman's daughter-in-law, Lady Strafford, to such a degree that she found it difficult to keep a straight face when in the former's company.[3]

Having recovered from the loss of her 'poor charming' Fubs, Lady Wentworth went to see her son's collection of 'great wolf dogs' in March 1710. She thought them very attractive creatures on the whole, although a little intimidating to be around, which was probably part of their intended function. Sir Ralph Verney of Claydon House considered smaller breeds of dog to be the most effective at guarding real estate and possessions in the mid-seventeenth century, pointing out to his son, Edmund, that 'rogues have tricks to quiet mastiffs, but none can quiet these little barking currs.' While canine aggression was certainly viewed as a desirable quality under the right circumstances, in some situations it could prove problematic. Sir Simonds D'Ewes' infant daughter 'escaped a miraculous great danger' in 1632 when a mastiff kept at his townhouse in Islington one day lunged at a nursemaid holding the toddler and 'rent her clothes'. The maid's skin was punctured as a result, with D'Ewes believing that the dog would have 'spoiled' both of them if 'some company present had not instantly prevented it'.[4] Anne, Lady North, faced a similar, and equally terrifying, predicament at Tostock in July 1679, which she recounted in a letter: 'My dog Tugg ran mad; but my servants did not believe it at first, and loved her so well they would try several things to her, so that they have all been "slabered" and "blodied", some of them she bit, and two of my little dogs she tumbled about, but whether she bit any we know not.'[5]

When it was safe to do so, dogs might be punished appropriately by aristocrats for their disobedience or general misbehaviour. Speed, Nicholas Blundell's agile greyhound, would hopefully learn a valuable lesson at Crosby Hall in May 1711 after being whipped by his master for 'taking a shoulder of mutton off the spit' without permission.[6] Such discipline, alas, did not stop the dog from running off one night and never being heard of again.

A dog's basic diet in the households of the Stuart aristocracy could consist of biscuits and stale bread or unwanted pieces of meat that would otherwise be thrown away. Nicholas Blundell, for instance, boiled the carcass of a bull calf and fed it to his dogs when the animal was discovered dead in a field in August 1709, with no whipping required on this occasion.[7] For cats, which are mentioned rarely in contemporary accounts, there was undesirable meat to be had, too, as well as whatever the felines could find on their independent jaunts around country and urban estates. Records indicate that Rachel Bourchier, Countess of Bath, owned a pet cat in the 1640s, although next to nothing is known about the animal. The legendary black and white cat of Henry Wriothesley, 3rd Earl of Southampton, however, was painted alongside her owner in a famous portrait of the nobleman completed in 1603, staring quizzically out of the frame to the left of the picture. The animal was called Trixie, and seems to have kept the earl company in the Tower of London while he was imprisoned there for taking part in a failed rebellion during the reign of Elizabeth I.

Horses were an intrinsic component of the aristocratic lifestyle in Stuart England, facilitating both fast transportation and several forms of outdoor recreation. Yet they could also be admired and appreciated for their own sake, as pets. In 1680, the writer William Waller had this to say about the animal:

> What a noble generous creature is this? and how answerable to that character of a brave goodly horse, which was delivered by God himself out of the whirlwind? His crest seems to be clothed

> with thunder; the glory of his nostrils is terrible; he swalloweth the ground with fierceness and rage; and saith among the trumpets ha, ha; he mocketh at fear; he paweth, and rejoyceth in his strength.[8]

In the 1610s, Edward Herbert, 1st Baron Herbert of Cherbury, owned a Spanish jennet to which he was utterly devoted, originally brought over from France. 'No horse yet was so dear to me,' he recollected in later life, 'whose love I had so gotten, that he would suffer none else to ride him, nor indeed any man to come near him, when I was upon him.' Herbert noted that the said steed would neigh happily and lick his hands – sometimes even his cheeks – as soon as he appeared in the stable, revealing that a picture of the two of them even hung in his private chapel. So widely esteemed was this horse that Sir Thomas Lucy of Charlecote Park in Warwickshire reputedly offered Edward £200 for the beast at one stage. 'I would not accept.'[9]

At the approach of the Georgian era, birds of various species were increasingly kept as pets by the English aristocracy, with two bird cages, one large and the other small, referred to at Belton House in the late seventeenth century. Here, in the grounds of the Lincolnshire mansion, peacocks sporting iridescent fans of blue and green feathers were also bred, for sheer ornamentation rather than any practical purpose. Lady Mary Verney, wife of Sir John Verney, acquired a pet blackbird in the 1690s that sang cheerfully to its mistress whenever the gentlewoman came into sight, being continuously supplied with a good provision of meat and drink. At the turn of the eighteenth century, there were songbirds in residence at Dyrham Park, the picturesque seat of William Blathwayt, which were kept in ornate cages suspended by strong pulleys '[so] as not to deface the ceiling'. Even birds from far-off lands could be found squawking and chattering in the recesses of some aristocratic households, to the immense satisfaction of guests and visitors. Rachel Bourchier, Countess of Bath, gave a shilling to the maid who brought her a parrot in 1644, and Lady Strafford mentioned a parrot owned by her mother-in-law in 1711, which she described, along with the rest of Lady Wentworth's animals, as a 'dumb creature'.[10]

A remarkable menagerie of beasts was maintained by Jemima, Countess of Sandwich, in London in the 1660s, her collection comprising at the very least a parrot, a civet, and an undisclosed number of apes. Possessing such exotic animals was another way of demonstrating prosperity and sophistication in the Stuart period. We hear of monkey chains being acquired for use at Lyme Hall in the early seventeenth century. The aristocratic Leghs paid handsome sums of money to have these creatures included at their Cheshire seat, parting on one occasion with a substantial £60 in the name of exoticism. Although clearly chained up around the estate for some of the day, the animals on the whole appear to have been treated well here, with one sick monkey being operated on in the late 1600s at a cost of five shillings.[11]

Pet monkeys were an unexpectedly routine addition to aristocratic properties at this time, with Lady Wentworth jumping on the bandwagon herself in the capital in the early 1700s. Her monkey was called Pug. In 1706, she wrote the following to her son, the 3rd Baron Raby:

> Mr Charles Arundell has got a monkey, he got it on shipboard, and it is exactly like my Pug, only mine is very pert, and full of devertin tricks, and the other is so kept under it dares not stir but just as they bid it; the eyes of mine sparkle like two diamonds, and is perter than ever you see her, and fuller of tricks, but it must be when she has a mind to it.[12]

However fiercely Lady Isabella Wentworth might fight Pug's corner, the evidence suggests that this monkey was generally unpredictable and given to sudden fits of energy that could be frightening, especially for young children. Isabella's niece, for instance, was 'very much afraid' of her aunt's foreign pet, treating Pug as kindly as the next animal, 'but at great distance'. To nobody's great surprise, Lady Wentworth only had love for the mollycoddled monkey, and broke down once again when the time came to say goodbye in December 1712. 'I think I ought not to have wrote so long a letter to you today, for I am sure you'll have a very long one from Lady Wentworth with very great lamentation; for her monkey is dead,' Lady Strafford briefed her husband that month. She had been banned from laughing at the request of her mother-in-law following the loss, although she privately admitted to Thomas that the monkey's passing was no great loss to her. As a coping mechanism, Lady Wentworth had immediately engaged a suitable artist to capture the late Pug's likeness in two separate portraits, 'one large and the other in miniature'.[13]

Horrific cases of aristocrats completely losing control of their pet monkeys were occasionally documented. Sir William Hooker's wife knew of a respectable family who had tragically lost a child in this way in the later seventeenth century, relating the gruesome story to John Evelyn in November 1683. One evening, she recounted, when the infant had been put to bed and the nurse 'was a little absent', a monkey living in the house had found its way into the chamber and 'bitten out its eyes, torn the face, and eaten the head into the brain'. Having listened to this tale, Evelyn came to the conclusion in his diary that such 'mischievous animals' should be kept away from young families at all costs.[14]

Riding and hunting

Taking one's horse out on a clear, bright day, with the grass crunching underfoot in cold weather and the trees stirring seductively during the summer months, was considered an ideal recreational activity by the Stuart aristocracy. 'All this week I spent at my work and sometimes riding abroad,' Lady Anne Clifford noted in her diary in June 1619. A month earlier she had accompanied her husband, the 3rd Earl of Dorset, and some others of considerable distinction for a gentle ride through 'Whitby Wood', causing supper to be pushed back that evening to 9:00pm. The 1st Baron Herbert of Cherbury, who as we know took great pleasure in horses, offered some advice on 'graceful' riding in the early seventeenth century. The rider should always look through the horse's two ears, he wrote, with the 'rod' placed over the left ear to turn him 'every way, helping himself with his left foot, and rod upon the left part of his neck, to make the horse turn on the right hand, and with the right foot and help of his rod also ... to turn him on the left hand'.[15]

In the countryside, horses were popularly used for hunting. During a tour of England at the beginning of the period, a foreign commentator observed: 'The English hold the chase in high esteem; there is scarcely any royal residence, or even a nobleman's house, which has not at least one deer park – sometimes two, or even three, may be found.'[16] This was indeed the case. Aristocrats valued hunting above almost every other form of recreational activity in the seventeenth and early eighteenth centuries, not only for its obvious connotations of grandeur and affluence, but also for its ability to thrill and excite. Sir Christopher Guise of Elmore Court in Gloucestershire could not praise the sport highly enough in the memoirs he drew up of his ancient family in the 1600s:

> Hunting is a kind of waking trance or a pleasing dream; for so long as the sport is on foot, it doth so amuse the mind and so earnestly busy all its faculties that I have been as much concerned for the death of a hare as some would be in the event of a "battayle", and have as earnestly wish't sometimes to find or start a hare as if therein had consisted a considerable part of my welfare... Hunting is no ill recreation for men of plentiful fortunes; it is good exercise, it clears the mind, it hardens the body for weather.[17]

If happening across an aristocratic hunt in the reign of James I, one might typically discern a party of well-dressed men on horseback, a pack of eager hounds, and should the day's events be progressing nicely, a herd of deer running furiously in the opposite direction. Often the setting for the sport was an aristocrat's deer park, which might even persuade the participants of the event to hunt on foot with weapons. While deer certainly seemed to be the primary target of large hunting parties in Jacobean England, they were not the only animal to be earmarked for slaughter. Foxes, otters, hares, rabbits, and ducks could easily find themselves being chased by yapping dogs and shouting men, and were particularly vulnerable around Downham in Lancashire, where the esquire Nicholas Assheton appeared willing to kill any creature that crossed his path. 'Hunting the otter; killed one; taken another', he wrote in his journal on 2 May 1617. Exactly a month later, the esquire recorded that he had 'tried for a fox, but found none'. Foxes succeeded deer as the chief quarry of the aristocracy in the later seventeenth century, in part due to the mounting expense of keeping deer in country parks. After a dramatic fox hunt in January 1702, the baronet Sir Robert Burdett was left 'miserably fatigued' at Bramcote in Warwickshire, with all but one of his hounds lost in the confusion of the chase.[18]

Hunting dogs could be difficult to control outside of the kennel, and in the first place were bred very carefully by aristocrats to ensure maximum efficiency in the field. Sir Robert Burdett described one pack of hounds as 'very poor' in March 1699, with many of the beasts apparently being too old, 'some very small, others large. I doubt there will not be any fit to breed on.'[19] To help men like Burdett on their way, the ideal hunting dog was meticulously outlined in a work entitled *The Gentleman's Recreation* in 1686. The head ought to be 'of middle proportion, rather long than round; his nostrils wide; his ears large; his back bowed; the fillets great; the haunches large; the thighs well trussed; the ham straight; the tail big near the reins, and the rest slender to the end'. In another treatise by the same writer, there were a few words on the best hunting horses, which were either to be bought from a reputable breeder or acquired at one of the great fairs held in northern England, for example Malton or Ripon. Ideally, a hunting horse's head should be broad and long, it was noted, while its ears were better small and 'pricked'; if the eyes were wide, bright, and attentive, and the nostrils sufficiently flared, this was preferable, too. According to the author, the colour of the animal also mattered.[20]

The inherent dangers of tearing helter-skelter towards prey on the back of a horse meant that accidents were an occupational hazard. Sir Robert Burdett admitted to injuring himself numerous times while engaged in the sport, commenting in one letter dated 1698 that he chased foxes 'to the hazard of my neck, having bruised my shoulder by tumbling over a slough, and ventured drowning' in a single day. In August 1619, the future baronet and knight Capell Bedell of Huntingdonshire ended up riding into a tree after pursuing a stag too frantically, the resulting blow being so violent that he was left 'sore battered and bruised', and even feverish.[21] Both baronets got off lightly compared to John Holles, 1st Duke of Newcastle, however. Having taken a tumble from his horse during a routine hunt near Welbeck Abbey in July 1711, the nobleman received such extensive injuries that he ended up dying from them a few days later.

If the risk of broken bones or death did not sit well with aristocrats, particularly those of a nervous disposition, they could always try ferreting instead. This more sedate activity worked well on smaller animals that dug homes underground, such as rabbits, and involved human participants first frightening the said creatures into their burrows by making a loud noise. Nets were next laid at the exits to the tunnels before the ferret was introduced. The ferret's job was to coax the conies (or whatever they might be) into leaving their burrows again, hopefully in the direction of the waiting traps. Before being set loose in the earth to carry out their claustrophobic assignment, ferrets were usually muzzled and fitted with little bells around their necks. Many Stuart aristocrats employed warreners to carry out such a form of hunting, for it was often seen as a necessity as opposed to a hobby, but even then, an earl or esquire might involve himself in the process when the fancy took him. Nicholas Blundell of Crosby Hall, for instance, jotted in his diary that he had helped his warreners kill four rabbits using a combination of ferrets and dogs in January 1705.[22]

Another type of hunting that provided an alternative to the perils of the deer and fox chase was hawking, or falconry. Birds of prey primarily targeted ducks and other waterfowl found in parkland and fields. A properly accoutred hawk or falcon was fitted with short leather straps called jesses, an additional leather strap called a bewit, which was tied to the leg and from which a shrill bell or bells were hung, and a leather hood to keep the bird calm when not flying. The falconer 'must use his hawk in such manner, that he may make her grow familiar with him alone or in company, and to that end he must often unhood and hood her again', it was advised in *The Gentleman's Recreation*. Training up a bird of prey to hunt on command took a fair amount of work and patience and could require many practice sessions. When Sir Richard Cholmley of Yorkshire obtained a new goshawk in July 1619, he made a point of getting up before sunrise one morning to begin training the bird, 'but all to little'. Towards the end of the seventeenth century, English aristocrats began to lose interest in hawking altogether, although the conservative William Russell, 5th Earl of Bedford, was spending more money than ever on the sport at Woburn Abbey after 1660. Here all manner of interesting raptors were to be found swooping through the air and leaping from the earl's fist, coming from Scotland, Ireland, Nova Scotia, New England, and North Africa.[23]

Outdoor and indoor games

There was lots of fun to be had in the gardens of aristocratic mansions. 'Burley Breaks' was sometimes played by Lady Anne Clifford and Richard Sackville at Knole in the 1610s, an outdoor game that involved three competing couples attempting to catch each other. In this garden one could also while away the time playing bowls, with most elite houses across the country possessing a manicured bowling green in the seventeenth century. Sir Richard Cholmley bought various items from a 'bowl-maker' in London in 1620, including a 'round jack' and a bag to put it in, which were presumably to be used on a private bowling green in Yorkshire. Should there be no green to speak of at a house or an aristocrat fancied playing further afield, public bowling greens were available to use. This well-tended setting was described as a 'school of wrangling' in *The Compleat Gamester*, first published in 1674, 'for here men will wrangle for a hair's breadth, and make a stir where a straw would end the controversy.' Sir Anthony Ashley Cooper visited his local bowling green in Dorset habitually as a young man in the 1630s, purportedly meeting his 'enemy' Mr Rogers here.[24]

Besides Burley Breaks and the very popular bowls, tennis might be taken up by the aristocracy to engage or relax the mind, although it was rare for an aristocrat to own his or her own court. This game was also exclusively played indoors in the Stuart period, and featured rules that would in all likelihood leave modern-day tennis players scratching their heads at the net. It is possible that the 5th Earl of Bedford had built himself a tennis court at Woburn Abbey by the Restoration era, but whether or not he did, the nobleman is known to have greatly enjoyed the sport, his accounts showing that throughout his life he made purchases of rackets and other necessary equipment.

Billiards was played indoors by aristocrats in the later seventeenth century, with Charles Cotton noting in *The Compleat Gamester* that 'I cannot but commend this as the most gentile and innocent [game] of any I know, if rightly used.' A billiards table appeared for the first time at Lyme Hall in Cheshire in 1689, joining the good-looking table at Woburn Abbey that had been installed two decades earlier by the 5th Earl of Bedford's son, William, Lord Russell. Henry Howard, 1st

Earl of Northampton, kept a chess set at Northampton House in a cabinet of purple velvet in the early seventeenth century, with pieces that were laced with gold. Nicholas Blundell, meanwhile, stored his own board unceremoniously in a loft 100 years later at Crosby Hall, recording in December 1707 that he played the game with a Mr Aldred.[25]

Gambling and prostitutes

Two particular indoor games heavily associated with the vice of gambling in Stuart England were dice and cards. To the chagrin of moral commentators, the English aristocracy loved both. It was reported in May 1672 that Robert Greville, 4th Baron Brooke, had won the astonishing sum of £4,800 in a single night in London playing dice. Shortly afterwards he was said to have tripped descending his carriage and scattered the money across the ground. In the 1680s, even a family christening did not stop a group of aristocratic women from playing cards for money. The infant involved was Sir Richard Temple's daughter, Maria, who on the day was accordingly doused with holy water in the drawing room of a modest London townhouse. While the child's mother, Mary Temple, and her godmothers, Lady Gardiner and Lady Chaworth, had the courtesy to break up their game long enough to witness the important moment, as soon as the ceremony was over, they immediately returned to gambling. Not all aristocrats showed the same inexorable enthusiasm for these amusements, however. 'I am weary of my life; I have here no time for my soul. Cards we play at four hours every day,' the wife of the 1st Earl of Godolphin, Margaret Godolphin, complained during her time at court in the later seventeenth century.[26]

Following its banishment from England under the rule of Oliver Cromwell, elite horse racing and the gambling that went with it thundered back into existence at Newmarket and elsewhere in the 1660s, thanks largely to the actions of Charles II. The future baronet Thomas Isham gave a description of the races held at Rothwell in Northamptonshire in 1672:

> The course is well situated in a plain between the hills, 2000 yards in length, 500 in breadth; they go twice round before they reach the goal. Four horses ran... The prize, two silver candlesticks, being placed before them, they got on their horses, and holding their reins, await[ed] the signal; when the shrill horn sounded they started off without delay, and bounded for the goal. Shouts rent the air.[27]

At another event at nearby Harlestone the same year, Isham noted that many of the distinguished riders who had turned up were instead competing for a silver cup. Two participants fell from their horses and badly hurt themselves that day, with one of the injured having bet another gentleman five shillings that he would win his race. Bets could often be much larger than this relatively modest figure, needless to say. 'The English nobility take great delight in horse races,' the traveller Monsieur Misson observed late in the period, noting that it was 'pretty common for them to lay wagers of £2000 upon one race'.[28]

Open-air cockfighting drew in aristocratic gamblers just as much as horse racing did. 'To that foolish sport of cocking they were addicted,' the disgraced Sir George Sondes said of his sons, Freeman and George, in 1655. The best combative cocks, according to *The Compleat Gamester*, had a particular shape and colour, and were endowed with both courage and a 'sharp-heel'. A nameless servant of the 1st Duke of Buckingham was well rewarded by Roger Manners, 5th Earl of Rutland, in 1605 when he brought a suitable 'fyghtinge cocke' to Belvoir Castle in Leicestershire.[29]

In the eyes of God-fearing citizens and especially Puritans, the one aristocratic entertainment perhaps worse than mindless gambling was whoring. 'I thank heaven, no man can tax me for swearing, drinking, whoring, or gaming,' Sir George Sondes wrote in 1655, adding for good measure, 'I never was in [a] whore-house, or used whores.' The same could not be said for Sir Humphrey Mildmay of Danbury Place in Essex, who in

May 1639 confessed to 'playing the fool with two punks on the Thames till towards night'. The esquire also recorded paying sums to 'bawds', 'she friends', and self-professed pimps in the mid-seventeenth century, and revealed openly on one occasion that he had visited 'a place of wantonness'. That the man also drank significant amounts of alcohol in this last establishment is no great surprise. In 1673, rumours circulated in Northamptonshire that Sir William Haselwood of Maidwell had gone one step further than Mildmay and was regularly entertaining prostitutes and 'loose men' on his own property. Such slander had allegedly escaped from the lips of a drunk servant called Chapman, who, when Lady Haselwood learned of the unspeakable things being said about her husband, was thrown out of the house by her.[30]

Dancing, masques, and balls

Margaret Cavendish, Duchess of Newcastle, admitted in later life that she was not one for the 'graceful art' of dancing, believing it to be an activity best suited to singletons. It was 'too light an action' for spouses, she argued, and sat badly with the 'gravity' and sacredness of marriage. While the noblewoman was entitled to her opinions, one can safely say that most other aristocrats did not hold this view in Stuart England. For the majority, there was no harm in letting one's hair down every once in a while, married or otherwise. The general rule of thumb in elite circles seemed to be that, if dancing was indeed planned for the evening, it should be sustained with fervour and enthusiasm until dawn. Sir Humphrey Mildmay and his relatives accordingly danced 'till morning light' at Danbury Place in July 1640, between the Short and Long Parliaments. Likewise in November 1700, Sir Walter Calverley of Esholt in Yorkshire dined and then danced through the night at Sir William Hawkesworth's house.[31]

For those aristocrats who spent much of their time at court, and who were lucky enough to find favour with the royal family, exciting opportunities arose to take part in masques or attend balls. Masques were a curiously popular form of entertainment at the court of James I and Anna of Denmark in the early seventeenth century, being a mixture of imaginative disguises, breathtaking set designs, biblical and classical themes, dancing, and original music that created a stimulating and sometimes surreal spectacle.[32] Theatrical performances in all but name, often they were written by notable playwrights such as London's Ben Jonson, who in a short space of time penned both *The Hue and Cry After Cupid* and *The Masque of Beauty*. The former masque was performed following the wedding of John Ramsay, Viscount Haddington, and Lady Elizabeth Radclyffe, a daughter of the 5th Earl of Sussex, in February 1608, showing 'Venus with her chariot drawn by swans' coming in a cloud 'to seek her son'. *The Masque of Beauty* had been staged a few weeks earlier in the wake of Twelfth Night, with Alethea Howard, Countess of Arundel, taking part. The countess appears to have practised for the role rigorously beforehand, and rightly so, for the end result comprised a glittering array of sixteen dancing ladies garbed in orange, silver, and 'sea-green' costumes, headed by Queen Anna herself. The occasional hiccup during a final performance was of course unavoidable, no matter the level of work put in. According to the courtier Sir John Harington, almost every aspect of the masque performed at Theobalds House in Hertfordshire in 1606 that could have gone wrong, did go wrong. One woman playing the Queen of Sheba tripped and fell directly at Christian IV of Denmark's feet, spilling the contents of a casket into his lap, before the Danish monarch himself tumbled over and had to be carried out of the room to recuperate. Harington reported that though 'the entertainment and show went forward' after these incidents, 'most of the presenters went backward, or fell down; wine did so occupy their upper chambers.'[33]

Masques, understandably termed 'strange pageantries' by Sir John Harington, continued unabated into the reign of Charles I, with the Mildmays of Danbury Place attending such a spectacle on 14 February 1635. All good things must inevitably come to an end, however, and as seventeenth-century aristocratic tastes changed and evolved, masques were gradually confined to the pages of history. Majestic balls with which the modern reader might be more familiar took their place, the grandest of them coinciding with state occasions and royal birthdays. The court of Charles II threw a ball nearly every week during his merry reign, with one event hosted by James Scott, Duke of Monmouth, for Queen Catherine, described in 1665 by Denis de Repas:

> There was not a dozen of persons in the room besides the ladies and gentlemen who did dance; yet I was there from the beginning to the last amongst all the nobility and the beauties. There was above four or five hundred people at the door, but none could get in. They did begin to dance about eight of the clock at night. The queen came half an hour after and went away at eleven. The rest did dance till between one and two. The queen danced all the while she was there with an extraordinary great modesty. They did dance altogether country dances, and did jump and leap as those creatures which live upon ... mountains.[34]

A ball held decades later in November 1684, just before Charles II passed away, was perhaps more inclusive, featuring guests attired in fine gowns and expensive 'shoulder knots'. The Duchesses of Norfolk and Grafton were said to have danced excellently at this event, although Lady Margaret Pembroke, wife of Thomas Herbert, 8th Earl of Pembroke, reportedly stole the show with her confident performance.[35]

The theatre

A trip into town to see the latest play helped Stuart aristocrats to remain cultured and informed in a country that was bursting with artistic talent. Over a few short months in 1634, Sir Humphrey Mildmay made it his business to watch three different plays in London, the first a comedy of manners by Shirley entitled *The Gamester*, the second a tragicomedy called *The Faithful*

Shepherdess, which was performed at Blackfriars Theatre, and the last a play by the name of *Lasander and Calista*.

Theatres suffered a predictable setback during the Cromwellian years, but just like horse racing and other forms of entertainment, they were to make a triumphant return with the Restoration in 1660, particularly in the capital. Everybody who was anybody flocked to venues such as the Duke's Theatre in Lincoln's Inn Fields and the Theatre Royal on Bridges Street in the early reign of Charles II. Samuel Pepys recorded seeing John Wilmot, 2nd Earl of Rochester, and the 1st Duke of Ormond's son, John Butler, at a performance of *Heraclius* at the Duke's Theatre in February 1667. The Irish aristocrat Butler received a standing ovation when he entered the pit in the play's final minutes. At the end of the reign of Queen Anne, the aristocratic appetite for theatre-going seemed to be just as ravenous, with Lady Strafford informing her husband in 1712 that she had recently been to see a play called *The Distressed Mother*, an adaptation of a French tragedy attributed to Ambrose Philips. 'I think it's a very good one,' she remarked simply.[36]

The eagerness of the aristocracy to get the very most out of their theatrical excursions could lead to senseless altercations on occasion. Sir John Reresby noted a heated encounter at the Theatre Royal in March 1678, involving himself and a gentleman called Mr Symons, who was dissatisfied with the afternoon's seating arrangements.[37] Put simply, Symons liked the look of Reresby's seat better than his own, and therefore he attempted to do a trade with the baronet using the excuse that an acquaintance of his was sitting nearby. Reresby, realising that his position in the theatre was far superior to that of Symons, repeatedly refused to move. The would-be negotiator, who had been drinking, aggressively accused Reresby of being 'uncivil' in his obstinacy, prompting Reresby to call Symons a 'rascal' in return. Tensions by now were dangerously high, with both men ready to use their fists to settle the matter. The argument happened to be overheard by the Cornish baronet Sir John

Trelawny, who jumped in before any blows were delivered and put his hand between the two opponents, calling for peace. For Reresby, though, this was not the end. Once Trelawny had disappeared into the crowds again, he told Symons in little more than a whisper that he should follow him out of the theatre to resolve the dispute permanently. The baronet, however, had not whispered quietly enough, for presently they were reported to the Captain of the Yeomen of the Guard, who by chance was attending the performance that afternoon. Before either man knew what was happening, they found themselves answering for their actions in the presence of the Duke of Monmouth. The intervention at length produced a truce, and when Sir John came across Mr Symons later on in the street, the latter gentleman thrust nothing in his face but an apologetic bottle of wine.

Other amusements

On the death of William Cavendish, 1st Duke of Devonshire, in 1707, it was noted reflectively that he had 'great skill in languages, was a true judge in history, a critic in poetry, and had a fine hand in music', as well as having 'an elegant taste in painting, and all politer arts'. At the beginning of the period, Lady Anne Clifford engaged in various recreational activities at Knole that were then chiefly regarded as feminine. One of these, needlework, kept the noblewoman occupied on many a dreary afternoon. 'I wrought very hard and made an end of one of my cushions of Irish stitch work,' she noted in her diary in June 1616. Dame Lucy Reynell of Forde House in Devon also liked to sew in her spare time, sometimes making 'coverings of tapestries', or creating articles of clothing for her own family.[38]

For a select few gentlemen, it was past events and the perusal of historical manuscripts that made the ideal hobby. The future Duke of Chandos, James Brydges, could think of nothing better than spending time sifting through old documents with his acquaintance Mr Tyrrell. In 1623, the Suffolk aristocrat

Sir Simonds D'Ewes also began to study historical manuscripts, initially out of necessity but then for sheer pleasure, with his first find at the Tower of London being a charter written during the time of Edward the Confessor in the eleventh century. 'From this day forward,' he wrote in his autobiography, 'I never wholly gave over the study of records; but spent many days and months about it, to my great content and satisfaction.'[39] In time, D'Ewes claimed that he could spot transcription errors made by the Tower clerks instantly, so well versed had he become in this niche field.

Aristocratic libraries or studies in England could contain hundreds, if not thousands, of volumes. In the cluttered study at Hanbury Hall in Worcestershire, the home of the esquire Thomas Vernon, there were 122 books to be found in the early eighteenth century. These included both volumes of Clarendon's *History of the Rebellion*, five thick volumes of Roman history, a copy of the English dictionary, the Old and New Testaments, *An Amount of Remarkable Things in Travelling* by Gilbert Burnet, and a tome entitled *History of Vegetables*. The great library at Woburn Abbey housed around 152 books in 1700, with a further 247 volumes and manuscripts kept pristinely at the Russells' townhouse in London. Both collections, however, were eclipsed by the impressive library of 1,400 books left by Francis Willoughby of Wollaton Hall when he died aged thirty-six in 1672. While Lady Anne Clifford had books read to her at Knole in the 1610s, one of which concerned 'the government of the Turks', most other aristocrats probably flicked through publications themselves.[40] Early newspapers added to the quantity of reading material available in the final years of the period, with Sir Daniel Fleming regularly purchasing *The London Gazette* and *Flying Post* between November 1698 and July 1699.

The emergence of new technologies and ideas, especially in the latter half of the Stuart epoch, occupied the idle minds of forward-thinking aristocrats such as Sir Thomas Isham of Lamport Hall. The Northamptonshire gentleman, for example, took great interest in the news that a telescope had recently been invented that was 'far superior to any other' in January 1672. A few months later, his thoughts were on another new device developed by the mathematician Sir Samuel Morland, being in essence a primitive form of megaphone called 'a stentorophonic trumpet'. Discovering that Sir William Langdale of Walgrave had acquired one in London, Isham and some others at once rode in a carriage to the knight's house in Northamptonshire to hear the instrument for themselves. 'Mr Richardson took it and went to the mill,' the gentleman recorded in his diary, 'but we remained near the bowling green, which is a mile off, but we could hear distinctly and articulately what Richardson said through the trumpet.'[41]

It was the Royal Society, an innovative scientific institution founded in London in November 1660, that entranced the future 1st Duke of Chandos, James Brydges, in the 1690s. He became an official member of the organisation in 1694 while still in his early twenties, and by 1702 the gentleman had already dined with his fellow enthusiasts an impressive forty-three times.[42] Even in the early years of the seventeenth century, male English aristocrats were leaving traces here and there of a fascination with the sciences and complex mathematics. An inventory drawn up at Bramfield in Suffolk showed that the esquire Arthur Coke had in his possession a selection of mathematical instruments upon his death in 1629, including a quadrant, a sector, and a circumferentor for measuring horizontal angles, the forerunner of the theodylite. The same year, another inventory of goods taken at Earls Croome in Worcestershire revealed that the esquire Leonard Jefferies had kept an 'astrologe' at home, a multipurpose device that was used either 'for fixing one's position using the stars' or 'for working out horoscopes'.[43]

8

TRANSPORT AND TRAVEL

Rain pounded the English countryside with considerable fury in February 1710 as Sir Thomas Cave and his wife approached the inviting outline of a coaching inn. This establishment, known as the 'Mag Pye', marked the halfway point in a routine journey the couple were making, from Claydon House in Buckinghamshire, where they had been staying with Lady Margaret's family, to the ornate Stanford Hall in Leicestershire, Sir Thomas's newly built country seat. The trio of aristocrats, including Margaret's cousin, Peg Adams, needed little encouragement to board the vehicle waiting for them in the inn's yard, which would be carrying them the remainder of the way to Stanford. In no time its dark form had rattled away from the Mag Pye again and disappeared into the encircling gloom, leaving behind only the faint sound of horses' hooves. What came next could not have been predicted, however. Very soon into the journey the weather deteriorated further and the roads became flooded, causing the bottom of the coach to dramatically fill with water. To make things worse, by the time the coachman had guided his horses to an unassuming ford that was to be crossed at Coton, the deluge of rain had left it near-on impassable. A coach, certainly, could not possibly have navigated the rushing current without being swept away.

In the end, Sir Thomas and Peg Adams braved the wild channel of water on horseback, while Lady Margaret, having no horse herself, was forced to cross the stream using a plank of wood as a kind of makeshift bridge. The gentlewoman by all accounts tried her utmost to reach the far side of the foaming, roaring stream without incident or injury, but ultimately the small plank on which she walked proved too hazardous a platform. Eventually, the elegant mistress of Stanford Hall, who was no doubt the envy of so many who kept company with her, slipped over into the filthy water. Coming to the unhappy traveller's aid almost immediately was the sodden coachman, an individual of some courage it would seem, who scooped her limp body into his arms as carefully as he could and made straight for the indistinct bank Lady Margaret had desperately been trying to reach. Here Sir Thomas and Peg Adams were already waiting with their steeds, drenched themselves and no doubt suffering from shock. By a stroke of luck, perhaps the only to be had that day, a lonely house was presently spotted nearby with a candle burning in one of its windows. The building was to be the coach party's salvation, although getting to this refuge first required an uncomfortable – and probably by this point unwelcome – climb 'over a hedge'.[1]

Of course, the ordeal undergone by the Caves and their coachman in 1710 was hardly reflective of the average aristocratic journey. It is fair to say that most Stuart aristocrats travelled in uninterrupted comfort during the seventeenth and early eighteenth centuries, with the promise at the end of equally comfortable destinations. Be it on foot, on horseback, or in a coach exuding convenience and opulence, the trips that elite men and women made were very rarely unpleasant affairs; some journeys, in fact, were regarded so positively or with such reverence that they were recalled many years later. Lady Anne Clifford, for instance, noted in her diary sometime in 1676: 'I remembered how this day was 60 years [since] my first Lord and I did go out of Little Dorset House in London Town onwards on our journey northwards.' While longer passages could by their very nature be more tedious than short rides between locations, often this was a non-issue. Young aristocratic men eager to begin touring the continent after years of endless study in England would certainly have been unfazed by the prospect of a lengthy trek across France, Italy, and other European countries. Indeed, the eighteen-year-old son of Sir Heneage Finch, Daniel, behaved so enthusiastically on his way to Florence in November 1665 that he ended up hurting his leg, to the 'great apprehension' of his parents.[2]

Modes of transport

Aristocrats were not above using their legs to get around in Stuart England, particularly if the distance to be covered was sufficiently short or adverse weather conditions rendered a horse or coach inappropriate. The esquire Nicholas Assheton of Downham recorded that his cousin went 'on foot' to see the knight Sir Peter Middleton one day in January 1618, 'there being a frost'. The impoverished Elizabeth Cary, Viscountess Falkland, on the other hand, chose to walk everywhere in London to 'avoid occasion of further debt by keeping or hiring a coach' in the 1630s.[3] Cary's relative destitution had come about through the actions of her father, Sir Lawrence Tanfield, and later those of her estranged husband, Sir Henry Cary, both of whom – albeit for different reasons – had taken the decision to cut her off financially. She married Sir Henry Cary in 1602 and travelled with him to Ireland, where he served as lord deputy from 1622 to 1629. In 1625, she returned to London and became a high-profile convert to Roman Catholicism in 1626. Her conversion encouraged her husband to seek a separation, and she led the remainder of her life in some poverty in London, seeking both financial redress and custody of their children. (Four of Cary's six daughters became Benedictine nuns at Cambrai, and her two youngest sons also professed in French religious houses, but returned to Protestantism later on.)

Those aristocrats who travelled on horseback also did so if the journey was expected to be a brief one, although extended rides covering many miles were similarly undertaken. In December 1616, Lady Anne Clifford spent the entire day on the back of a horse after setting off from the now ruinous Brougham Castle in the direction of London. This distance amounted, according to the noblewoman in her diary, to twenty-seven miles. Such an achievement would be bettered in 1663 by the esquire Richard Legh of Lyme Hall, who is said to have travelled all the way from Cheshire to London on horseback accompanied by his steward and two other servants. The significant levels of prestige and skill involved in journeying on horseback undoubtedly appealed to gentlemen like Legh, while for younger aristocrats there could have been nothing more thrilling in life than riding to destinations in the open air. When it was time for Edmund Verney's son, Ralph, to attend school at Winchester College in the late 1670s, the sixteen-year-old boy pleaded with his father to set aside the family's usual means of transportation for the journey south. 'My boy Ralph having lost his ague, keeps a great deal of begging at me to go on horseback, pretending that he is always sick in a coach.' He eventually gave in and agreed to his son's request, riding down to Winchester from their country abode with the teenager and two attendants. Edmund's deceased mother, Lady Mary Verney of Claydon House, had represented a minority of Stuart aristocrats who were open about their dislike of travelling in this manner. 'Yesterday I came very late to town and very weary,' she informed her husband, another Ralph, from London in 1647, 'for by reason I came all ye way but six miles on horseback … and I rid upon a cruel trotting horse to boot.'[4]

A coach and horses was the standard mode of transport for longer routes, with many aristocratic families possessing their own personal model and animals for the purpose. Lady Anne Clifford and Richard Sackville took two coaches 'with four horses apiece' when they embarked on a lengthy journey north to visit the former's ancestral lands in 1616, which was likely to have been broken up into sections to ease the couple's passage.[5] The husband of the illegitimate child of Charles II, Lady Mary Tudor, Countess of Derwentwater, however, would call upon his own coach and horses in the early eighteenth century for short distances. For this, he became an object of great ridicule: 'Lady Derwentwater's new husband comes every day to the coffee house in his fine coach and two footmen to wait of him, and the coach waits at the coffee house, and all else here walks to it, so he is laughed at for it.'[6] So noted Lady Isabella Wentworth from the capital in September 1707, who herself was one for keeping up appearances.

Elegant coaches, and all that came with them, were indeed something to be shown off by the nobility and gentry. Just over a year earlier in March 1706, Lady Wentworth had been most taken with the coach horses owned by one Charles Arundell, presumably some relation of the Arundell esquires of Stoke Park in Northamptonshire, which were the 'prettiest' the gentlewoman had ever seen. She described them as 'very dark, almost like black, with white manes and long white tails', and as having a majestic trot that encouraged 'all people from the highest to the lowest [to] stare after them'. Lady Wentworth wished that her son, who was in Berlin at the time, had the handsome animals for himself.[7]

Aristocratic coaches could be just as pretty as the creatures that dutifully pulled them. Although earlier designs in the reign of James I might appear altogether clumsy and imposing, with their black leather exteriors, square bodies, and heavy curtains or flaps, coaches emerging in the middle years of the seventeenth century were by contrast sleek, contoured, and delicate.[8] These latter vehicles were sometimes gilded or had their doors painted with an aristocratic family's coat of arms, housing tasteful interiors that might be upholstered in velvet or decorated with yards of ribbon. Gilt coaches were such a regular sight at Hyde Park in London from around 1660 that Charles II famously ended up banning them early in his reign, believing that the gold paint could be better used elsewhere.

One new feature of cabs considered both sophisticated and practical during the Restoration, and that would not be going anywhere for centuries, was glass windows. They replaced the curtains or flaps that had covered the openings of previous coaches, and in theory provided aristocrats with a securer interior that was better at keeping bad weather out. As with all things, this development pleased some and made sceptics of others, such as the dubious 1st Viscount Fermanagh in the summer of 1704, who was 'sensible that a glass chariot is an inconvenient way of travelling in the month of August'. A coach with glass windows disagreed entirely with an ailing female relative of Sir Edward Harley, the 1st Viscount Townshend informing his 'kinsman' in January 1669 that the gentlewoman was unable to ride in one without fainting on the spot.[9]

The cheapest coach Sir Edward Harley could find for his family in February 1665 was £38, equivalent to the sum of about £4,000 today. That these structures were so expensive to purchase in the first place, and the fact that suspension in them was supposedly improving, makes it all the more surprising to discover that mishaps and even serious accidents involving coaches did happen. Sir John Verney's coach had to be dragged home in March 1699 after one of its front wheels – not for the first time – malfunctioned and left the Buckinghamshire gentleman stranded in the middle of London. 'Now Richard tells me one of the hind wheels is broke and he believes none of the wheels will last down,' he wrote angrily. The fashionable model belonging to the baronet and politician Sir John Pelham of Sussex overturned and killed him four years later in 1703. Such unfortunate episodes taking place during coach journeys did not always pertain to structural failure, as Charles Sackville, 6th Earl of Dorset, would learn a short while after John Verney's wheel fiasco in the capital. Riding between Fulham and Chelsea one Saturday night in July 1699, the earl's coach suddenly found itself being set upon and robbed by ten soldiers on horseback, who stole sixty guineas, a gold watch, a gold snuffbox, and a sword.[10]

An alternative to the standard coach and horses towards the end of the Stuart period was the chaise, a light vehicle with two wheels and an open top, which might be pulled by two horses at most. Often considered 'too slight' to travel any great distance by aristocrats, but very fast, this mode of transport was admired by the courtier Sir Thomas Coke's brother, John, at the beginning of 1704, who was impressed by the fact that they 'all hung on shafts'.[11] For convenient, though not necessarily speedy, transportation around London in particular, the sedan chair made a welcome appearance in England in the 1630s. These nifty contraptions were introduced from France by Sir Saunders Duncombe, and consisted of two sturdy poles that held aloft a small, basic cab for a single aristocrat to sit in. The poles were lifted and carried by dedicated 'chairmen' positioned at either end of the structure. Alice Sherard, Lady Brownlow, paid two chairmen five shillings a day to take her around the capital in a sedan chair in the early 1690s, sometimes giving them a shilling extra to purchase a drink *en route*. When it was dark and the gentlewoman happened to find herself occupying her suspended seat, another shilling was spent on torches to light the way. The sedan chair used in London by Wriothesley Russell, 2nd Duke of Bedford, and his wife Elizabeth Russell in the early eighteenth century was richly finished like their many coaches, being painted, lined with crimson and white velvet, and boasting three glass windows.[12]

If all else failed, one could always turn to a public stagecoach for transport. Robert Harley, son of Sir Edward Harley, opted to use one to get to the Inner Temple in London in October 1692. That he began a subsequent letter to his father with 'I arrived here safely this evening' speaks volumes, the gentleman further commenting:

> The company in the coach were two women, one a Londoner, her sister married to Motly, a dancing master in Ludlow; the other taken up at Broadway, an innkeeper's wife in Bishopsgate Street. The two men were a Frenchman, a student of Divinity, and a very tall elderly gentleman, in face like the family of the Howards, very well bred and a good scholar.[13]

The danger of riding in a stagecoach was made more apparent in another letter written by Harley to his father in October 1693, when he had again employed public transport to make his way down to the capital from Worcester. This time his travelling companions included a Catholic man, apparently married to a Protestant, and 'another man, I suppose in orders'; these individuals, however, were not what made the journey perilous that day. Harley noted that 'ten or twelve coaches kept together from Uxbridge for fear of thieves,' intimating that stagecoach robberies were perhaps more of a problem than for private vehicles. This seemed to be the case, although thievery on the highways was without doubt a widespread problem in Stuart England.[14]

In the event that a significant expanse of water featured on the planned route of an aristocrat, or travelling by water was considered the most effective way of getting somewhere, there were of course boats. While some aristocrats simply took a ferry up and down the River Thames in this period to make their way across London, such as the Brownlows of Belton House in the reign of William III, others owned exclusive private barges in the capital, which were moored on the river when not in use. Francis Russell, 4th Earl of Bedford, kept his luxurious barge on the bank opposite the original Bedford House in the Strand in the early seventeenth century, usually employing it to cruise up to Whitehall for business or pleasure. In May 1696, the potential pomp of such barge journeys along the Thames was exhibited in a short voyage made by Henry Howard, 7th Duke of Norfolk, during which several members of the nobility and a refined band of Venetian ambassadors were lavishly entertained with a 'variety of music' and a 'noble banquet'.[15]

Given the uncertain nature of water and its tendency to mirror the mood of the weather, good or bad, boats carrying aristocrats might infrequently run into danger, wherever they were situated in the country. In 1640, Sir Henry Slingsby and some already nervous relatives boarded a vessel that was to ferry them across the Humber in eastern England from Hull to Barton. Unfortunately, the boat encountered markedly fierce winds during its river crossing and even collided with a larger boat as it approached the opposite shore, which left Slingsby's son 'so affrighted with ye waters that he gave not over crying, and cried so vehemently as if he would have burst himself, and prayed as heartily'.[16]

Destinations

For what reasons did aristocrats travel? For many, like Lady Anne Clifford, journeys were made to visit or stay at various properties around the country. In July 1667, the great noblewoman left Barden Tower in Wharfedale after spending around half a year there, making for another of her northern piles in Westmorland, the rugged and now derelict Pendragon Castle. Here she stayed for only eight days before setting off with her household again, this time heading for Appleby Castle on the banks of the River Eden. The widow made herself reasonably comfortable at Appleby until the middle of October, when she rode off into the countryside once more to visit her medieval mansion of Brougham Castle near Penrith. It was usual for aristocratic families with a London townhouse to travel to them for an extended stay at least once a year, with the Russell family tending to leave Woburn Abbey for Bedford House in late winter or early spring. They were normally back in rural Bedfordshire by the end of June. The effective relocation of the Earl of Bedford and his entire household required a considerable level of coordination in the days before the Russells themselves boarded their coaches and began the journey south, especially from the steward and the clerk of the kitchen. The two servants systematically oversaw the loading of furniture and other domestic necessities onto waggons and hired carriers, which would all be sent to Bedford House ahead of the family in preparation for their arrival.

Another reason Stuart aristocrats travelled was of course to visit family, friends, and acquaintances. Though Sir Simonds D'Ewes' ultimate destination was his country abode of Stow Hall in Suffolk in June 1624, he first made a significant detour:

> On Monday, June the 21st, I went out of London towards Northamptonshire, where having stayed till Monday morning,

> June the 28th, I visited Sir Euseby Isham, aged about seventy years, the near kinsman, and Sir John Isham, the only brother of the Lady Denton, whom my father had married, both inhabiting and residing in that shire; I went from Orlingbury the said Monday morning, where Mr Tanfield sojourned, to Cambridge, and lay there that night, visiting divers of my friends there; having also in my way thither, between Spaldwick and Huntingdon, escaped some danger in a fall I had from my horse. The next day, being Tuesday, and the 29th day of June, I came from Cambridge to Dalham Hall, in the county of Suffolk, where Sir Martin Stuteville resided ... and was welcomed by them with many real and affectionate expressions far beyond that entertainment I had received from the Ishams in Northamptonshire. We had not discoursed long, before my father, the same Lady Denton, and the rest of his family arrived safe at Dalham also, which he took in his passage home from London to Stow Hall; so as we enjoyed a great deal of harmless mirth and content together there the residue of this afternoon, and the ensuing Wednesday morning.[17]

Wriothesley and Elizabeth Russell, Duke and Duchess of Bedford, journeyed frequently in their coach to pay visits to friends and family in the early eighteenth century, on one occasion travelling to Chatsworth House in Derbyshire to see the duke's sister, Rachel, Duchess of Devonshire. The esquire Richard Legh of Lyme Hall in Cheshire could often be found careering towards either Croxteth Hall or Knowsley Hall in the 1660s to catch up with his Liverpudlian neighbours.

Business and professional appointments demanded further aristocratic excursions. Cassandra Willoughby of Wollaton Hall, who would eventually profit from an advantageous marriage to James Brydges, future Duke of Chandos, visited tenants at Gainsborough and Muskham as part of her travels in 1697. A stately journey to Cambridge from Woburn Abbey in 1689, meanwhile, was undertaken by William Russell, 5th Earl of Bedford, due to his business commitments at Trinity College, although the nobleman also called in on old friends while staying in the area.

If English aristocrats went abroad, often this was to fulfil ambassadorial duties, as was the case in 1619 when Edward Herbert, 1st Baron Herbert of Cherbury, left England for the continental delights of Paris. In this city he was to be the English ambassador, at first taking a house in Faubourg Saint-Germain that was richly furnished and large enough to accommodate 'all my train'. From Faubourg, Herbert made an initial visit to Tours in the Centre-Val de Loire region of France, where the French court was then in residence. On his return to Paris, the eventual baron 'gave the best order I could concerning the expenses of my house, family, and stable, that I might settle all things as near as was possible in a certain course'. Such matters involved buying in meat, including beef, mutton, veal, pork, and pheasant, along with sourcing a selection of pies and tarts 'after the French manner'.[18]

The ambassadorial obligations of James Brydges, 8th Baron Chandos, took him across Europe to Istanbul in 1680, where he stayed for seven years as a representative of the Levant Company. There is a record of his children joining him in Turkey in October 1681, which no doubt eased any separation anxiety experienced. Spain and Portugal were the foreign destinations to which the baronet Sir Richard Fanshawe of Ware Park and his wife Ann Fanshawe travelled in the 1660s, with the former having been appointed an ambassador to both countries by Charles II. In March 1664, the couple found themselves being ostentatiously welcomed by local dignitaries and members of the nobility to the Spanish city of Seville, who took their guests with stupendous pomp to the Royal Alcázar, the site of their apartments for the duration of the diplomatic visit. 'We were lodged in a silver bedstead, [the] quilt and the curtains and vallances and counterpanes of crimson damask, embroidered richly with flowers of gold; the tables of precious stones and the looking-glasses bordered with the same, the chairs the same,' Ann, Lady Fanshawe, recalled in her memoirs. Every entertainment imaginable was provided for the Fanshawes at the Royal Alcázar, including singing, dancing, and theatrical performances staged inventively on water. The diplomat and his wife were also presented with a variety of gifts by their accommodating hosts, namely 'a very fine horse' worth £300, 'a great quantity' of chocolate and sugar, napkins of sarcenet, a large silver pot, and twelve 'very fine cups'. Incredibly, a 'young lion' was gifted to Lady Ann personally, who 'did not accept of it, saying I was of so cowardly a make I durst not keep company with it'.[19] A year later, business had taken Sir Richard Fanshawe to Madrid, again with his wife, where the couple enjoyed several bullfights over a number of months in the company of Philip IV of Spain.

Edward Herbert had already been to France before his appointment as the English ambassador to Paris in 1619, as a foreign tourist. He brought with him on this introductory trip a talented gentleman called Aurelian Townshend, who could speak French, Italian, and Spanish 'in great perfection', together with two liveried footmen and three horses.[20] The party began in Calais and drifted south to Paris, finally arriving at the wealthy district of Faubourg Saint-Germain in the city, where Herbert would later take up residence. In such a distinguished location, the Englishman soon acquired an assortment of friends in high places and was even a guest of Henri de Montmorency at his princely *château* of Mello.

From the mid-seventeenth century onwards, it became the done thing for young, elite Englishmen to travel abroad for the sole purpose of playing the tourist, the rite of passage being known to future generations as the Grand Tour. Such a tour was considered a good way of rounding off a teenager's education, and by that logic occurred in the majority of cases as soon as the well-to-do boy had finished up at either Oxford or Cambridge. In November 1665, Sir Heneage Finch, 1st Earl of Nottingham, was explicit in what he hoped his son would gain from a tour around Europe:

> You are now where all your friends wished you... All your former studies were full of pains and difficulties and the close pursuit of

them might impair your health. Now all your employments tend to health and exercise, and your chiefest study will be conversation and to understand men.[21]

Daniel Finch had reached Florence by this stage, where he would go on to be tutored in dancing as well as gentlemanly decorum. Two years later in September 1667, the boy was still abroad, having thus far followed a circular route around Europe that had taken in Frankfurt, Munich, Venice, Florence, Naples, and Rome. Now in France and seemingly with no immediate plans to cross the Channel, Sir Heneage wrote to inform his son unequivocally that it was high time he came back. 'There is scarce one day in the week wherein your mother and I do not heartily wish you at home, the two years allowed for your whole voyage being now expired, and we think the rest of that precious time which you spend abroad can add little more either to your satisfaction or improvement.' The patriarch seems, however, to have softened slightly in a letter composed soon afterwards, admitting to Daniel that spending some time learning French 'as far as will be necessary for conversation' might not be such a bad thing. Whether this is what the twenty-year-old Daniel was really up to in France is open to speculation.[22]

Sir Ralph Verney of Middle Claydon embarked on a tour of the continent in 1651, aged thirty-seven, when so-called Grand Tours were still in their infancy. Like many other aristocrats, what drove the man to travel abroad was a desire to see more of the world and to find inspiration in the things he came across, be they people, places, or historical monuments. In Ralph's case, however, there was also the issue of the recent death of his beloved wife, formerly Mary Blacknall. It was felt that a gentle sojourn in mainland Europe might finally help to focus the Buckinghamshire knight's mind elsewhere, which had until then been entirely consumed by the loss he had suffered. 'I confess till now I never knew what sorrow was, [for] this, oh this, far exceeds all my other misfortunes, and hath put me upon so many several resolutions that I know not what to resolve,' he wrote miserably in September 1650, in response to her untimely passing.[23] Sir Ralph took the plunge and began his own version of the Grand Tour in March 1651, accompanied by his son Edmund and another travelling companion called William Gee. Passing first through France and stopping off at Bordeaux, Toulouse, Carcassonne, and Lyon, the party then made their way eastwards towards the treacherous Italian border, eventually reaching Pisa in central Italy and shortly afterwards the city of Florence. Rome was next and the Verneys arrived at Naples just after Christmas; here in southern Italy father and son were able to admire the fearful Mount Vesuvius and the islands of Capri and Ischia.[24] Sir Ralph's return journey took in Venice, and Frankfurt and Cologne in modern-day Germany, before the widowed traveller arrived at Antwerp in September 1652.

Pomp on the road

English aristocrats, as we have already seen, seldom travelled alone in the Stuart period. If a journey was expected to be lengthy, or an elite individual was heading somewhere that would require the presence of servants, attendants would be a likely addition on the road. The nine-year-old Lady Alethea Compton, granddaughter of Lady Anne Clifford and only surviving daughter of the late Isabella Compton, Countess of Northampton, rode to Pendragon Castle to visit her grandmother accompanied by four gentlewomen, a gentleman, and 'other servants' in 1670, along with a resident of Skipton in Yorkshire by the name of Colonel Carr. As might be expected, the infinitely wealthy Lady Anne Clifford was not one to travel lightly herself. In April 1672, the noblewoman journeyed from Pendragon Castle to Brough Castle in Westmorland with several gentlewomen and maidservants 'attending me in my coach', manservants following on horseback, and also 'a great many of my tenants and neighbours', all of whom were invited to see Brough's refurbished hall before departing 'to their several homes'. Two years earlier in October

1670, Anne even had members of the local gentry in attendance when she 'came safe and well I thank God into my castle of Brougham', with neighbours and tenants also present.[25]

Sometimes there was simply not enough room for every servant of an aristocratic family to travel with the main cavalcade. When making arrangements for the return of his family to Claydon House in Buckinghamshire in June 1697, for instance, Sir John Verney deduced that his three maids would have to go it alone and take the stagecoach separately as far as Aylesbury. How they would get from there back to Middle Claydon, the gentleman did not know. Whether the trio of maids ended up travelling conveniently with the Verney coaches or using public transport, the passage ahead would invariably have been a drawn-out affair. While stagecoaches were notoriously sluggish and moved at an average speed of just five miles per hour in seventeenth-century England, Verney himself admitted of his own transportation in April 1703 that 'we are a large family and great bodies move slowly.'[26]

With regard to coaches in particular, coachmen, postilions, and at times outriders were all necessary components of an aristocratic journey. Increasingly, these attendants were decked out in liveries to add to the spectacle of travelling. Both the coachman and the postilion in the employment of William Russell, 5th Earl of Bedford, were given frieze coats to wear in the later seventeenth century, with the postilion, who rode up front, also being presented with a specific 'frock' and a pair of smart trousers to don.[27]

Wayward and unpredictable coachmen and postilions could appear in the households of Stuart aristocrats from time to time. The diarist John Evelyn commented in March 1669 that his own and the 5th Duke of Norfolk's coachman had been plied with drink so remorselessly during a visit to Sir William Ducie's house in London, they both 'fell off their boxes' on the return journey. The story emanating from Leez Priory in Essex, one of the residences of Mary Rich, Countess of Warwick, was much more sobering a year earlier in March 1668. Approaching the red-brick building after a trip away, the noblewoman was stopped on the road by the baronet Sir Richard Evarard of Much Waltham, who informed her of the distressing news that a postilion in the service of the Earl of Warwick had recently drowned himself in a pond in the grounds.[28]

The examples given previously of the manner in which Lady Anne Clifford travelled in the 1670s hint at the celebratory aspect of homeward journeys in particular, where there might be an organised welcome for an aristocrat to a property. Having married at Heythrop in Oxfordshire to the jovial sound of church bells, the esquire Nicholas Blundell and his new wife Frances Langdale set off for Crosby Hall in Lancashire in good spirits in June 1703. The festive atmosphere did not wane upon their arrival at Blundell's northern seat a few days later, for musicians aplenty had been hired to herald the approach of the couple to their marital home, while friends and neighbours also stood waiting with presents and good wishes. When Rachel Bourchier, Countess of Bath, who had married a man twice her age, travelled to the 5th Earl of Bath's country pile at Tawstock for the first time in 1639, church bells instead of musicians announced her arrival.[29] This had been done, according to the meticulous compiler of the couple's extensive accounts, on the orders of the countess herself.

Sir James Forbes wrote to Lady Rachel Russell in August 1693 to tell the stalwart widow about the recent journey undertaken by her daughter, Catherine Russell, to Belvoir Castle. She had just married John Manners, future Duke of Rutland. Believing it to have been more akin to 'the progress of a king or queen through their country than that of a bride and bridegroom's going home to their father's house', Forbes noted that the couple were first met in Leicestershire by the high sheriff and 'all the gentlemen of the country', who complimented the bride on her appearance and paid their respects to both individuals. From Market Harborough onwards, the 'train' steadily grew in size and splendour, with cheering crowds lining the roads in their thousands as the attractive newly-weds drew ever closer to the Manners' famed seat. Forbes continued:

> I cannot better represent their first arrival at Belvoir, than by the Woburn song that Lord Bedford liked so well; for at the gate were four-and-twenty fiddlers all in a row; four-and-twenty trumpeters, with their tan tara ra ra's; four-and-twenty ladies, and as many parsons; and in great order they went in procession to the great apartment, where the usual ceremony of saluting and wishing of joy passed, but still not without something represented in the song, as very much tittle-tattle, and fiddle-fiddle.[30]

The journey really extended well into that evening, culminating in the couple moving once again 'in procession' to the great hall at Belvoir, where healths were drunk liberally and light-heartedly from silver cups.[31]

As part of his large travelling party in 1689, William Russell, 5th Earl of Bedford, had bell-ringers, trumpeters, and even harpists to keep him entertained all the way up to Cambridge.[32] There did not seem to be a particular reason for the degree of pomp and circumstance seen on this occasion in Bedfordshire, Hertfordshire, and Cambridgeshire, only that the Earl of Bedford was making a journey that covered some distance. The total mileage from the gates of Woburn to the halls of Trinity College, however, was hardly considerable.

9

COMPLAINTS AND CURES

Illness, both fatal and chronic, plagued members of the Stuart aristocracy across the seventeenth and early eighteenth centuries. In 1603, Thomas Sackville, 1st Earl of Dorset, made an assessment of his health that was typical of the entire period, writing to Robert Cecil that 'since your last being with me I have endured a far more dangerous but never a more painful sickness. My cold increased so mightily that with continual coughing all my breast came into an extreme soreness.' He continued dejectedly, 'I take physic on Friday and must again on Sunday. I know not when I shall be clear.' Chronic pain of varying degrees was just as unremitting as sickness, with Sir Nathaniel Bacon of Culford Hall in Suffolk informing his wife matter-of-factly in a letter dated 1624 that he was 'still accompanied with my constant companions, the toothache and headache, of whose society I begin to grow so weary that I shall not any longer give them quiet entertainment'.[1] In short, there was rarely a moment when elite men and women did not feel out of sorts to some extent, just like everybody else in early modern England.

Whether or not it was of any real benefit, what the aristocracy did have over a large chunk of the population in Stuart England was ready access to healthcare. Aristocratic patients, unlike their tenant farmers, could afford to see reputable physicians and even a select number of women with sound medical knowledge when unwell or in pain, and their coffers could also buy them any number of remedies from a list that was practically endless. All was to be in vain in the curious case of Abigail Bramston, daughter of Sir John Bramston of Skreens in Essex, however. Falling sick in the early 1690s, she was examined by every 'eminent' physician going in London at the request of her concerned father, yet none could convincingly determine what exactly it was that ailed the gentlewoman. The services of respectable apothecaries and a host of recommended medicines were tried, but did not help. Sir John, who relied on Abigail to be his housekeeper, was left exasperated by the lack of progress being made:

> After all this expense, and the trial of so many medicines, doctors, and apothecaries, there was not found any medicine that gave any present ease, no, not the laudanum and other opiates; a plain demonstration her disease was known by none of the doctors. Lister said she had an imposthume [an abscess], Cole said an ulcer, or some mortification in the bowels. Her apothecary thought there might be some stone in the kidneys. Radcliffe laughed at him, and said it was an imposthume, but thought her in a deep consumption, and that she would come to vomiting of blood, and so die; indeed, from the first time he saw her, he said it was a thousand to one if she recovered.[2]

Unfortunately for the desperate Bramstons, Radcliffe, presumably the noted physician Dr John Radcliffe, was right on the money. Abigail ultimately did not survive whatever had incapacitated her for so long. When she found herself close to the end in July 1694, the patient was said to have murmured knowingly, 'God have mercy on me, I am dying.'[3]

Some remedies administered to Stuart aristocrats, while not killing them, in fact did more harm than good in the long run. Sir William Waller of Osterley Park, being 'ill of his eyes' in later life, took certain pills to 'purge his head' one day in 1660, although he probably wished in the days after that he had not. His wife, Lady Anne Waller of the Paget family, remarked of the occasion in her diary that the pills in question 'made him so ill that I greatly feared [for] his life'. At the Inns of Court in London in the early seventeenth century, meanwhile, a surgeon hired to cure Sir Hugh Cholmley of his debilitating sore throat could only suggest the application of liquid mercury to ease the Yorkshireman's discomfort. Cholmley only realised later on how risky this treatment had been. 'By God's mercy it succeeded well,' he wrote in hindsight in his memoirs, 'some physicians told me since, "the remedy was as dangerous as the disease".'[4]

Plague

Outbreaks of bubonic plague tended to affect the whole country in seventeenth-century England. During its various eruptions in the 1600s, however, most English aristocrats could avoid the worst of the infection by escaping to their isolated seats in the countryside, where cases would either be fewer or non-existent. The 1625 outbreak in London encouraged the esquire Paul D'Ewes, a Clerk in Chancery and father of Simonds D'Ewes, to 'hasten away' from the capital as soon as term had ended in July.[5] Simonds himself took a leaf out of his father's book and followed the clerk out of the city the same day, choosing to escape by water. Eventually the pair were reunited at the relatively safe New Place in Essex, the home of a relative, while the rest of Paul's family accordingly retreated to Stow Hall in deepest Suffolk.

Following the first significant visitation of plague in Stuart England, in the summer of 1603, the thirteen-year-old Lady Anne Clifford and her privileged kin also ran from London, initially to Hampton Court Palace with the rest of the country's frightened courtiers, and then to the quieter Norbury Park in rural Surrey, the seat of the Stiddolph family. At Hampton Court, there were genuine fears that Lady Anne had actually contracted the pestilence, 'but within two or three days I grew reasonably

Lady Anne Clifford, from a portrait by Daniel Mytens.

Richard Sackville, 3rd Earl of Dorset, from a miniature by Isaac Oliver.

Left: The late fifteenth-century gatehouse at Berry Pomeroy Castle. (Author's collection)

Below: The ruins of the Elizabethan house at Berry Pomeroy Castle, built in the 1560s. (Author's collection)

The frontage of Longford Castle in Wiltshire, drawn by John Buckler. (Yale Center for British Art)

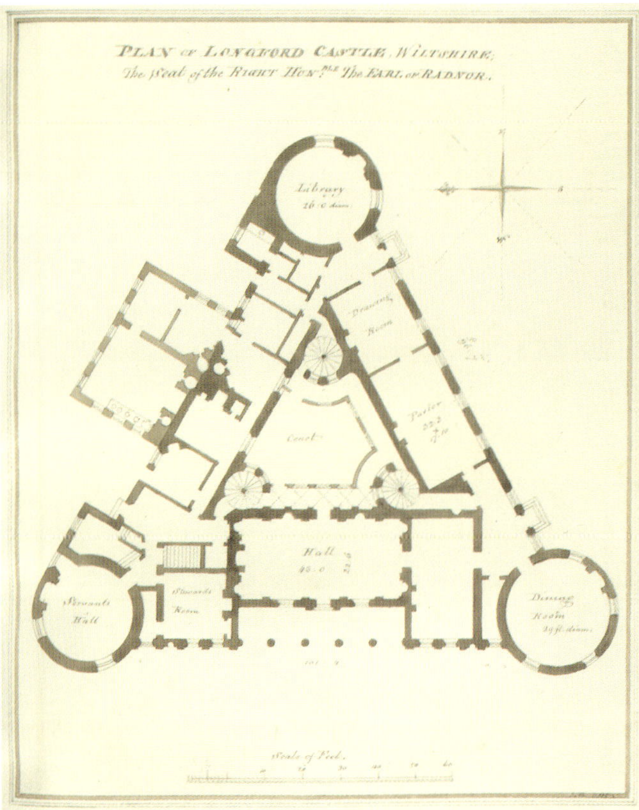

Plan of Longford Castle in Wiltshire, drawn by John Buckler. (Yale Center for British Art)

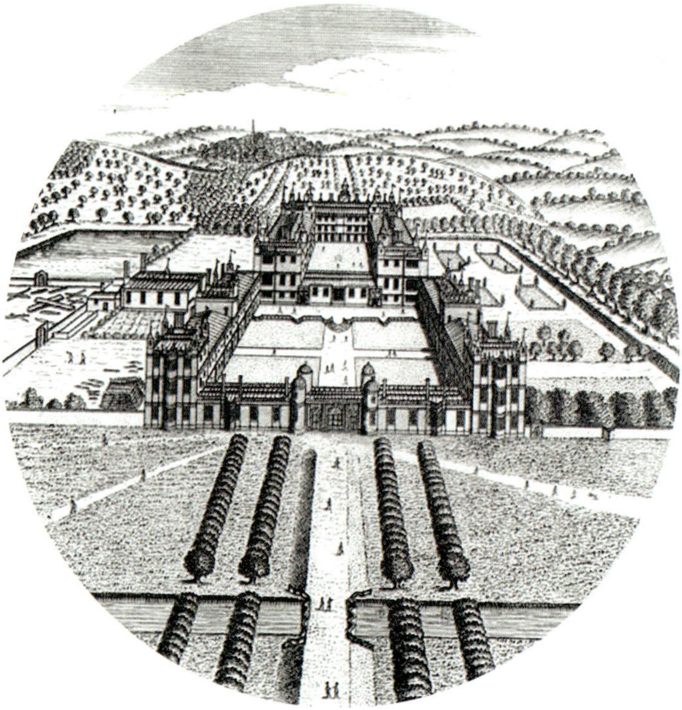

Above: Audley End House 'in its splendour' in the seventeenth century. (New York Public Library)

Below: Chatsworth House and its sprawling, manicured gardens, *c.* 1708, drawn by Kip and Knyff. (Rijksmuseum)

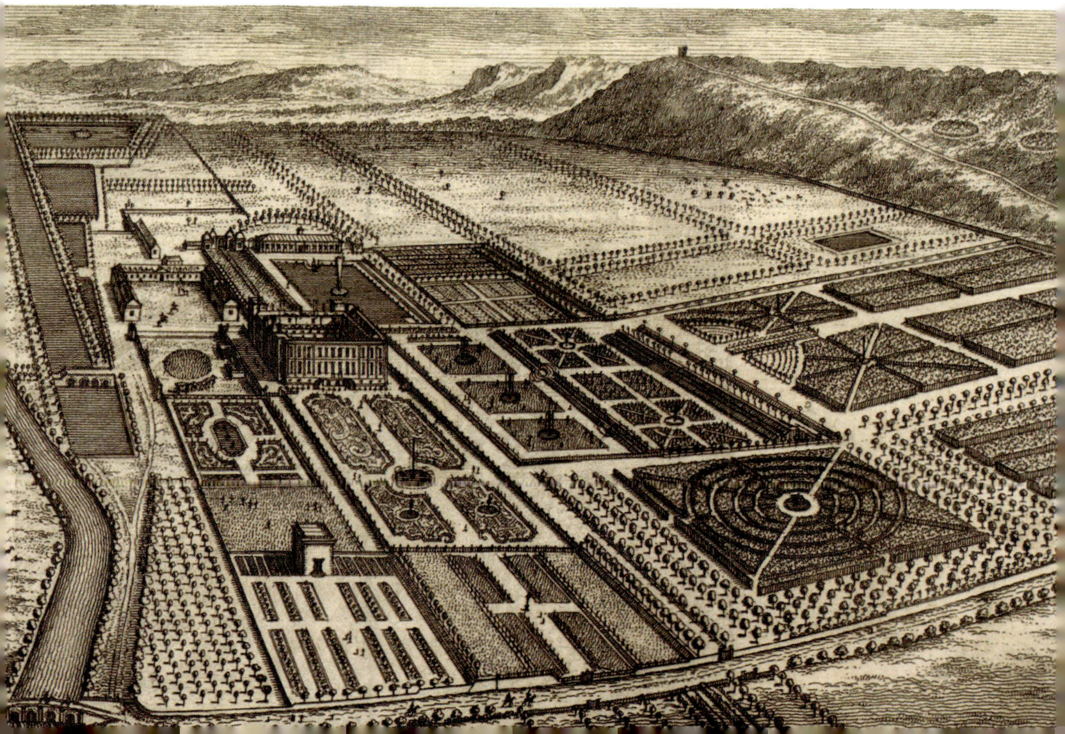

Northumberland House, formerly Northampton House, as it appeared in London in 1752, by William James after Canaletto. (Yale Center for British Art)

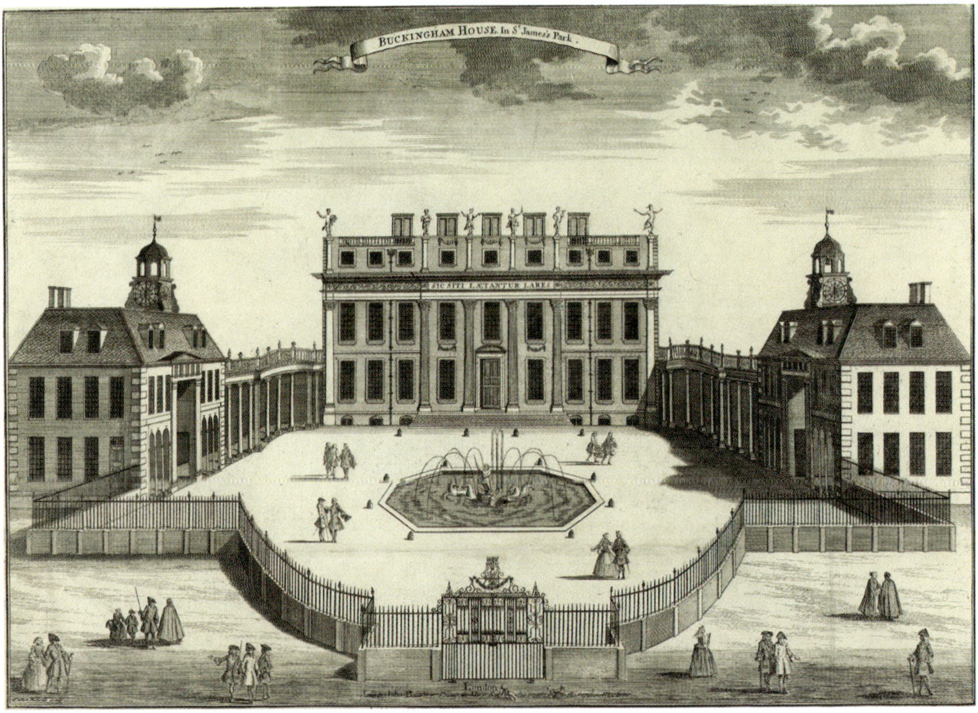

Buckingham House in London following its completion in the early eighteenth century. (Yale Center for British Art)

Left: Elizabeth Cary, Viscountess Falkland, early seventeenth century, by Paul van Somer. (Museum of Fine Arts, Houston)

Below left: A work by Gonzales Coques thought to depict Margaret Cavendish and her husband, William Cavendish, 1st Duke of Newcastle. (Gemäldegalerie)

Below right: The original Thomas Wentworth, 1st Earl of Strafford, by Alexander Browne after Anthony van Dyck. (Rijksmuseum)

Right: Mary Rich, Countess of Warwick, from the frontispiece of Mary Palgrave's biography of her.

Below: Alethea Howard, Countess of Arundel, 1620, by Peter Paul Rubens. She is painted with her dog and some attendants. (Alte Pinakothek München)

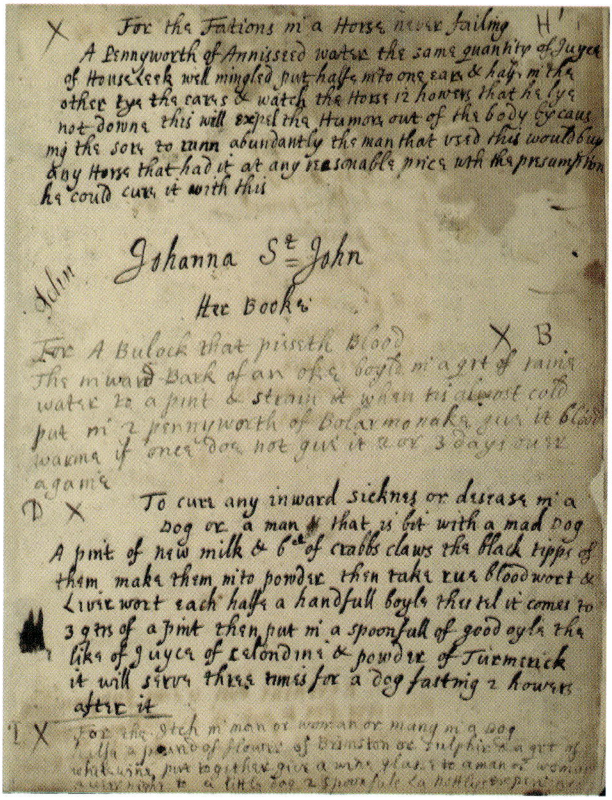

For the Fations in a Horse never failing H'
A Pennyworth of Annisseed water the same quantity of Juyce of Houseleek well mingled put halfe into one eare & halfe in the other tye the eares & watch the Horse 12 howers that he lye not downe this will expell the Humour out of the body because in the sore to runn abundantly the man that used this would buy any Horse that had it at any reasonable price with the presumption he could cure it with this

Johanna St John
Her Booke

For A Bulock that pisseth Blood X B
The inward Bark of an oke boyle in a qrt of raine water to a pint & strain it when tis almost cold put in 2 pennyworth of Bolarmonake give it blood warme if once doe not give it 2 or 3 days over againe

D X To cure any inward sickness or disease in a Dog or a man that is bit with a mad Dog
A pint of new milk & 6d of crabbs claws the black tipps of them make them into powder then take rue bloodwort & Liverwort each halfe a handfull boyle these til it comes to 3 qrts of a pint then put in a spoonfull of good oyle the like of Juyce of celondine & powder of Turmerick it will serve three times for a dog fasting 2 howers after it

I X For the Itch in man or woman or mange in a Dog halfe a pound of flower of Brimston or Sulphire & a qrt of whitwine put together give a wine glass to a man or woman [illegible] to a little Dog 2 spoonfulls [illegible]

Left: A page from one of Johanna St John's famous recipe books. (Wellcome Collection)

Below: Hawking in the later seventeenth century, as depicted in Nicholas Cox's *The Gentleman's Recreation* (1686). (Tufts University)

well and was sent away.' It was comparatively rare for a Stuart aristocrat to catch the most feared disease in human history, but unconfirmed and confirmed cases amongst the elite were known, nonetheless. In August 1603, the colossally influential Lucy Russell, Countess of Bedford, had to be 'carried from the court' when she came down with a fever that some suspected to be plague; that the noblewoman lived on until 1627 makes this diagnosis unlikely, though not impossible.[6] The baronet Sir William Pennyman of Marske Hall in Yorkshire, on the other hand, very probably died of plague at Oxford in August 1643. With its virtual disappearance from English shores after the Great Plague of the mid-1660s, this mortal disease became even less of a concern for the aristocracy, who were by now fighting off other infections.

Smallpox and the measles

Unlike plague, smallpox remained in England constantly throughout the seventeenth and early eighteenth centuries. It was a particularly common infection amongst Stuart aristocrats, bringing with it an array of unpleasant symptoms. Discomfort began in the head for the most part, consisting of an aggressive and sudden fever, blinding headaches, and sometimes projectile vomiting. Loss of appetite and sleepless nights might join these physical manifestations, which in time would be followed by a sea of red spots on the face, hands, and forearms that blistered after just a few days. A relative of the Oxenden baronets of Deane, James Oxenden, commented on his personal experience of smallpox in a letter dated 1640: 'Truly for my own part I not long since was so infected with the smallpox that I did verily think I should have never wrote unto you again, being so sore troubled with them that for the space of three weeks I did very little stir out of my bed.'[7]

This was a typical response to the illness, which could render even the healthiest individuals bedridden for many weeks. What was decidedly abnormal, however, were the actions of the baronet

Sir John Chichester of Raleigh in Devon when he contracted smallpox in late 1667. According to one source, the disease made Chichester so violently unwell that he fell into a kind of deranged frenzy as a result, which led him to stab a young, pregnant woman to death with a sword that he had first politely asked her to 'put into his hands'.[8] He died not long after this incident, and his mental anguish perished with him.

Smallpox's mortality rate was estimated by some to be as high as sixty per cent, so no wonder it was so feared by members of the aristocracy. If contracted, the disease could kill very quickly. Margaret Brownlow, daughter of the late Sir John Brownlow of Belton House, had her wedding outfit made and was shortly to marry Peregrine Bertie, Lord Willoughby, in August 1710, before smallpox intervened and ensured that the gentlewoman would never walk down the aisle. As a consolation, Willoughby ended up wedding Margaret's sister, Jane, instead. In 1641, the 4th Earl of Bedford, Francis Russell, also came to a swift end due to smallpox, with the nobleman confined to his bed at Bedford House in a half-conscious state, but aware of those around him, for a couple of days only before succumbing on 9 May. The rest of the family were in another part of the mansion at the time of Russell's passing, having been ordered there by the patient himself to keep them at a safe distance from the notoriously contagious malady.

In terms of how aristocrats dealt with smallpox, measures were preventative rather than curative. Sending family members to other houses or into the countryside when the disease was thought to be present was a standard move, being the response of Sir George Hastings, 8th Earl of Huntingdon, upon discovering that his sibling might be at risk of developing the 'pox' in June 1701. 'For the love of God send for my sister to your house,' he wrote feverishly to Thomas Coke of Melbourne Hall. 'She never has had them, and they have proved fatal to our family.' Dorothy Spencer, Countess of Sunderland, acted equally as promptly in the knowledge that she herself had caught smallpox in August 1661, choosing to pack off her daughter, Lady Penelope, not to another abode, but instead to the stables at Rufford Abbey where they were then residing. Forty odd years later, having been made aware that one of his maids was similarly incapacitated, Sir John Verney's main concern was keeping anything and everything touched by the servant away from Middle Claydon. 'None of it must come to my house to be wash't, that being dangerous, nor anything that is used about the sick body until the maid be recovered and the things well aired,' he instructed his steward, John Coleman.[9]

Recovery from smallpox was a cause for celebration in elite circles, given its potential lethality. Relatives might write to give their treasured kin a metaphorical pat on the back for escaping death and could even turn the recent ordeal into a positive if they were feeling particularly sanguine. On 5 August 1661, Lady Anne Chicheley of Wimpole Hall sent a letter to her adult stepson, Tom, in which she anticipated that he had battled smallpox and won:

> Dear Son, I hope by this time I may congratulate your perfect recovery of a disease that few escape their whole life from, and therefore 'tis a blessing to have passed it and it often is a means of better health by clearing the body of those humours that foment distempers, especially where they purge well after it as I hope you have done.[10]

Lady Abigail Harley was likewise upbeat in 1675 when every single member of the Harley household at Brampton Bryan recovered from smallpox, viewing the 'many speckled faces' around her as 'marks of God's goodness in sparing the lives of all'.[11]

For many aristocratic individuals, though, 'speckled faces' were a terrible misfortune. Pockmarked skin left over from smallpox was considered unsightly and therefore had the potential to do great harm to the overall appeal of a person, especially a woman. Lady Isabella Wentworth certainly feared that her youngest daughter's 'market would be spoiled' by a bout of the disease in the early eighteenth century, who was not yet married. Similar anxieties were expressed by Samuel Pepys in 1668, the famous diarist noting with distress that Frances Stewart, Duchess of Richmond, was suffering so badly from smallpox in London that 'all do conclude she will be wholly spoiled.' This, he believed, was a prime example of the fleeting nature of beauty, for the duchess was known to have been amongst the most attractive noblewomen in Stuart England. In another diary entry written a few days later, Pepys came across a picture of the duchess as a 'young maid', which made him even sadder. 'It would make a man weep,' he remarked, 'to see what she was then, and what she is like to be, by people's discourse, now.'[12]

While oftentimes appearing in children, the measles were known to occur in aristocratic adults, too. This disease was, like smallpox, characterised by fever, headaches, and raised spots, and could similarly kill, given the right set of circumstances. Sir Simonds D'Ewes' wife, Anne Clopton, appeared to contract the measles in March 1628, with 'little pimples' erupting on 'divers parts of her body' following several days of ill health. At first smallpox was suspected by the physician who came to examine her at Stow Hall, until the learned man had observed his patient long enough to assure Sir Simonds that it was not quite so serious. That both complaints were frequently confused with each other is further evident in a letter dated 1667 upon the decease of Lady Grace Castleton, who, it was written, either 'died of the measles or smallpox'. One grotesque fact the author of the letter could confirm, however, was that the unlucky Lady Castleton 'continued bleeding from the nose' until her last breath.[13]

The spleen and the stone

Problems with the spleen were regularly reported by Stuart aristocrats. The baronet Sir Henry Slingsby's wife, Barbara, 'felt a heaviness in her side, and a fume to [then] rise out of her left side' in 1639, which turned out to be, according to the physician at any rate, a malady originating from this particular organ. Such issues with the spleen, located in the upper part of the abdomen, had a very odd effect indeed on Mary Rich, Countess of Warwick, in the

1650s, who described the general complaint in her autobiography as 'a very long and dangerous sickness'.[14] The countess's head shook over and over again as a consequence of the disorder, while other strange symptoms experienced by the noblewoman included talking nonsense for hours on end, sporadically laughing or crying for no reason, and falling into semi-conscious states that made identifying other people in the room impossible.

It is not surprising to discover that the Countess of Warwick went on to survive her ordeal. The range of remedies available to help with this condition in the seventeenth century was particularly extensive, meaning that amongst the scores of questionable treatments was bound to be at least one effective restorative for elite patients. Dame Barbara Slingsby took 'steel pills' each day to encourage her own recovery in 1639, together with 'a dish of thin broth with cream of tartar in it, dissolving one of ye papers of tartar in ye broth for one draught'. Later, she moved on to wine that had been heated a little (with a drop of beer to be drunk straight afterwards), 'Castor' pills, and 'Rubard' powder. Lady Eliza Cornwallis sent her mother, Jane, Lady Cornwallis Bacon, a barrel of Seville olives in 1634, which were also said to be 'very good for the spleen, if they be eaten in a morning fasting, and digested by some exercise', while Sir John Oglander's own method for 'purging and opening the spleen' at around the same time involved the consumption of a rhubarb electuary.[15]

Remedies to combat 'the stone' were perhaps even more plentiful. This painful complaint, whereby stones appeared in the bladder or kidneys, afflicted the Stuart aristocracy just as much as disorders of the spleen. Charles Rich, 4th Earl of Warwick, was said to have been 'violently ill of the stone' in July 1667, which appeared so agonising to his wife, Mary Rich, that she pleaded with God to grant her husband some temporary relief from his suffering. God obliged on this occasion and allowed Charles to sleep for 'two hours together', although the man's suffering, as will be discovered later, was certainly not over.[16] When it came to the selection of a remedy to ease or eradicate the stone, one had to be especially careful that the benefits of pursuing a given treatment outweighed the risks. In June 1653, Edward Conway, 2nd Viscount Conway, wrote to Edward Harley of Brampton Bryan to give him a piece of advice on the subject:

> If your father suspect stone in the bladder he would do well to be searched, which may easily be done and without danger. He would also do well to take heed of violent medicines and of such as are given to break the stone, for they bring down violently gravel and cause very ill accidents and often death.[17]

Most medicines seemed harmless enough. One mode of treatment advocated by English aristocrats in the 1620s called for a couple of pieces of toasted rye bread, which were to be coated in a thick layer of black soap and then applied to the genitals 'so hot as you are able to abide it'. Another remedy merely made use of distilled milk and white wine, again for pain relief, which was to be mixed together and drunk in the mornings for three days in a row. The aged George Manners, 7th Earl of Rutland, paid for two 'gree stones' in 1640 to aid him in his evident struggles with the stone, costing £3 5 shillings in total.[18] Interestingly, an agreement was reached with the provider that, should the said stones prove ineffective after twelve months of use, Manners would be able to make further purchases of the mystery object at a discount.

Gout

Too much good living caused many Stuart aristocrats to develop gout as they grew older. On 15 May 1681, Sir John Reresby 'was visited with a rheumatism, which first began like the gout in my foot, and after seized on one part of me after another, that I had scarce any part of me free'. The gentleman was confined to his bed for a whole month consequently, being so weak that he could not even turn himself over. In terms of how gout might manifest itself, one of the best surviving descriptions comes from Lady

Anne Waller in November 1657, who wrote that her husband, Sir William Waller's feet 'swelled to a very great bigness, and began to discolour so much, that I apprehended some danger of a gangrene'.[19] It is fair to say that gout could be incredibly painful for sufferers, with its tendency to produce hot, swollen, irritated skin in the feet and hands, and sometimes as far up as the elbows and knees. The ailment forced the frustrated 1st Viscount Fermanagh to walk morosely about Claydon House on crutches in 1713, which required him to have a servant on hand at all times. Moreover, the Buckinghamshire patriarch found it impossible to get his stockings and shoes on in the mornings, so inflamed were his feet and legs.

Gout seems to have contributed at least in part to some aristocratic deaths in this period, including that of Charles Rich, 4th Earl of Warwick, in 1673. His was an ordeal twenty years in the making, having been recorded in eye-watering detail by his long-suffering wife in her pious diary. 'In the morning, as soon as up, I retired into the wilderness,' Mary Rich wrote on one occasion in 1669, 'being very melancholy, because my lord had one of the saddest nights of pain that ever I remember him to have had, not sleeping at all, but continually roaring out.' Charles' frequent outbursts of anger, a direct result of the agony with which he had to live for so long, was something Mary found difficult to adjust to over the course of the couple's very unstable marriage. Towards the end of his life, when gout and other unidentified ailments had taken hold of the Earl of Warwick completely, the man was probably begging for eternal rest. On his deathbed at Leez Priory in August 1673, Charles had finally lost the use of his limbs, could not feed himself, and was 'so weakened and wasted that he was like a mere skeleton'.[20] Such a fate was deemed unacceptable to the baronet and Member of Parliament Sir John Brownlow of Belton House, who also suffered badly from gout. He made the bold decision to free himself of the excruciating pain earlier than God intended in July 1697, aged just thirty-eight, by putting a pistol to his temple and pulling the trigger.[21] The

Lincolnshire knight left behind a doting widow and five young daughters, which was proof enough that his condition was beyond intolerable.

Help was at hand for those aristocrats who were willing to continue resisting the horrible effects of gout. If of the general opinion that any medicine was better than no medicine, trying one of Sir John Oglander's interesting remedies dreamt up on the Isle of Wight in the early seventeenth century might be the way to go. The first treatment noted in his commonplace book necessitated plucking 'a score' of snails from a garden wall, pulverising them, and mixing the debris with chopped rue (a perennial evergreen shrub), before boiling the concoction in badger grease and applying it 'warm to the place affected'.[22] A further remedy listed was much simpler, and involved oysters only, which were to be bound to the swollen skin with a cloth. One more of Oglander's treatments is worth quoting from the knight's notebook in full:

> Take the pissell of a great boar and tie it fast before you kill him, so that no urine may be lost. Then take the flick of the boar and put it into the neck of the bladder and mingle it with the urine. Let the bladder hang a month. Then pierce it and therewith anoint the place infected with the gout.[23]

One assumes that these were tried-and-tested therapies, although there is no record of their proven efficacy in Sir John's detailed notes. Turning to Sir John Reresby for advice and guidance, therefore, might have been preferable for aristocratic patients in search of relief later in the period. In May 1681, the Thrybergh baronet claimed that drinking both cow's and ass's milk had unequivocally cured him of his gout, writing in his memoirs that he 'recovered to a miracle'. Whatever the preferences of the elite sufferer, one medicine to be avoided at all costs was that given to Henry Jermyn, 1st Baron Dover, in the spring of 1698, whose head and face, as a result of taking the potion, were both left 'extremely swelled'.[24]

Toothache and headaches

Chronic pain that seemed to radiate from the very bones of an aristocrat was a widespread problem in Stuart England, with long-term toothache being particularly distressing. Elizabeth Hervey's painful tooth constantly kept her awake at night in the 1690s, which drove the gentlewoman to have the thing removed entirely in December 1696, after two horrific attempts at 'pulling' by the practitioner. Sadly, the extraction of the tooth only led to more misery for the matriarch of Ickworth over the Christmas season. 'I must give you an account of my illness since I wrote last, when I told you I had my tooth drawn, and hoped to be better, but instead of that have grown worse and worse,' she began in a letter to her husband, John Hervey, on 29 December. In summary, the draught Elizabeth had been given to help her sleep following the procedure had not worked, and so instead she had spent the first night soothing her jaw with a series of warm objects. By morning, it was clear that this action had apparently done more harm than good, for the inside of her mouth had swelled monstrously, the unsightly inflammation extending 'quite up to my ear… I kept my bed most part of Sunday.' A physician was sent for on the advice of her father, who 'found my jaw not broke, only some splinter of it'. Even so, the mere act of eating remained too agonising for the incapacitated Elizabeth, who estimated that she had consumed little more than the equivalent of a chicken since the tooth's removal.[25]

Extraction at the hands of a professional was just one way in which chronic toothache could be dealt with by aristocrats. As ever, Sir John Oglander had his own, quirky remedy for the condition in the early seventeenth century, which required the employment of six cloves of garlic, burnt alum, burnt brimstone, aquavitae, and 'as much pepper, beaten small, as will lie upon a sixpence'. These ingredients were to be mixed together, shaped into little balls, covered in lawn cloth, and then applied to the throbbing tooth to provide some kind of temporary relief to the sufferer.[26] Failing Oglander's method, one could simply resort to tobacco or alcohol. Half a pound of tobacco appeared to see Sir John Brownlow through the worst of his regular battles with toothache in the

1690s, though in the end it would do the troubled man no good. Sir Richard Newdigate of Arbury Hall, on the other hand, found himself miraculously cured of his dental pains in October 1682 by drinking a glass or two of sack. Heartfelt prayer, which Newdigate decided to try on a separate occasion, and which reportedly worked just as well as wine, came free of charge.

Persistent headaches marred the day-to-day existence of Sir Edward Harley of Brampton Bryan when he wrote agitatedly to his physician for advice in December 1682, as they had done since at least the mid-1660s. His remedies up to that point, which seem to have been somewhat helpful, included 'senna, rhubarb, tartar, pearl, crab's eyes, and coral'. No medicine, however, could mitigate the near-constant agony Dame Dorothy Ogle of Suffolk experienced in her head in 1626. As reported by Sir Simonds D'Ewes, every morning the gentlewoman would develop a 'most violent and dreadful' headache that lasted at least four or five hours, described by Dame Ogle herself as the pain one might feel if a dagger was driven deep into one's skull. She further noted of the complaint that 'if God would deliver her of that torment ... she should account all her other afflictions light and small.'[27]

Medical practitioners

A 'suitable' physician according to seventeenth- and early eighteenth-century aristocrats was one who had been rigorously and professionally trained, having ideally attended university and attained a good degree in medicine. A proven track record in administering successful treatments was likewise a plus, as well as the possession of an illustrious client list that might include one or two names of national renown.

Many elite patients in England vied for the medical attention of the celebrated practitioner Sir Théodore de Mayerne in the early 1600s, who was an attractive candidate both for his role as physician to the English royal family and, from 1616 onwards, for his connections with the Royal College of Physicians. Sir Henry Slingsby managed to enlist the esteemed assistance of de Mayerne around 1640, when his wife's sickly condition had gotten so severe that it was thought to be hopeless. The Yorkshireman described the physician's private study in London in minute detail in his diary, which he tended to visit at 7:00am for quick consultations. It was by all accounts a large, comfortable room, filled with countless shelves of books and innumerable rows of pictures, the latter including a prominent likeness of the Greek physician Hippocrates, the supposed 'Father of Medicine'. An ornate desk occupied the space, too, standing somewhere amongst the ocean of tomes, austere portraits, and wood panelling, behind which Sir Théodore would sit importantly to listen to the concerns of his clients. The table in question, along with accommodating the Genevan practitioner and whichever distinguished individual had come to him for medical advice, also bore the wax figurine of a man, 'to set forth ye ordure and composure of every part [of the human body]'.[28] Slingsby noted generally that all patients, apart from members of the royal family, came to de Mayerne for treatment, and never the other way round. This arrangement, the esquire suspected, was due largely to the man's obesity and pomposity.

There was an appreciation in most well-to-do households that, without doubt, the very best physicians of the Stuart period were to be found in London. Nowhere else in the country, as far as noble and gentle persons were concerned, produced such fine and reliable talent. In June 1641, Frederick Cornwallis wrote to his mother, Jane, Lady Cornwallis Bacon, to remind her of the fact:

> Madam, I hear by my sister ... that your Ladyship is inclinable to a dropsy. I need not tell you how dangerous that disease is, if not timely prevented; but, Madam, give me leave to desire you most humbly, if not for your own sake, yet for your children's sake, for my poor children's sake, nay, even for God's sake, that you will be pleased to come up to this town and ask the advice of our physicians here.[29]

Physicians based in London who were more accommodating, and probably less busy, than Sir Théodore de Mayerne might even travel to aristocratic patients in the countryside to offer advice and administer treatments. In 1604, one Dr Mumforde, a practitioner usually operating in the capital, was paid £15 by Roger Manners, 5th Earl of Rutland, to visit his sick wife at Belvoir Castle in Leicestershire.

With supposedly great medical talent came even greater medical costs, both within and outside of London. Before approaching de Mayerne to help him cure his spouse Dame Barbara Slingsby in 1640, who was himself an expensive option, Sir Henry Slingsby had rested his hopes on another costly physician by the name of Dr Frires, a man 'of great fame for his skill and cures, which he doth not a little brag of'.[30] Frires' remedies, quite absurdly, were priced variously between £50 and £100. Parting with such vast sums of money might be considered a worthwhile endeavour if a physician went on to deliver outstanding results, but in the event that a practitioner's advertised prowess turned out to be substandard, extraordinary expenses could be hard to justify. Indeed, many Stuart aristocrats were either suspicious of, or wholly sceptical about, the abilities of reputable physicians such as de Mayerne and the enigmatic Frires, including Sir Henry:

> They may be said to sell medicinal drugs, but that they are physicians no man can truly say; and as one saith, they make such descriptions of our infirmities, as doth a town crier, who cryeth a lost horse, or a dog, and describeth his stature, his hair and ears, with other marks and tokens; but bring him to either, and they know him not; they promise much but perform little, and less than all other arts do they show ye effects of what they do profess.[31]

Lucy Russell, Countess of Bedford, was likewise extremely reluctant to 'punish herself' by taking a 'course of physick' prescribed by Sir Théodore de Mayerne in March 1626, being 'very incredulous that it can prevent my having more fits of the gout'.[32]

An alternative to the male physician was the female healer, or 'skilful woman' as she was sometimes called, who could often be found plying an informal trade nearby to a country estate. As well as being infinitely cheaper than a London professional, this type of practitioner might genuinely offer learned advice to aristocrats, and to boot have compelling medicines up her sleeve that one would not ordinarily come across in the medical stores of a university-educated man. When Sir Richard Cholmley of Yorkshire 'fell sick in a grievous fit of the stone' at Saxton in May 1619, it was a local skilful woman, not a physician, to whom he turned for help. The healer's name was Jane Pennythorne; her individualistic solution, more to the point, was to give the esquire a powder to drink, which was to be taken with white wine. Inevitably, there were those Stuart aristocrats, such as Sir Henry Slingsby and his wife, who were less than impressed with the work of female practitioners. The couple were pointed in the direction of one such woman by Sir Lionel Tollemache of Helmingham Hall in Suffolk in 1639, who over the space of two decades had reportedly 'practiced chemistry and out of that art had extracted certain oils and salts, which she applied to all diseases'. Her forte was curing disorders of the spleen, which is why she was deemed a particularly good fit for the ailing Dame Barbara. The Slingsbys, however, begged to differ after a month of testing the woman's unconventional remedy, for it seemed to have made no difference to Barbara's overall health whatsoever. Similar disappointment could be discerned at Crosby Hall in Lancashire in July 1707, when one Mrs Bootle, who possessed certain medical knowledge and skills and was a neighbour of the Blundell family, administered a quantity of 'phisick' to Mary Blundell that failed to ease the young girl's suffering.[33]

Other Stuart aristocrats had mixed feelings about the abilities of skilful women, but crucially did not dismiss them out of hand. Edmund Verney of Claydon House was approached by a female healer called Clark in 1664, who claimed that for £20 she could cure his wife of her mental sickness. While his father, Sir Ralph, decided in the end that his distressed daughter-in-law was better off looking elsewhere for treatment, the great baronet nonetheless acknowledged that 'I confess divers women have very good receipts, and good success too, and frequently have cured those that the doctors have not.'[34]

Female healers with a knack for dressing wounds and tending to physical injuries were particularly valued by the aristocracy. In May 1631, Sir Gilbert Gerard of Flambards in Harrow on the Hill enthusiastically informed his mother-in-law, Lady Joan Barrington (formerly a Cromwell, and aunt of the future Lord Protector, Oliver Cromwell), that his lame leg had been healed with the excellent assistance of a woman chirurgeon 'of your breeding', a possible indication that he was, in fact, referring abstractly to his own wife. Whether it was Mary Gerard or some other individual who had ultimately seen to the affliction, the knight commended the nameless practitioner for having 'dressed me so neatly and so tenderly that I cannot tell whither I took more pleasure and contentment in her pains with me or sorrow for my pains of it'.[35]

At Woburn Abbey in the later years of the seventeenth century, female 'nurses' were a customary addition to the Russell sickbed, should it ever be inhabited. Anne, Countess of Bedford, seems to have had such a caregiver in her presence constantly towards the end of her life in the 1680s, with the noblewoman eventually slipping away at Woburn just a few months after the death of her high-profile son, William, Lord Russell, who had been executed for treason at Lincoln's Inn Fields in July 1683. Many of those taking up the role of nurse in Bedfordshire came conveniently from within the Russells' own ranks, being relatives of the various men who worked on the large estate. Mrs Field, it would appear, was especially sought after by more than one generation of the family, being the wife of Woburn's resident gardener, John Field. Indeed, such was her reliability and aptitude that the humble woman might even be summoned to London or further afield if a Russell family member became unwell away from the main house.[36]

Spas

Although waters originating from mineral springs had long since been thought to possess healing properties, it was only in the first decades of the seventeenth century that spa resorts truly began to take off in England. The most popular of these retreats amongst the Stuart aristocracy were Bath and Tunbridge Wells, where one could drink and even bathe in the restorative waters, or, as was so often the intention of elite visitors, enjoy the accompanying entertainments. While Tunbridge Wells in Kent was considered the more respectable and fashionable of the two destinations, Bath as a spa resort had age and tradition on its side. In May 1612, arguably the most powerful aristocrat in England, Robert Cecil, 1st Earl of Salisbury, who had been secretary of state under two monarchs since 1596, travelled to 'take the waters' there. His reason for making the long journey from London to Somerset was, very simply, that he was sick and eager to be rid of the disease that had been causing him such discomfort. Unfortunately, the liquid remedy had little effect on the great statesman's probable cancer, which encouraged him to make 'all the haste he could out of that suffocating sulphurous air'.[37]

Like Tunbridge Wells, the resort of Bath had lots to offer an aristocrat looking for a good time. Lady Margaret Cave of Stanford Hall, a few months prior to her horrendous ordeal on the road from Claydon House in February 1710, gave a description of the place to Sir John Verney:

> This town is extreme full of company, and highly entertained with singing and music, by the famous Nicoleno and Valentinio, besides plays, baths, puppet-shows, ladder dancing, and some gaming, but I don't see much of that, high amongst the ladies, being but few of quality at this place now. I sometimes take the air on horseback, and otherwise am a gazing spectator.[38]

In terms of the waters, she found them to be most agreeable, for they had given her 'a much better appetite than I had before'.[39]

Tunbridge Wells as a spa resort for the aristocracy came into existence following the experience of Dudley, Lord North, in 1606, who, journeying back to London from a hunting lodge at Eridge, stumbled across a water supply in the area that appeared to restore the diseased nobleman to full health. By the reign of Charles II, having been visited by the highest echelons of society and then the world and his wife, the Kent retreat was so popular in England that it had begun to divide opinion amongst its many frequenters. 'That Tunbridge is the most miserable place in the world is very certain, and that the ladies do not look with very great advantage at three of the clock in the morning is as true,' the courtier Henry Savile wrote disdainfully to Lady Dorothy Savile in around 1665.[40] Another commentator, Antoine Hamilton, was a little less scornful in his own assessment of the place, which he made in the early eighteenth century when compiling the memoirs of his brother-in-law, Philibert de Gramont. Referring to Tunbridge Wells as a resort of 'mirth' and 'pleasure', he went on to write:

> Constraint is banished, familiarity is established upon the first acquaintance, and joy and pleasure are the sole sovereigns of the place. The company are accommodated with lodgings in little, clean, and convenient habitations, that lie straggling and separated from each other, a mile and a half all round the Wells, where the company meet in the morning: this place consists of a long walk, shaded by spreading trees, under which they walk while they are drinking the waters: on one side of this walk is a long row of shops, plentifully stocked with all manner of toys, lace, gloves, stockings, and where there is raffling: on the other side of the walk is the market; and, as it is the custom here for every person to buy their own provisions, care is taken that nothing offensive appears on the stalls. Here young, fair, fresh-coloured country girls, with clean linen, small straw hats, and neat shoes and stockings, sell game, vegetables, flowers and fruit: here one may live as one pleases: here is, likewise, deep play, and no want of amorous intrigues.[41]

The mind boggles to imagine what exactly Hamilton meant by certain parts of his comprehensive description, but what is clear from the man's observations is that a considerable number of aristocrats who turned up at Tunbridge Wells were not there for the benefit of Lord North's waters alone.

For those aristocratic frequenters of Bath and Tunbridge Wells, and other spa resorts in England besides, who were genuinely interested in using the spring waters to rid themselves of ailments, there were a number of things one could do to get the most out of a retreat visit. Multiple bathings might be recommended if a malady was grave, or considered especially difficult to cure; or there was repeated drinking from the springs, should an aristocrat not wish to bathe. Lady Mary Coke, daughter of the 2nd Earl of Chesterfield and wife of the courtier Sir Thomas Coke, drank a quart of water at Bath one summer morning in 1703, but resorted to gulping down two more for good measure when a 'fit' suddenly overcame her later in the day. Rest periods between taking the waters, in particular directly after bathing, were similarly advised by elite men and women who believed themselves in the know, including the future 1st Earl of Nottingham, Sir Heneage Finch. In August 1662, the vigilant father advised his son, Daniel, who was planning a recreational trip to Bath with his tutor, to find comfortable, proper lodgings in the city, because the teenager would surely need to sleep for 'an hour or two' following a spell at one of the bathhouses.[42]

As to the overall effectiveness of taking the waters, Stuart aristocrats had, as usual, conflicting views on the subject. Lady Mary Coke was of the impression that drinking three quarts of water at Bath had been on the whole beneficial in June 1703, with the gentlewoman's physician, Dr John Radcliffe, further assuring her that 'here is my only remedy'. In his attempts to cure himself of an unspecified illness in September 1664, Sir Robert Harley of Brampton Bryan (Sir Edward's brother) also felt optimistic after his tenth bathing session at Bath, noting that he was 'somewhat strengthened by it, so as to sit upright with greater ease and to go with a little more steadiness'. George Savile, 1st Marquess of Halifax, however, could not be entirely persuaded in the 1680s.

'I confess I have a lower opinion of the virtue of waters than is fashionable for a man to have, the doctors in vogue having declared so much for them,' he wrote to his brother Henry Savile in 1686.[43]

The marquess, known for his sagacity and his unapologetic scrutiny of the social world in which he lived, was not alone in feeling this way. Clearly, Robert Cecil, 1st Earl of Salisbury, who as we know came across no remedy whatsoever for his cancer at Bath in May 1612, left the place with his entourage wishing he had never bothered going. This was no doubt the conclusion drawn by Lady Margaret Elmes upon vacating the 'nasty' spa at Knaresborough in the 1660s, who, by the tone of her letters, seemed to think the whole experience had done her more harm than good. '[We] have now begun to drink the horrid sulphur water,' she recounted to her brother, Sir Ralph Verney, during her visit, 'which although as bad as is possible to be imagined, yet in my judgment pleasant, to all the doings we have within doors.' Margaret went on to complain about the dining room, which 'sure hath never been well cleaned nor aired these dozen years[;] It makes me much more sick than the nasty water.'[44]

Mental health

A handful of aristocrats in Stuart England suffered from various forms of psychological illness, poorly understood at this time and therefore difficult to deal with effectively. The troubled mind of Dame Dorothy Ogle in the early seventeenth century left Sir Simonds D'Ewes feeling somewhat disturbed and uncomfortable. While the Suffolk gentleman regarded Dame Ogle's ordeal as a bout of 'extreme despair' in his autobiography, twenty-first-century commentators might be inclined to describe it as clinical depression, brought on by her husband's colossal debts and her dramatic descent into poverty. Such a depression, alas, eventually caused Dorothy to become suicidal. In Ludgate Hill in about 1616, the gentlewoman slipped a knife into bed with her and proceeded to slash her own throat when the maid in the room had finally fallen asleep. The attendant woke with a start to the sounds of 'struggling and groaning', and immediately ran downstairs to find help, which was given by a surgeon who happened to be passing in the dark street outside.[45] D'Ewes noted that Dorothy, having survived that night, vowed on a number of subsequent occasions to try and kill herself again.

No member of the Verney family in the later seventeenth century could ignore the fact that the spouse of Sir Ralph's eldest son, the 'tall' and 'slight' Lady Mary Verney, was tormented by a mental affliction, which, in the modern world, might be interpreted as a schizoaffective or personality disorder. The gentlewoman's behaviour could be so alarmingly erratic that it could leave her own servants in floods of tears. This was the outcome on one notorious occasion in the early 1670s, when Edmund Verney returned to the couple's Buckinghamshire home full of cheer from a hunting expedition at nearby Addington, and found the building in complete disarray. The mistress of the house, with a fist that was very soon to be dripping with blood, had apparently gone from room to room smashing every window she could find. Along with destroying property, Mary was known to sleep with sharp objects, such as scissors and knives, and records indicate that at least once she swallowed a jagged piece of glass and a silver thimble. Additionally, the woman might scream or cry for no particular reason, attempt to starve herself, or get up without warning in the middle of a church service and purposefully distract the congregation. Edmund Verney was, sadly, the direct recipient of verbal and physical abuse from his wife at times, although the crude insults appeared to be more painful than the punches.

Finding a remedy for Lady Verney was no easy task for the dutiful husband, who craved an end to the irrational outbursts and unpredictable actions that frequently made his life a misery. Various solutions were suggested over the course of the gentlewoman's long-lasting 'melancholy', including, in quick succession, 'a secret powder that sends people to sleep for three or four days and nights ... after which they awake cured', tying the wrapped skull of a hare to Mary's head and leaving it there for half a week, and ardent prayer for six successive Sundays, but none of these made any difference to her condition.[46]

10

CHURCH AND CHARITY

> The first thing to be considered, is religion: it must be the chief object of your thoughts, since it would be a vain thing to direct your behaviour in the world, and forget that which you are to have towards Him who made it. In a strict sense, it is the only thing necessary: you must take it into your mind, and thence throw it into your heart.[1]

It was not just George Savile, 1st Marquess of Halifax, who believed that religion was one of the most important parts of life. The vast majority of Stuart aristocrats, whether they were Protestant or Catholic, would have agreed that there was no greater duty on earth than serving God to the best of one's ability. On a day-to-day basis, the aristocracy engaged with Christianity in a number of different ways, with worship the most obvious and widely practised act of piety. Christian charity from a place of privilege, which could come in a variety of forms, was also popularly enacted. In the 1630s, Sir Hugh Cholmley of Whitby fed a 'certain number of old people, widows, and indigent persons' from his own gates twice a week, every week, dispensing to the needy on each occasion a hearty combination of bread and pottage made with beef. Sir Nathaniel

Barnardiston of Kedington fed, clothed, and even left bequests of money to the poor living near him in Suffolk in the early seventeenth century.[2]

Worship

Virtually all aristocrats attended church every Sunday over the seventeenth and early eighteenth centuries, which was standard practice across the entirety of English society. Many elite individuals, though, worshipped in between as well. Where grand households had a resident chaplain, the family might gather for prayers and godly sermons on a daily basis, as they did with due diligence at Wollaton Hall in Nottinghamshire in the late 1680s. Prayers tended to take place in the mornings here, between 8 and 9am, with staff members expected to participate alongside the revered Willoughby dynasty. If any servant failed to show up for this important observance, and worse, had no good reason for their absence, they were made to fast until dinner by the master or mistress of the house.[3] Prayers were held earlier still at the Yorkshire abode of Sir Hugh Cholmley in the 1630s, beginning at 6am sharp and again occurring every day of the week; the practice, furthermore, was repeated twice more before dinner and supper. Even prominent noblemen occupying high offices in London might still find the time in their busy schedules to pray with close relatives and a personal chaplain each day. It was a ritual that Anthony Ashley Cooper, 1st Earl of Shaftesbury, insisted on wholeheartedly while serving as lord chancellor in the early 1670s. A contemporary of the statesman noted that Cooper never missed morning prayers with his family during term-time, which commenced at 7am, and he was seldom absent from their late morning and evening devotions either.

Dismay might be caused and, sometimes, alternative arrangements made if aristocrats found themselves unable to attend a religious service, or believed they were in danger of missing one. This was particularly the case on Sundays and festival days. Sir John Bramston of Skreens, a veritable relic of the Stuart period who was now in his late eighties, developed a cold in the weeks before Christmas Day in 1699, and was greatly 'in fear I should not have been able to go to church'. Fortunately, the heavens smiled on the ex-politician once 25 December arrived; 'I thank God I went,' he wrote afterwards, 'received the Communion at the rails, and I praise God I have been free from the cold ever since.' Sir Ralph Verney also made it to Claydon church one Sunday morning in August 1696, even though, at the admirable age of eighty-two, he was said to have been 'as weak as a two year old child'. For this reason, he was forced to abandon the service halfway through, which seemed to upset the gentleman enormously. While stoically insisting at the time that the ladies present in the church should continue to listen to the preacher's pious words, later he was to be discovered at Claydon House in a 'most lamentable' state as a result of having to excuse himself. Whenever Lady Anne Clifford felt she did not have the strength to leave her chamber on a Sunday to go to church, which happened time and again towards the close of her life at Brougham Castle in the 1670s, she sent her servants along instead. 'My two gentlewomen and most of my menservants went and three of my laundry maids to ye church of Ninekirks where Mr Grasty ye parson preached a good sermon to them and the rest of the congregation,' she wrote in her diary on one such day.[4] Ninekirks, or St Ninian's church as it was and is officially known, had been restored by Lady Anne Clifford in the mid-seventeenth century.

Elite women especially might completely immerse themselves in religious thought and teachings for days on end, which left little room in their schedules for other, quotidian activities, save for the basic acts of eating, drinking, and sleeping. Lady Margaret Hoby of Hackness in Yorkshire appeared to set the trend for such dedicated, female worship in the Stuart period, with her diaries in and after 1603 reflecting a near-constant engrossment in prayer and religious literature. 'After private prayers I went about until prayer time: and after dinner went into the garden, until I returned to private prayer and reading,' the gentlewoman noted in one diary entry of 1605. Lady Anne Clifford in the early years of her married life to Richard Sackville appeared similarly preoccupied with godly endeavours, although not to the same degree as the devout Mary Rich, Countess of Warwick, in the Restoration era. As well as worshipping extensively herself, Rich also passionately encouraged others to do the same. Riding home in a coach with her husband, the 4th Earl of Warwick, one afternoon in 1670, she suddenly turned to the nobleman and told him 'how much thankfulness we owed to God, who had given us such sweet parks and accommodations; and that we should serve him with cheerfulness of heart in that plenty and abundance of all things which we enjoyed'. Servants were certainly encouraged to worship, too, with Mary spending one morning in September 1671 'catechizing some of the poor weeders' and 'stirring them up to look after their souls'. As for her own devout activities, the Countess of Warwick's day invariably involved much prayer, soul-searching, and deep meditation. The latter could last for three hours at a time.[5]

If the sources are to be believed (and, of course, one should probe all historical documents), for some elite males, worship also became akin to a lifestyle. A biography of Sir Nathaniel Barnardiston of Kedington written some thirty years after his death in July 1653 considered the man a 'saint in all places and relations', because he was said to have followed a devout life that saw him worshipping, or interacting with God and His teachings, at every opportunity. The man prayed privately at least three times throughout the day, according to the biography's author, Samuel Clarke, while he could forever be found studying passages from the Bible. 'He ever made sure work to begin and close up with prayer, that he might obtain the blessing of God thereon.'[6]

It took other male aristocrats until they reached the sombre environment of their own deathbeds, with the world to come staring them straight in the face, to commit to religion in a similar way. William Cavendish, 1st Duke of Devonshire, assumed an uncharacteristically and consistently pious air when he took to his bed for the last time in London in August 1707, having been struck down by a fatal complaint. 'He confessed his being troubled, being very much troubled, for the lateness of his repentance,' it was noted during the nobleman's funeral service, 'which he hoped was sincere... He professed himself to be truly sorrowful for all the many great sins and errors of his life, and did humbly and earnestly beg forgiveness of God for them.' Once the moment arrived for the Duke to slip into eternal rest, therefore, he purportedly 'fell asleep, not merely like an ancient Roman, but rather like a good Christian'.[7]

Fasting

Abstaining from certain foods and drink in the name of religious observance was practised by a fair few of the Stuart aristocracy from time to time. Aside from the normal strictures of Lent, fasting might also be resorted to by aristocrats if widespread sickness was crippling the nation. Lady Margaret Hoby of Hackness fasted in response to a serious outbreak of plague in England in the latter part of 1603, noting on 7 October that she had refrained from eating or drinking anything at all until the evening. Instead, the gentlewoman had concentrated her efforts on 'begging of the Lord that blessing which yet I want'. Margaret was a little less strict with herself two days later on 9 October, choosing to pick at some bread in the morning before determinedly setting off to church to perform certain 'exercises' intended to slow the spread of the contagion.[8] Decades later, in August 1666, we find Mary Rich, Countess of Warwick, also fasting at Leez Priory in Essex, in the hopes that the Great Plague, the last epidemic of its kind in England, would disappear from the country and never return. Every 30 January, moreover, the noblewoman set aside nourishment to observe the anniversary of the death of Charles I, beheaded outside the Banqueting House in London in 1649 for treasonous crimes against the people.

Sir Simonds D'Ewes' wife, Anne Clopton, joined her new husband in giving up certain foods while still a teenager in 1627:

> Monday, December the 17th, my dear wife, who had in her young and tender age, being not yet full fifteen years old, practised most religious and pious duties that concerned a Christian, upon her own earnest entreaty and desire, joined with me in fasting and humiliation, beginning also to draw most blessed and certain signs of her own future happiness after death from several graces: which assurance she afterwards finished upon other her like days of humiliation and fasting in which we two alone joined together.[9]

Surrendering a hefty percentage of one's diet was not always an easy ask for elite individuals used to having satisfied stomachs and overflowing cups. Sir Richard Newdigate of Arbury Hall took to fasting for several days in 1683, eating one morning just a single crust of bread and drinking only water. This made him 'listless and weary' at chapel, and afterwards in the gardens at Arbury he was unable to stop himself from enjoying a generous quantity of homegrown fruit. The Warwickshire gentleman was nonetheless proud that he had managed to abstain for seventy-two hours from 'eating one grain of salt with my meat, which is very insipid, especially roast venison, without it'.[10] He hoped that such a sacrifice, which was clearly very significant to him, would be enough to enrich his spirit and bring him closer to God.

During Lent, many Christians, both high- and low-born, replicated Christ's forty days of fasting in the desert, or at least followed a version of fasting. The Catholic Elizabeth Cary, Viscountess Falkland, fasted through Lent without fail during her lifetime, as did many other aristocrats up and down the country under the rule of the Stuarts. In Cary's case, butter and milk were dispensed with for the two months that made up the observance, along with 'sugary' meats. Elizabeth was even more sparing when in the company of Protestants over this period, which included her own husband, Henry Cary, 1st Viscount Falkland, and children. On these occasions, she chose to forgo all foods except nettle porridge 'without butter' and 'cakes made only of flour, water, and salt, baked on the hearth'.[11]

The poor

The nobility and gentry were in a unique position, with their wealth and privilege, to be able to fulfil the Christian act of relieving the destitute. Naturally, some examples of aristocratic giving were more Christianly than others. According to the esquire William Blundell, one repeat beggar at Crosby races in the later seventeenth century, who infuriated noble racegoers no end with his incessant flattery and over-the-top compliments, eventually had a shilling thrown at his head to get rid of him. 'A pox o' God take thee!' the provider of the coin was said to have bellowed.[12] In general, however, assisting the poor appeared to come from a place of genuine compassion, with aristocrats keen to show the rest of society that they were sympathetic, charitable, and benevolent human beings.

The most common way in which the elite relieved the poor in this period was through offerings of food and money. If food was involved, often the items would be distributed from the gates of a country house or townhouse, comprising either leftovers from meals or sustenance prepared specially for the impoverished. At Melford Hall in Suffolk in the early 1600s, there was accordingly a 'back-gate for the beggars and the meaner sort of swains to come in at'. In times of particular hardship or during a religious holiday, food might be directed further afield by proactive aristocrats to those unfortunate individuals who were considered most in need of feeding.

Robert Harley wrote to his father, Sir Edward Harley, to thank him 'for the care you have taken to send beef and corn to the poor of Radnor' in December 1690, just before Christmas, but thought that the Brampton Bryan man could circulate his offerings more widely still.[13] Operating from Charlecote Park in Warwickshire in the years leading up to her death in 1648, the Puritan Lady Alice Lucy was always quick to respond should there be shortages of food in the local area. A description was given of her charitable instincts some forty-five years after the gentlewoman's passing:

> In those times of scarcity, every week she sent many loaves of bread to many neighbour towns. She caused her corn to be sold in the markets (as it were) by retail, in such small quantities as might not exceed the poor's abilities to purchase.[14]

Lady Alice even invited members of the poor into her own stately mansion at Charlecote for meals, welcoming especially people 'whose empty bellies were discernible in their pale faces'. Witnessing a healthier complexion return to their cheeks, it seems, brought the widow of Sir Thomas Lucy much joy. The Dowager Countess of Arundel, Anne Howard, also had destitute persons over for dinner or supper before her death in April 1630, the noblewoman following the ancient custom of 'the better sort' entertaining their neighbours at 'Christmas or such other times'. This she would apparently do in an affable manner, without pretentiousness or detachment, allowing her guests to dine with her in the hall or parlour of Shifnal Manor. Each of the people the dowager summoned, furthermore, would be spoken to in turn, 'so that they departed ever well contented, and conceiv'd a love and esteem of her'.[15]

Where money was concerned, alms might simply be tossed to poor persons and vagrants wandering the highways if an aristocrat was travelling in a coach or on horseback. There were, however, more formal processes in place. Many eminent benefactors gave annual sums to their local parishes in the Stuart period, which were to go towards relieving the poor specifically. These were called 'benevolences' by Francis Manners, 6th Earl of Rutland, and his steward in early seventeenth-century Leicestershire, with £2 handed over in 1620 'to the use of the poore' of St Martin's parish, presumably in Leicester. Special or significant occasions in the lives of aristocrats might warrant one-off payments to the local impoverished throughout the year, which, when arising, tended to be handed out in an ecclesiastical setting. In 1628, for instance, on the fifty-first anniversary of Lord William Howard's long marriage to Lady Elizabeth Dacre, the latter arranged for fifty-two 'poore folkes' to receive alms to commemorate the nuptials, one for each year of the couple's marital union. So, too, elite funerals were a time for doles. The aforementioned William Howard's burial in October 1640 featured a dole for the poor of the parish of Greystoke worth a not inconsiderable £5 18 shillings, although collective offerings at these events could easily reach in excess of £20.

It would seem that for some needy individuals, being presented with hard cash by a social superior, in whatever context, was a difficult concept to come to terms with. The esquire William Blundell of Crosby Hall noted one encounter in July 1684 that he appeared to find particularly amusing, involving a nameless poor woman with significant familial responsibilities. Blundell asked her how many children she had, to which the poverty-stricken female replied, 'six'. At this, the sympathetic esquire offered the mother some money, saying, 'here is sixpence for them.' The woman immediately misunderstood the benefactor, such was her confusion and obvious suspicion of his intentions. She answered, 'No sir, I will not sell my children.'[16]

Together with bestowing food and money on the poor, the aristocracy might also help to clothe them. 'Ask the poor ... who daily attended her door in flocks: who put off their hunger with their rags ... how often they came naked and went away clothed,' a contemporary account declared in relation to the charitable Dame Lucy Reynell of Forde House, who died in 1652. Dame Reynell even helped to make the many clothes that were given by her household to the destitute, the gentlewoman purportedly being responsible for 'all kinds of garments for them'. While the Dowager Countess of Arundel earlier in the seventeenth century did not physically sew the garments she distributed to the poor around Shifnal Manor in Shropshire, she was very much responsible for the purchase and organisation of the required materials. Each year, the Howard noblewoman arranged for certain amounts of 'northern woollen cloth' and 'coarser linen' to be brought to her household, which she then paid to have transformed into basic clothing.[17]

Almshouses for those with absolutely nothing were frequently founded by aristocrats across the Stuart period, having been a common feature of the English landscape since before 1066. Lady Anne Clifford recorded with immense satisfaction the moment the very first stone was laid at her new almshouse in Appleby-in-Westmorland in 1651; two years later, in 1653, she wrote again in her diary that the building was 'quite finished' and would be housing eleven widows and an injured maid. In the Newton Abbot area in around 1640, Dame Lucy Reynell set up her own almshouse for four ministers' widows to live in, 'if any should come to be reduc'd to that distress'. It was said to be a 'fair' edifice upon completion, split presumably into four dwellings for each of the poor women to inhabit, with every lodging possessing three rooms and a garden plot. The quartet of widows, moreover, were to receive the annual sum of £5 each until they died.[18] Though the available evidence appears to suggest that noble and gentle females did much of the heavy lifting when it came to poor relief in the seventeenth and early eighteenth centuries, there were in fact some aristocratic men who founded almshouses. A notable example is Henry Howard, 1st Earl of Northampton, the man who left in his wake such splendour at Northampton House in London upon his demise in 1614. In the years leading up to his death, Howard founded no fewer than three almshouses in various parts of the country, one in Shropshire in 1607, another in Norfolk in 1609, and a third in Greenwich in 1613, known as Trinity Hospital. The latter almshouse offered twelve places for poor males living in Greenwich itself, while a further eight spaces were reserved for impoverished men hailing from Shotesham in Norfolk, the earl's own birthplace.[19]

When consideration was given to the very youngest members of the English poor, it is clear that Stuart aristocrats believed above all else that they should enjoy a decent education. In some instances, the elite might revert to money once again in an attempt to give underprivileged children this opportunity. In February 1608, Roger Manners, 5th Earl of Rutland gave a 'poor scholar' from Grantham, by the name of William Allen, twenty shillings 'for his better furtherance' to Cambridge University. A solution that was becoming steadily more popular, however, involved those with wealth and influence founding their very own schools for the indigent of a particular parish. In 1624, following the death of his son, Henry, the knight Sir William Borlase created one such institution at Marlow in Buckinghamshire, which was to gain its funding from land with a rent value of £14 per year. Within this place, a schoolmaster earning an annual salary of £12 would aim to teach twenty-four poor children to 'write, read, and cast accounts'.[20]

The baronet Sir Thomas Rich knew he would never live to see his own school for the poor be realised in the later seventeenth century, having only made provision for it in his last will and testament. The idea was for the establishment to be run from Rich's own townhouse in Gloucester, 'for the entertaining and harbouring of twenty poor boys and their maintenance, with diet, lodging, washing, clothing, and other necessaries'. The boys were to have a uniform, consisting of blue coats and caps, which emulated the dress code seen at Christ's Hospital in Newgate Street, London, and none of them were to be below the age of ten or over the age of sixteen. Furthermore, the baronet instructed that four students every year were to be apprenticed in the capital to 'some honest handicraft trades there and with honest masters, not adhering in their opinions to the novelties of the times'. The school opened in 1668, a year after Sir Thomas' death. In Battersea in 1700, another educational institution for destitute youngsters was established by a

Stuart aristocrat, in this instance the baronet Sir Walter St John of Lydiard Tregoze in Wiltshire. His was a school that would welcome twenty more poor boys into the potentially lucrative world of reading and writing, some of whom would eventually go on to be apprenticed elsewhere.[21] As ever, though, there were no girls to be found in the elite man's establishment.

The sick

Tending to the sick was likewise seen as a Christian duty by aristocrats in this period, with sufferers who were given assistance not always comprising members of the poor. Whenever Lady Alice Lucy's personal physician was in residence at Charlecote Park in the early seventeenth century, she made sure that all and sundry in the local area knew that the practitioner was visiting her, should any amongst them require medical assistance. 'But at all times when any wanted health,' a contemporary account of the gentlewoman stated, 'she presently had intelligence of it, and most cheerfully communicated whatsoever she conceived conducible to their recovery.'[22] Lucy, apparently, had a great number of medicines at her disposal, and knew how to administer many of them herself.

Anne Howard, Dowager Countess of Arundel, was also happy to aid sick individuals from various backgrounds. A contemporary text celebrating her life, and that of her distinguished husband, noted:

> Another kind of alms [consisted of] medicines, salves, plasters, and other remedies to all kind of people who either wanting will, or means to go to doctors and chirurgeons, came to her for the curing of their wounds and distempers. And her charity herein was so famous, that not only neighbours, but several out of other shires, twenty, forty, and more miles distant did resort unto her to that end, and scarce a day passed in which many did not come, sometimes more than threescore have been counted in one day: and to every one that came besides advice and medicines if the matter

> did require it, she usually gave some alms in money if they were poor, as many were... A hundred marks every year she assigned for her private purse, and the greatest part thereof was distributed either by herself, or some of her gentlewomen to such kind of patients or other distressed people.[23]

Treating the incapacitated poor was particularly important to the Catholic dowager, however. When they did not come to her for medical assistance, she might be determined enough to seek them out instead, however long the journey. On one occasion in the London area, this is exactly what the noblewoman did, following the appearance of a frantic woman at her doorstep in Acton who claimed that a destitute female in labour needed help immediately. The mother-to-be in question lived in Hammersmith, which was three miles away from Anne's property. Even with no coach to speak of at this time, the dowager was not to be put off, going with the messenger on foot at once to locate the expectant woman. While this example admittedly occurred at the close of the reign of Elizabeth I, it is nonetheless worth mentioning for its representation of Anne Howard's charitable character.[24]

In a work entitled *The Saintly Life of Mrs Margaret Godolphin*, John Evelyn wrote endlessly of the gentlewoman's benevolent interactions with the sick and infirm in London. The well-bred wife of the future 1st Earl of Godolphin, Margaret was said to have braved dingy backstreets and 'obscure places of the town' just to reach those who needed her help, giving them 'physic' that she had brought along all by herself. When a patient was close to death, moreover, she did not hesitate to send for a minister to 'prepare them for the Sacrament', and even received it with them as the light slowly left their eyes. Margaret found such joy in tending to the indisposed of the capital, according to Evelyn, that she often chose visiting them over 'gay and public company' and 'the greatest entertainments'.[25] If this is indeed a true statement (and one must remember that Evelyn and Godolphin were very close companions), then the woman is to be commended.

EPILOGUE

Pomp and piety are two themes that occur over and over in the daily existence of seventeenth- and early eighteenth-century English aristocrats. The significant presence of religion, or piety, is evident not only in the last chapter on worship and charitable acts, but also in many of those that come before it. Pomp, ceremony, and privilege, one trusts, are easily discerned throughout the volume. The coexistence of ostentation and devoutness in the lives of the Stuart aristocracy is revealed for a final time in the following excerpt. It comes from the diary of Lady Anne Clifford, written when she was in London in November 1617:

> The 2nd being Sunday I went to church with my Sister Sackville to St Bride's and afterwards my cousin George and I went and dined with my Lady Ruthven, where I met my Lady Shrewsbury... All the time I was at court I wore my green damask gown embroidered without a farthingale. The same day I sent the Queen by Lady Ruthven the skirts of a white satin gown all pearl and embroidered with colours which cost me fourscore pounds without the satin.[1]

Appendix

THE MAIN CHARACTERS

The following aristocrats featured in this book are listed by their most senior ranks, and in alphabetical order.

BLUNDELL, Nicholas, esquire (1669–1737)
Blundell was the grandson of the esquire and civil war veteran William Blundell. He had taken over the family seat of Crosby Hall by the early eighteenth century, following the death of his father, another William, in 1702. Nicholas chose Frances Langdale for his wife and had two daughters.

BOURCHIER, Henry, 5th Earl of Bath (*c.* 1587–1654), **and Rachel, Countess of Bath** (1613–1680)
This noble couple married in December 1638, when Henry was around fifty years old and Rachel (a Fane by birth) exactly half his age. Henry had inherited the earldom of Bath in 1636, which brought with it many privileges and assets, including Tawstock Court in Devon. The two lived there and in London over the course of their married life, until the the death of the earl at Tawstock in August 1654. Rachel married for a second time in 1655 and lived on for several decades until her own death in November 1680.

BRAMSTON, Sir John, knight (1611–1700)
Given the suffix 'the younger', Bramston was born in London in 1611 to his namesake, Sir John Bramston 'the elder', who was for a time Chief Justice of the King's Bench, and Bridget Moundeford. Bramston 'the younger' eventually took over the family pile of Skreens in Essex, although he spent much of his time living in nearby London, where he practised law and dabbled in politics. He married Alice Abdy in 1635, having with her a number of children – both sons and daughters – before she died in 1647. Bramston was knighted in 1661 and lived as Sir John for a further four decades; he was succeeded by his son, Anthony, upon his death in February 1700.

BROWNLOW, John, 3rd Baronet (1659–1697)
Brownlow lived at Belton House in Lincolnshire, the son of Richard Brownlow, 2nd Baronet, and Elizabeth Freke of Stretton in Dorset. In 1676, John married Alice Sherard of Lopethorp, who gave him a succession of daughters. The baronet died in July 1697, aged thirty-eight.

CALVERLEY, Walter, 1st Baronet (1670–1749)
Calverley hailed from Yorkshire and was created a baronet in 1711. He married the daughter of another baronet, Julia Blackett, in 1707, with the couple eventually taking up residence at Esholt Hall near Bradford two years later.

CAVENDISH, Margaret, Duchess of Newcastle (*c.* 1623–1673)
Cavendish came from the modest Lucas family, who had a manor house in the grounds of St John's Abbey in Colchester. She married above her station in 1645, her husband William Cavendish, then Marquess of Newcastle, whom she had met in Paris while travelling with Queen Henrietta Maria. When William became a duke in 1665, Margaret accordingly assumed the illustrious position of a duchess. Having written prolifically throughout her life, she died at Welbeck Abbey as a woman of literary renown – both good and bad – in December 1673.

CHOLMLEY, Hugh, 1st Baronet (1600–1657)
Cholmley was the son of Sir Richard Cholmley of Whitby and Susanna Legard. He married Elizabeth Twysden in 1622, who gave him several children, and was made a baronet in 1641.

CHOLMLEY, Sir Richard, knight (*c.* 1579–1631)
Cholmley, the son of Sir Henry Cholmley, came from an ancient family that could trace its roots back to Cheshire. He was knighted in 1603 and set up an estate for himself in Whitby.

CLIFFORD, Anne, Countess of Pembroke, Dorset, and Montgomery (1590–1676)
Known throughout her life as Lady Anne Clifford, this noblewoman was born at Skipton Castle in Yorkshire in the late sixteenth century to George Clifford, 3rd Earl of Cumberland, and his wife, Lady Margaret Russell. She had two brothers, Robert and Francis, who both died young. In February 1609, following a match orchestrated by Thomas Sackville, 1st Earl of Dorset, Anne married the nineteen-year-old aristocrat Richard Sackville, who was then on the verge of succeeding his father as 3rd Earl of Dorset. Two surviving girls were produced by the Sackvilles' largely unhappy marriage, Margaret and Isabella, with a further three sons all dying as children. This left the Earl of Dorset without male issue when he himself died in London in 1624, the death reducing Anne to a bereaved but eligible widow at the relatively young age of thirty-four. She remarried some six years later, on 3 June 1630, taking for her second husband the widower Philip Herbert, Earl of Pembroke and Montgomery, who already had several sons from his first marriage. When the supporter of Parliament also died in 1650, Anne turned her attention fully to the Clifford estates she had inherited in northern England from her father's family. Having constantly moved between her Yorkshire and Westmorland properties in the final years of her life, she eventually died at Brougham Castle in March 1676, aged eighty-six.

COKE, Sir Thomas, knight (*c.* 1674–1727)
Coke's family called Melbourne Hall in Derbyshire their home. He was born and baptised there in about 1674, and in later life inherited the country estate from his father, John Coke. A prominent Member of Parliament and in time a member of the privy council, Thomas married Lady Mary Stanhope in 1698, who was a daughter of Philip Stanhope, 2nd Earl of Chesterfield. When she died prematurely, the Member of Parliament married again, taking as his second wife Elizabeth Hales.

COOPER, Anthony Ashley, 1st Earl of Shaftesbury (1621–1683)
Cooper was born at Wimborne St Giles in Dorset to the baronet Sir John Cooper and his wife, Lady Anne Ashley. Appointed lord chancellor in 1672, he was accordingly made an earl the same year. In the early 1680s, after getting caught up in a political scandal at home, the nobleman escaped to mainland Europe, dying in Amsterdam in January 1683.

D'EWES, Simonds, 1st Baronet (1602–1650)
D'Ewes was a Suffolk man, born to Paul D'Ewes of Stow Hall, near Bury St Edmunds, and his wife Cecelia Simonds. He inherited his father's estates when the esquire died in 1631, further enhancing his status ten years later upon becoming a baronet. Simonds married twice over the course of his life, his first spouse being the heiress Anne Clopton of Kentwell Hall, who died in 1641.

FINCH, Heneage, 1st Earl of Nottingham (1621–1682)
Finch could boast an illustrious and ancient lineage, being born to Sir Heneage Finch and Frances Bell of Beaupré Hall in Norfolk. He made a name for himself in politics in the later seventeenth century and consequently became lord chancellor in 1675, a post that he would gladly hold for a number of years. During his tenure as chancellor, Heneage was made 1st Earl of Nottingham. He married Elizabeth Harvey in 1646 and had several children by her, one of whom, Daniel, would succeed him in 1682 as 2nd Earl of Nottingham.

FLEMING, Sir Daniel, knight (1633–1701)
Fleming was born to a prominent landowner by the name of William Fleming in the reign of Charles I. When his father died in 1653, he inherited substantial lands in Westmorland, which included the stately Rydal Hall. Daniel was eventually knighted at Windsor in 1681, increasing his prestige and social standing to an even greater degree. His sons, a product of his marriage to Barbara Fletcher of Hutton, went on to become baronets.

HARLEY, Sir Edward, knight (1624–1700)
Harley was the son of Sir Robert and Lady Brilliana Harley of Brampton Bryan Castle in Herefordshire. He was married twice, first to Mary Button in 1654, then in 1661 to Abigail Stephens of Eastington. Abigail gave him a son, Robert, who would go on to be Earl of Oxford and Mortimer.

HARLEY, Robert, 1st Earl of Oxford and Mortimer (1661–1724)
Harley's parents were Sir Edward Harley of Brampton Bryan and Lady Abigail Stephens. Robert managed to outrank his deceased father in 1711 as a result of his political successes and appointments, becoming in that year Earl of Oxford and Mortimer. He lived intermittently with his two successive wives at Brampton Bryan Hall in Herefordshire, inherited from Sir Edward in 1700. This building was constructed to replace the earlier castle, which had been largely destroyed during the English Civil War.

HERBERT, Edward, 1st Baron Herbert of Cherbury (*c.* 1582–1648)
Herbert was an Anglo-Welsh aristocrat, born in the reign of Elizabeth I to Richard Herbert of Montgomery Castle. He married a cousin in 1599 and had several children by her, with the man constantly flitting between Wales, England, and even France, where he was for some time an ambassador. Edward was knighted in 1603 by James I and was given an English barony in 1629.

HERVEY, John, 1st Earl of Bristol (1665–1751)
Hervey was born to Sir Thomas Hervey of the Ickworth estate in Suffolk. He succeeded his father in 1694, accruing in 1703 the title of 1st Baron Hervey, and then in 1714 1st Earl of Bristol. The eventual earl married twice, with his second wife, Lady Elizabeth Felton of Playford Hall, giving him as many as seventeen children.

HOWARD, Anne, Dowager Countess of Arundel (1557–1630)
Anne was born a Dacre in the reign of Mary I, but quickly adopted the great Howard name when she married the 13th Earl of Arundel in the early 1570s. By the Stuart period, she had become Dowager Countess of Arundel, having lost her husband, Philip Howard, in October 1595. A famous Catholic convert, she spent her final years of widowhood at Shifnal Manor in Shropshire.

HOWARD, Henry, 1st Earl of Northampton (1540–1614)
This illustrious nobleman was born at Shotesham in Norfolk, to Henry Howard, Earl of Surrey, and his wife, Lady Frances de Vere. By the middle years of the reign of James I, Henry had become a member of the privy council, First Lord of the Treasury, Lord Warden of the Cinque Ports, and Earl of Northampton, possessing as a result a number of elegant properties. He had no wife or children when he died in 1614, and therefore the earldom of Northampton perished with him.

HOWARD, Thomas, 14th Earl of Arundel (1585–1646)
Howard was the son of Anne, Dowager Countess of Arundel, and Philip Howard, 13th Earl of Arundel. He inherited the earldom of Arundel only when his recusant family were reinstated at court in 1604, his Catholic father having died a decade earlier in the Tower of London. Thomas found a match in Lady Alethea Talbot the following year, who gave him several sons and a happy marriage. The nobleman was a great traveller and art enthusiast, known for his vast collection of paintings that had come from across Europe. He died a Catholic, like both his parents, in Padua in 1646.

HOWARD, Lord William (1563–1640)
Howard was born at Audley End in Essex, son of Thomas Howard, 4th Duke of Norfolk, and Lady Margaret Audley. He married his stepsister, Elizabeth Dacre, very young in October 1577, aged thirteen, and eventually lived with her at Naworth Castle in Cumberland. Here, from about 1607 onwards, the couple oversaw aspects of their grandchildren's upbringing. William died at Greystoke Castle in Cumberland in 1640, while fleeing the Scottish.

ISHAM, Thomas, 3rd Baronet (1657–1681)
Isham was the third in a short line of baronets occupying Lamport Hall in Northamptonshire. His parents were Justinian Isham, 2nd Baronet, and Lady Vere Leigh, a granddaughter of Sir Thomas Egerton, 1st Viscount Brackley. Thomas took over at Lamport Hall following his father's death in 1675, but died himself in 1681, aged just twenty-four, before he could make much of an impression on the estate. He never married.

MANNERS, Roger, 5th Earl of Rutland (1576–1612)
Manners became 5th Earl of Rutland following the death of his father, John Manners, in February 1588, at the age of eleven. His principal residence as earl was Belvoir Castle in Leicestershire, where he lived with his wife Lady Elizabeth Sidney, whom he had married in 1599. The union produced no children, and both spouses died in 1612.

MILDMAY, Sir Humphrey, knight (1592–*c.* 1666)
Humphrey came from a branch of the Mildmay family inhabiting Danbury Place in Essex. He was knighted in July 1616 and by the early 1630s had inherited the quaint country seat to the north-east of London. Not long after he was knighted, Humphrey married the daughter of Sir John Crofts of Little Saxham in Suffolk, who was either called Joan or Jane. The precise year of his death is not clear, although 1666 has been suggested.

NEWDIGATE, Richard, 2nd Baronet (1644–1710)
Newdigate was the son of a baronet, also called Richard Newdigate. He inherited the family seat of Arbury Hall in Warwickshire in 1678 upon the death of his father, and in doing so became a baronet himself. Richard's two wives were Mary Bagot and Henrietta Wigginton; the former gave him seven children.

OGLANDER, Sir John, knight (1585–1655)
Oglander came from the Isle of Wight, born to Sir William Oglander of Nunwell and Ann Dillington. He took over Nunwell House following his father's death in 1609 and was knighted in 1615. Sir John held a number of high offices on the Isle of Wight over the course of his life, including deputy governor in the 1620s. He married Frances More early in the seventeenth century, who bore him several children.

RERESBY, John, 2nd Baronet (1634–1689)
Reresby was a Yorkshireman whose country seat was at Thrybergh, near Rotherham. He became a baronet in 1646 upon the death of his father, another John Reresby, and went on to marry the daughter of a humble barrister, Frances, in 1665.

REYNELL, Sir Richard, knight (1558–1634), **and Dame Lucy** (1577–1652)
This gentle couple were married in 1600 and lived at Forde House in Devon. Sir Richard was knighted in 1622 and died some sixteen years before his wife, Lucy. They had one surviving daughter called Jane.

RICH, Mary, Countess of Warwick (1624–1678)
Rich originally came from Ireland, having been born to Richard Boyle, 1st Earl of Cork, and his second spouse, Catherine Fenton. She met and fell in love with the future 4th Earl of Warwick, Charles Rich, in the early 1640s, marrying him without delay in 1641. This was to the mild chagrin of her father, who nonetheless

ensured that his 'unruly' daughter was financially prepared for her new life across the Irish Sea. Unfortunately, Mary's marriage to Charles was beset with difficulties from the very start, their relationship increasingly suffering due to the earl's ill health and continued grief for his two children, who both died young. The couple spent a good proportion of their married life at Leez Priory in Essex, although they could also frequently be found at Warwick House in London. The earl died in relative agony in August 1673, while Mary followed him five years later, wholly enveloped in religious preoccupations.

RUSSELL, William, 1st Duke of Bedford (1616–1700)
Russell was born to Francis Russell, 4th Earl of Bedford, and his wife, Lady Catherine Brydges, whose country seat was Woburn Abbey in Bedfordshire. He became 5th Earl of Bedford in 1641, having married the heiress Lady Anne Carr four years earlier in 1637. Between them, they had many children who survived into adulthood, including the traitorous William, Lord Russell, who was to meet his end in 1683 at the hands of the executioner Jack Ketch. The earl was elevated to the rank of duke in 1694; he died at Bedford House in London at the turn of the eighteenth century, aged eighty-four.

RUSSELL, Wriothesley, 2nd Duke of Bedford (1680–1711)
Russell was the son of William, Lord Russell, and Lady Rachel Wriothesley, and more importantly the grandson of the 1st Duke of Bedford. Following his father's execution in 1683, he became heir apparent to the dukedom of Bedford, which he inherited when his grandfather died in 1700. Wriothesley had married the heiress Elizabeth Howland in May 1695, whom he predeceased in 1711 aged only thirty. They had six children.

SLINGSBY, Henry, 1st Baronet (1602–1658)
Slingsby was born to an earlier Henry Slingsby and his wife, Frances Vavasour. He made Red House in Yorkshire his principal seat, where he lived comfortably with his children and spouse,

Barbara Belasyse, who was the daughter of Viscount Fauconberg. Henry was made a baronet in 1638, but, following the defeat of Charles I in the 1640s, his fortunes took a turn for the worse. A diehard supporter of the Royalist cause, the baronet found himself imprisoned in 1655 as a result of his suspected – but unconfirmed – involvement in the Penruddock Uprising, which aimed to destroy Cromwell's Protectorate and re-establish the monarchy in England. His arrest led to his execution on Tower Hill in June 1658, just three months before Oliver Cromwell's own death from malaria.

VERNEY, John, 1st Viscount Fermanagh (1640–1717)
Verney was a son of Ralph Verney of Middle Claydon and succeeded to his father's baronetcy in September 1696. He became 1st Viscount Fermanagh in 1703. The nobleman was married twice, first to Elizabeth Palmer in 1680, and then in 1692 to Mary Lawley, who would become Viscountess Fermanagh.

VERNEY, Ralph, 1st Baronet (1613–1696)
Verney lived in Claydon House in Buckinghamshire for fifty-four years, from 1642 to his death in 1696. He married Mary Blacknall in 1629 and had six children by her, with the couple enjoying an affectionate relationship until the latter's death in France in 1650. Ralph was made baronet of Middle Claydon in 1661.

WENTWORTH, Isabella, mother of the 1st Earl of Strafford (*c.* 1653–1733)
Isabella Apsley, daughter of the soldier Sir Allan Apsley, married Sir William Wentworth in the later seventeenth century. When William died in 1692, she was supported emotionally and financially by her eight surviving children, relying particularly on her son Thomas, who acquired various titles and significant wealth at an early age. While Thomas was abroad fulfilling his role as English ambassador, Isabella spent a good deal of her time at his house in Twickenham, called Mount Lebanon, where she played hostess to the elite of London and lived very well. She died at Twickenham in 1733.

WENTWORTH, Thomas, 1st Earl of Strafford (1672–1739), and Anne, Countess of Strafford (1684–1754)

The Thomas Wentworth mentioned in this book is not to be confused with the nobleman of the same name and rank who was executed on Tower Hill in 1641. Our Thomas Wentworth was born in September 1672, to Sir William Wentworth and his wife, Lady Isabella Apsley. Before marrying in 1711, he inherited the title of 3rd Baron Raby, was made the English ambassador to both Berlin and The Hague, and was created 1st Earl of Strafford. His wife was the heiress Anne Johnson, daughter of Sir Henry Johnson, who provided her husband with several children and wrote him many adoring letters when he was out of the country.

NOTES

Abbreviations

HMC	Historical Manuscripts Commission
RHS	Royal Historical Society
PCCRP	Prerogative Court of Canterbury and Related Probate Jurisdictions

Introduction

1. William Dougal Christie, *A Life of Anthony Ashley Cooper, First Earl of Shaftesbury, 1621–1683*, Vol. 1 (London: Macmillan and Co., 1871), p. xv.
2. Christie, *Cooper*, Vol. 1, pp. xv–xvii.
3. C. H. Firth (ed.), *The Life of William Cavendish, Duke of Newcastle* (London: J. C. Nimmo, 1886), p. 275.

1 Ceremonies and Celebrations

1. Samuel Margerison (ed.), *Yorkshire Diaries and Autobiographies in the Seventeenth and Eighteenth Centuries* (Durham: Andrews and Co., 1886), p. 111.

2. D. J. H. Clifford (ed.), *The Diaries of Lady Anne Clifford* (Stroud: Alan Sutton Publishing Ltd, 1992), p. 67; Margerison, *Yorkshire Diaries*, p. 62; Todd Gray (ed.), *Devon Household Accounts, 1627–59: Part Two* (Exeter: Devon and Cornwall Record Society, 1996), p. 262.
3. Gladys Scott Thomson, *The Russells in Bloomsbury, 1669–1771* (London: Jonathan Cape Ltd, 1940), pp. 62–3.
4. HMC, *The Manuscripts of His Grace the Duke of Rutland*, Vol. 4 (London: Mackie and Co. Ltd, 1905), pp. 446, 459.
5. Henry B. Wheatley (ed.), *The Diary of Samuel Pepys*, Vol. 1 (New York: Random House, pref. 1893), p. 350.
6. Gray, *Devon Household Accounts* 2, p. xli.
7. HMC, *The Manuscripts of His Grace the Duke of Portland*, Vol. 3 (London: Eyre and Spottiswoode, 1894), p. 505.
8. James J. Cartwright (ed.), *The Wentworth Papers, 1705–1739* (London: Wyman and Sons, 1883), p. 43.
9. Ibid., p. 149.
10. Augustus Jessopp (ed.), *The Autobiography of the Hon. Roger North* (London: David Nutt, 1887), p. 236.
11. Richard Griffin Braybrooke (ed.), *The Autobiography of Sir John Bramston* (London: John Bowyer Nichols and Sons, 1845), pp. 18–9.
12. James J. Cartwright (ed.), *The Memoirs of Sir John Reresby* (London: Longmans, Green, and Co., 1875), p. 366.
13. HMC, *Report on the Manuscripts of the Late Allan George Finch*, Vol. 2 (London: His Majesty's Stationery Office, 1922), pp. 3–4.
14. Narcissus Luttrell (ed.), *A Brief Historical Relation of State Affairs from September 1678 to April 1714*, Vol. 3 (Oxford: Oxford University Press, 1857), p. 476; Gladys Scott Thomson, *Life in a Noble Household, 1641–1700* (London: Jonathan Cape, 1950), p. 393.
15. Rev. W. D. Macray (ed.), *Beaumont Papers: Letters Relating to the Family of Beaumont* (London: Nichols and Sons, 1884), p. 34.

16. Norman Egbert McClure (ed.), *The Letters of John Chamberlain*, Vol. 1 (Philadelphia: The American Philosophical Society, 1939), pp. 496–7.
17. HMC, *Duke of Portland*, Vol. 3, p. 371.
18. C. B. Phillips (ed.), *Lowther Family Estate Books, 1617–1675* (Gateshead: Northumberland Press Limited, 1979), p. 169.
19. Margaret M. Verney, *Memoirs of the Verney Family*, Vol. 2 (London: Longmans, Green, and Co., 1904), pp. 366, 369.
20. Anon. (ed.), *The Memoirs of Sir Hugh Cholmley* (Publisher unknown, 1870), p. 24; Phillips, *Lowther Family*, p. 179.
21. Walter Bourchier Devereux, *Lives and Letters of the Devereux, Earls of Essex*, Vol. 2 (London: John Murray, 1853), pp. 468–70, 505–9.
22. Henry Granville Fitzalan-Howard (ed.), *The Lives of Philip Howard, Earl of Arundel, and of Anne Dacres, His Wife* (London: Hurst and Blackett, 1857), pp. 262–3. The title of this work spells Anne's maiden name as 'Dacres', not 'Dacre'.
23. Anon., *Hugh Cholmley*, p. 54.
24. Jessopp, *Roger North*, p. 229.
25. Verney, *Memoirs*, Vol. 2, p. 213; Rev. Robert Isham (ed.), *The Journal of Thomas Isham of Lamport* (Norwich: Miller and Leavins, 1875), p. 22; J. J. Bagley (ed.), *The Great Diurnal of Nicholas Blundell of Little Crosby, Lancashire*, Vol. 1 (Liverpool: The Record Society of Lancashire and Cheshire, 1968), p. 239.
26. Philip Lee Ralph, *Sir Humphrey Mildmay: Royalist Gentleman: Glimpses of the English Scene, 1633–1652* (New Brunswick: Rutgers University Press, 1947), p. 108; Clifford, *Anne Clifford*, p. 65.
27. Bagley, *Nicholas Blundell*, Vol. 1, p. 197; C. Roy Hudleston (ed.), *Naworth Estate and Household Accounts, 1648–1660* (Durham: Andrews and Co., 1958), p. 16.
28. Margerison, *Yorkshire Diaries*, p. 117; HMC, *Duke of Rutland*, Vol. 4, p. 464 (for example); Isham, *Thomas Isham*, p. 22; Bagley, *Nicholas Blundell*, Vol. 1, p. 240.

29. Rev. F. R. Raines (ed.), *The Journal of Nicholas Assheton of Downham* (Manchester: The Chetham Society, 1848), pp. 69, 120; Ralph, *Humphrey Mildmay*, p. 108.
30. Cartwright, *Wentworth Papers*, pp. 66–7.
31. Cartwright, *Reresby*, pp. 101, 228, 310.
32. Ralph, *Humphrey Mildmay*, p. 107.
33. Thomson, *Noble Household*, pp. 350–1; HMC, *Duke of Rutland*, Vol. 4, pp. 458–9; Mary F. S. Hervey, *The Life, Correspondence, and Collections of Thomas Howard, Earl of Arundel* (Cambridge: Cambridge University Press, 1921), p. 29.
34. HMC, *Duke of Rutland*, Vol. 4, p. 473; Blake Tyson (ed.), *The Estate and Household Accounts of Sir Daniel Fleming of Rydal Hall, Westmorland, from 1688–1701* (Kendal: Cumberland and Westmorland Antiquarian and Archaeological Society, 2001), pp. 163, 305.
35. Francis Bamford (ed.), *A Royalist's Notebook: The Commonplace Book of Sir John Oglander* (London: Constable and Co. Ltd, 1936), p. 5.
36. Clifford, *Anne Clifford*, pp. 54, 70; Margaret M. Verney, *Verney Letters of the Eighteenth Century*, Vol. 1 (London: Ernest Benn Ltd, 1930), p. 36.
37. Cartwright, *Reresby*, p. 454.
38. Braybrooke, *Bramston*, p. 410.
39. HMC, *The Manuscripts of His Grace the Duke of Rutland*, Vol. 2 (London: Eyre and Spottiswoode, 1889), p. 25; Margerison, *Yorkshire Diaries*, p. 81.
40. Clifford, *Anne Clifford*, p. 78; Anon. (ed.), *Letters of Rachel, Lady Russell*, Vol. 1 (London: Longman, Brown, Green, and Longmans, 1853), p. 88.

2 Children and Childhood

1. Gladys Scott Thomson, *The Russells in Bloomsbury, 1669–1771* (London: Jonathan Cape Ltd, 1940), p. 62; James Orchard Halliwell (ed.), *The Autobiography and*

Correspondence of Sir Simonds D'Ewes, Vol. 1 (London: Richard Bentley, 1845), p. 431.

2. J. J. Bagley (ed.), *The Great Diurnal of Nicholas Blundell of Little Crosby, Lancashire*, Vol. 1 (Liverpool: The Record Society of Lancashire and Cheshire, 1968), p. 67; Margaret Blundell (ed.), *Cavalier: Letters of William Blundell to His Friends, 1620–1698* (London: Longmans, Green, and Co., 1933), pp. 44, 79.
3. G. Davies (ed.), *Autobiography of Thomas Raymond and Memoirs of the Family of Guise* (London: RHS, 1917), p. 112.
4. Margaret M. Verney, *Memoirs of the Verney Family*, Vol. 1 (London: Longmans, Green, and Co., 1904), p. 380.
5. D. J. H. Clifford (ed.), *The Diaries of Lady Anne Clifford* (Stroud: Alan Sutton Publishing Ltd, 1992), p. 123.
6. Anon. (ed.), *The Memoirs of Sir Hugh Cholmley* (Publisher unknown, 1870), pp. 21–2.
7. Bagley, *Nicholas Blundell*, Vol. 1, p. 88; Anon., *Hugh Cholmley*, p. 22; Thomson, *Bloomsbury*, p. 63.
8. C. H. Firth (ed.), *The Life of William Cavendish, Duke of Newcastle* (London: J. C. Nimmo, 1886), pp. 278–9.
9. Ibid.
10. HMC, *The Manuscripts of His Grace the Duke of Portland*, Vol. 3 (London: Eyre and Spottiswoode, 1894), p. 319.
11. Richard Griffin Braybrooke (ed.), *The Private Correspondence of Jane, Lady Cornwallis, 1613–1644* (London: S. & J. Bentley, Wilson, and Fley, 1842), p. 253.
12. Firth, *Cavendish*, p. 278.
13. Augustus Jessopp (ed.), *The Autobiography of the Hon. Roger North* (London: David Nutt, 1887), p. 215.
14. Ibid.
15. Rev. Daniel Parsons (ed.), *The Diary of Sir Henry Slingsby* (London: Longman, Rees, Orme, Brown, Green, and Longman, 1836), p. 72; Lady Newton, *The House of Lyme: From Its Foundation to the End of the Eighteenth Century*

(London: William Heinemann, 1917), pp. 268–9; Clifford, *Anne Clifford*, p. 55.

16. HMC, *Duke of Portland*, Vol. 3, p. 213; Anon. (ed.), *Letters of Rachel, Lady Russell*, Vol. 1 (London: Longman, Brown, Green, and Longmans, 1853), p. 95; Thomson, *Bloomsbury*, pp. 63–4; Rev. Robert Isham (ed.), *The Journal of Thomas Isham of Lamport* (Norwich: Miller and Leavins, 1875), p. 8.
17. Anon. (ed.), *Letter-Books of John Hervey, 1st Earl of Bristol*, Vol. 1 (Wells: Ernest Jackson, 1894), p. 203.
18. Parsons, *Slingsby*, p. 53; Halliwell, *D'Ewes*, Vol. 1, pp. 61–2.
19. Anon. (ed.), *Memoirs of the Life of Colonel Hutchinson* (London: J. M. Dent and Co., 1913) p. 14.
20. Elizabeth Hagglund, "Cassandra Willoughby's visits to country houses". *The Georgian Group Journal* 11 (2001): p. 185.
21. Verney, *Memoirs*, Vol. 1, pp. 500–1.
22. Anon. (ed.), *The Memoirs of Ann, Lady Fanshawe* (London: John Lane, The Bodley Head, 1907), p. 22.
23. Firth, *Cavendish*, p. 280.
24. James J. Cartwright (ed.), *The Memoirs of Sir John Reresby* (London: Longmans, Green, and Co., 1875), p. 22; Anon., *Hutchinson*, p. 14.
25. Gladys Scott Thomson, *Life in a Noble Household, 1641–1700* (London: Jonathan Cape, 1950), pp. 72–3.
26. HMC, *Report on the Manuscripts of Allan George Finch*, Vol. 1 (London: His Majesty's Stationery Office, 1913), p. 244.
27. Verney, *Memoirs*, Vol. 1, pp. 507, 511.
28. J. V. Beckett, *The Aristocracy in England, 1660–1914* (Oxford: Basil Blackwell Ltd, 1986), p. 99.
29. George Sondes, *Sir George Sondes: His Plaine Narrative* (London: 1655), pp. 15–6.
30. Cartwright, *Reresby*, p. 22.
31. Davies, *Guise*, p. 115; Maurice F. Bond (ed.), *The Diaries and Papers of Sir Edward Dering* (London: Her Majesty's Stationery Office, 1976), p. 108; John Richard Magrath (ed.),

The Flemings in Oxford, Vol. 2 (Oxford: Clarendon Press, 1913), p. 254.

32. Halliwell, *D'Ewes*, Vol. 1, pp. 118–9.
33. John Richard Magrath (ed.), *The Flemings in Oxford*, Vol. 1 (Oxford: Clarendon Press, 1904), p. 17; Robert Parsons, *A Sermon Preached at the Funeral of the Right Honorable John, Earl of Rochester* (London: H. Hills, 1707), p. 5.
34. Magrath, *Flemings*, Vol. 2, p. 262; Ibid., Vol. 1, pp. 304, 318, 320.
35. Halliwell, *D'Ewes*, Vol. 1, p. 141; Davies, *Guise*, pp. 116–7.
36. Will H. Dircks (ed.), *The Autobiography of Edward, Lord Herbert of Cherbury* (London: Walter Scott, 1888), p. 56.
37. Clifford, *Anne Clifford*, p. 55; Anon., *Hervey*, Vol. 1, pp. 119, 127, 278, 370.
38. James Orchard Halliwell (ed.), *The Autobiography and Correspondence of Sir Simonds D'Ewes*, Vol. 2 (London: Richard Bentley, 1845), p. 146.
39. Anon., *Hugh Cholmley*, p. 22; Parsons, *Slingsby*, p. 30; HMC, *The Manuscripts of the Earl Cowper*, Vol. 1 (London: Eyre and Spottiswoode, 1888), p. 93.
40. HMC, *Duke of Portland*, Vol. 3, p. 449.
41. HMC, *Duke of Rutland*, Vol. 2, p. 48.
42. Verney, *Memoirs*, Vol. 1, pp. 505–6.
43. C. B. Phillips (ed.), *Lowther Family Estate Books, 1617–1675* (Gateshead: Northumberland Press Limited, 1979), p. 62.
44. Sydenham Hervey (ed.), *The Diary of John Hervey* (Wells: Ernest Jackson, 1894), p. 100.
45. Parsons, *Slingsby*, pp. 259–62.
46. Sondes, *Narrative*, p. 17; HMC, *Duke of Portland*, Vol. 3, p. 317.

3 Stately Piles and Possessions

1. Edmund Lodge (ed.), *Illustrations of British History*, Vol. 3 (London: John Chidley, 1838), pp. 214–5.

2. The will of Dame Priscilla Rolle, 1708, PCCRP: Will Registers, PROB 11/502/277.
3. Charles Kightly, *Berry Pomeroy Castle* (London: English Heritage, 2011).
4. John Prince, *The Worthies of Devon* (London: J. McCreery, 1810, originally printed 1701), p. 649.
5. J. T. Cliffe, *The World of the Country House in Seventeenth-Century England* (London: Yale University Press, 1999), p. 15.
6. Harold Spencer Scott (ed.), *The Journal of Sir Roger Wilbraham* (Publisher unknown, 1902), p. 66.
7. Austin Dobson (ed.), *The Diary of John Evelyn* (London: Macmillan and Co. Limited, 1908), p. 184.
8. Henry B. Wheatley (ed.), *The Diary of Samuel Pepys*, Vol. 2 (New York: Random House, pref. 1893), p. 674.
9. Catherine Parsons, "Horseheath Hall and Its Owners", *Proceedings of the Cambridge Antiquarian Society* 41 (1948).
10. Dobson, *Evelyn*, p. 271.
11. Matthew Walker, *Architects and Intellectual Culture in Post-Restoration England* (Oxford: Oxford University Press, 2017), p. 89.
12. Joan Johnson, *The Gloucestershire Gentry* (Gloucester: Alan Sutton Publishing, 1989), p. 114.
13. Richard Wilson and Alan Mackley, *Creating Paradise: The Building of the English Country House, 1660–1880* (London: Hambledon and London, 2000), p. 170.
14. White Kennett, *A Sermon Preached at the Funeral of the Right Noble William, Duke of Devonshire* (London: W. B., 1708), pp. 139–140.
15. Ibid., pp. 141–2.
16. Ibid., p. 143.
17. Dobson, *Evelyn*, p. 198.
18. Manolo Guerci, "The Construction of Northumberland House and the Patronage of Its Original Builder, Lord Henry Howard, 1603–14", *The Antiquaries Journal* 90 (2010).

19. Evelyn Philip Shirley (ed.), "An Inventory of the Effects of Henry Howard", *Archaeologia* 42, no. 2 (1870).
20. Gladys Scott Thomson, *The Russells in Bloomsbury, 1669–1771* (London: Jonathan Cape Ltd, 1940), pp. 34–5; Dobson, *Evelyn*, p. 235.
21. Edward Hatton, *A New View of London*, Vol. 2 (London: 1708), p. 623; Dobson, *Evelyn*, p. 288.
22. Hatton, *London*, Vol. 2, pp. 623–4.
23. Ibid., p. 624.
24. The will of Dame Johanna St John, 1705, PCCRP: Will Registers, PROB 11/480/286.
25. HMC, *The Manuscripts of the Earl Cowper*, Vol. 2 (London: Eyre and Spottiswoode, 1888), pp. 371, 390.
26. Ibid., p. 374.
27. Ibid., p. 375.
28. Ibid., p. 377.
29. Ibid., p. 378.
30. Anon. (ed.), *Memoir of Lady Warwick* (London: The Religious Tract Society, 1847), p. 125.
31. Dobson, *Evelyn*, p. 288; Prince, *Worthies*, p. 392.
32. Hatton, *London*, Vol. 2, p. 624; Rev. Daniel Parsons (ed.), *The Diary of Sir Henry Slingsby* (London: Longman, Rees, Orme, Brown, Green, and Longman, 1836), pp. 6–7; Parsons, "Horseheath Hall", p. 15.
33. Todd Gray (ed.), *Devon Household Accounts, 1627–59: Part Two* (Exeter: Devon and Cornwall Record Society, 1996), p. 117; Mary F. S. Hervey, *The Life, Correspondence, and Collections of Thomas Howard, Earl of Arundel* (Cambridge: Cambridge University Press, 1921), p. 93; Emily Griffiths (ed.), *Through England on a Side Saddle: The Diary of Celia Fiennes* (London: The Leadenhall Press, 1888), p. 4.
34. Parsons, *Slingsby*, p. 4; Prince, *Worthies*, p. 649; Johnson, *Gentry*, p. 114; James J. Cartwright (ed.), *The Wentworth Papers, 1705–1739* (London: Wyman and Sons, 1883), p. 64; Griffiths, *Fiennes*, p. 4.

35. Elizabeth Hagglund, "Cassandra Willoughby's visits to country houses", *The Georgian Group Journal* 11 (2001): p. 191; Hatton, *London*, Vol. 2, p. 624; Prince, *Worthies*, p. 392.
36. Anon. (ed.), *Letters of Rachel, Lady Russell*, Vol. 2 (London: Longman and Co., 1853), pp. 171–2.
37. Parsons, *Slingsby*, pp. 1–2; Anon., *Lady Warwick*, p. 247; J. J. Bagley (ed.), *The Great Diurnal of Nicholas Blundell of Little Crosby, Lancashire*, Vol. 1 (Liverpool: The Record Society of Lancashire and Cheshire, 1968), p. 22; Gray, *Devon Household Accounts* 2, p. 138.
38. James J. Cartwright (ed.), *The Memoirs of Sir John Reresby* (London: Longmans, Green, and Co., 1875), p. 66; Anon. (ed.), *Letters of Rachel, Lady Russell*, Vol. 1 (London: Longman, Brown, Green, and Longmans, 1853), p. 59; Bagley, *Nicholas Blundell*, Vol. 1, pp. 157, 159; Francis Bamford (ed.), *A Royalist's Notebook: The Commonplace Book of Sir John Oglander* (London: Constable and Co. Ltd, 1936), p. 226.
39. Margaret M. Verney, *Verney Letters of the Eighteenth Century*, Vol. 1 (London: Ernest Benn Ltd, 1930), p. 60; Bagley, *Nicholas Blundell*, Vol. 1, pp. 121, 130, 142, 153, 154.
40. William Waller, *Divine Meditations* (London: B. Griffin, 1683), p. 59; Norman Egbert McClure (ed.), *The Letters of John Chamberlain*, Vol. 2 (Philadelphia: The American Philosophical Society, 1939), pp. 90–1; Lady Newton, *The House of Lyme: From Its Foundation to the End of the Eighteenth Century* (London: William Heinemann, 1917), p. 65.
41. George Ornsby (ed.), *The Household Books of the Lord William Howard* (Durham: Andrews and Co., 1878), p. 62; Bamford, *Oglander*, p. 95.
42. Cliffe, *Country House*, p. 60–1.
43. Griffiths, *Fiennes*, p. 4.
44. Ibid., pp. 4–5.

45. Robert Plot, *The Natural History of Staffordshire* (Oxford: The Theatre, 1686), p. 339.
46. C. B. Phillips (ed.), *Lowther Family Estate Books, 1617–1675* (Gateshead: Northumberland Press Limited, 1979), p. 174; HMC, *The Manuscripts of the Earl Cowper*, Vol. 3 (London: Eyre and Spottiswoode, 1889), pp. 72–3.
47. Rev. T. Ellison Gibson (ed.), *A Cavalier's Notebook* (London: Longmans, Green, and Co., 1880), p. 157; Hagglund, "Cassandra Willoughby", p. 186; Griffiths, *Fiennes*, p. 140; Various, *Blenheim Palace World Heritage Site: Revised Management Plan 2017* (Norfolk: Historic Landscape Management Ltd, 2017), p. 17.
48. Hervey, *Thomas Howard*, pp. 255–6.
49. Ibid., pp. 97, 106; Wheatley, *Pepys*, Vol. 2, p. 232.
50. Hatton, *London*, Vol. 2, p. 624; Shirley, "Henry Howard", pp. 359, 360; Lyn Boothman and Richard Hyde Parker (eds), *Savage Fortune: An Aristocratic Family in the Early Seventeenth Century* (Woodbridge: The Boydell Press, 2006), p. 78; Malcolm Wanklyn (ed.), *Inventories of Worcestershire Landed Gentry, 1537–1786* (Worcester: The Worcestershire Historical Society, 1998), p. 190; Sydenham Hervey (ed.), *The Diary of John Hervey* (Wells: Ernest Jackson, 1894), p. 137; Phillips, *Lowther Family*, p. 252.
51. Griffiths, *Fiennes*, p. 141; Wanklyn, *Inventories*, p. 251; The will of Dame Penelope Osborne, 1695, PCCRP: Will Registers, PROB 11/427/174.
52. Margaret M. Verney, *Memoirs of the Verney Family*, Vol. 2 (London: Longmans, Green, and Co., 1904), p. 134; Shirley, "Henry Howard", p. 372; Mary F. S. Hervey, "A Lumley Inventory of 1609", in *The Sixth Volume of the Walpole Society*, ed. anon. (Oxford: Oxford University Press, 1918), p. 40.
53. Anon. (ed.), *The Memorandum Book of Sir Richard Cholmley* (Northallerton: North Yorkshire County Record Office, 1988), p. 36; Shirley, "Henry Howard", pp. 357, 358;

Hervey, "Inventory", p. 40. 'Cholmley' is spelled this way to be consistent with other references.

54. Verney, *Memoirs*, Vol. 2, p. 134; Shirley, "Henry Howard", pp. 354, 359, 373; Boothman and Parker, *Savage Fortune*, p. 78; Wanklyn, *Inventories*, p. 190.
55. Waller, *Meditations*, pp. 49–50; Anon., *Richard Cholmley*, p. 36; Wanklyn, *Inventories*, pp. 294, 328; Shirley, "Henry Howard", pp. 349, 356–7, 360–1.
56. Hervey, *Thomas Howard*, pp. 474–500.
57. Blake Tyson (ed.), *The Estate and Household Accounts of Sir Daniel Fleming of Rydal Hall, Westmorland, from 1688–1701* (Kendal: Cumberland and Westmorland Antiquarian and Archaeological Society, 2001), p. 231; Wanklyn, *Inventories*, p. 251; "Advertisements", editorial, *London Gazette* Nov 9, 1685, p. 2.
58. The will of Sir John Bolle, 1607, PCCRP: Will Registers, PROB 11/109/372; Anon., *Richard Cholmley*, p. 65; Boothman and Parker, *Savage Fortune*, p. 81.
59. Anon., *Richard Cholmley*, pp. 34, 35; The will of Dame Alicia Greaves, 1684, PCCRP: Will Registers, PROB 11/378/65; Will of Osborne.
60. Francis W. Steer (ed.), "The Inventory of Arthur Coke of Bramfield, 1629", *Proceedings of the Suffolk Institute of Archaeology and History* 25 (1951); Shirley, "Henry Howard", pp. 351–3; Wanklyn, *Inventories*, pp. 249–50; Will of Osborne.

4 Servants

1. George Savile, *Advice to a Daughter* (London: 1688), p. 82; J. T. Cliffe, *The World of the Country House in Seventeenth-Century England* (London: Yale University Press, 1999), p. 199; George Ornsby (ed.), *The Household Books of the Lord William Howard* (Durham: Andrews and Co., 1878), pp. 500–3; Gladys Scott Thomson, *Life in a Noble Household, 1641–1700* (London: Jonathan Cape, 1950),

p. 124; Rev. Daniel Parsons (ed.), *The Diary of Sir Henry Slingsby* (London: Longman, Rees, Orme, Brown, Green, and Longman, 1836), p. 26.

2. Cliffe, *Country House*, p. 114. While Cliffe appears to be talking about the gentry specifically here, it is probable that this was the standard wage received by all aristocratic stewards.
3. Henry Granville Fitzalan-Howard (ed.), *The Lives of Philip Howard, Earl of Arundel, and of Anne Dacres, His Wife* (London: Hurst and Blackett, 1857), p. 240; Anon. (ed.), *The Memorandum Book of Sir Richard Cholmley* (Northallerton: North Yorkshire County Record Office, 1988), p. 106; Lady Newton, *The House of Lyme: From Its Foundation to the End of the Eighteenth Century* (London: William Heinemann, 1917), p. 61.
4. Margaret M. Verney, *Verney Letters of the Eighteenth Century*, Vol. 1 (London: Ernest Benn Ltd, 1930), p. 232; Newton, *Lyme*, p. 343.
5. D. J. H. Clifford (ed.), *The Diaries of Lady Anne Clifford* (Stroud: Alan Sutton Publishing Ltd, 1992), p. 36.
6. Joseph Jacobs (ed.), *The Familiar Letters of James Howell* (London: David Nutt, 1890), p. 264. The authenticity of this source has been disputed, but it is still a useful portrait of footmen in the seventeenth century.
7. Mark Girouard, *Life in the English Country House* (London: Book Club Associates, 1979), pp. 140–1.
8. Thomson, *Noble Household*, p. 118.
9. Richard Griffin Braybrooke (ed.), *The Autobiography of Sir John Bramston* (London: John Bowyer Nichols and Sons, 1845), pp. 380, 382; Thomson, *Noble Household*, pp. 119–20.
10. J. J. Bagley (ed.), *The Great Diurnal of Nicholas Blundell of Little Crosby, Lancashire*, Vol. 1 (Liverpool: The Record Society of Lancashire and Cheshire, 1968), p. 69; Margaret Blundell (ed.), *Cavalier: Letters of William Blundell to His Friends, 1620–1698* (London: Longmans, Green, and Co., 1933), pp. 62–3; Clifford, *Anne Clifford*, p. 51.

11. Margaret M. Verney, *Memoirs of the Verney Family*, Vol. 1 (London: Longmans, Green, and Co., 1904), p. 525.
12. Jacobs, *Familiar Letters*, pp. 286–7.
13. Parsons, *Slingsby*, p. 24; Margaret M. Verney, *Memoirs of the Verney Family*, Vol. 2 (London: Longmans, Green, and Co., 1904), p. 303.
14. James Orchard Halliwell (ed.), *Ancient Inventories of Furniture, Pictures, Tapestry, Plate, Etc.* (London: J. E. Adlard, 1854), p. 18.
15. Thomson, *Noble Household*, p. 121; Ornsby, *Household Books*, pp. 27–8, 62, 200.
16. Francis Bamford (ed.), *A Royalist's Notebook: The Commonplace Book of Sir John Oglander* (London: Constable and Co. Ltd, 1936), p. 32; Anon. (ed.), *Letter-Books of John Hervey, 1st Earl of Bristol*, Vol. 1 (Wells: Ernest Jackson, 1894), p. 128.
17. Parsons, *Slingsby*, p. 64; Verney, *Memoirs*, Vol. 2, p. 41; Emily Griffiths (ed.), *Through England on a Side Saddle: The Diary of Celia Fiennes* (London: The Leadenhall Press, 1888), p. 98.
18. Bagley, *Nicholas Blundell*, Vol. 1, pp. 15, 18, 25, 196.
19. HMC, *The Manuscripts of His Grace the Duke of Rutland*, Vol. 4 (London: Mackie and Co. Ltd, 1905), p. 485; Todd Gray (ed.), *Devon Household Accounts, 1627–59: Part One* (Exeter: Devon and Cornwall Record Society, 1995), p. xxi; Todd Gray (ed.), *Devon Household Accounts, 1627–59: Part Two* (Exeter: Devon and Cornwall Record Society, 1996), p. 229.
20. "Advertisements", editorial, *London Gazette* Nov 21, 1687, p. 4.
21. Clifford, *Anne Clifford*, p. 275; Anon. (ed.), *The Memoirs of Sir Hugh Cholmley* (publisher unknown, 1870), p. 30; HMC, *The Manuscripts of His Grace the Duke of Portland*, Vol. 3 (London: Eyre and Spottiswoode, 1894), p. 408.
22. "Advertisements", editorial, *London Gazette* Apr 23, 1677, p. 2.

23. Clifford, *Anne Clifford*, p. 276; James J. Cartwright (ed.), *The Memoirs of Sir John Reresby* (London: Longmans, Green, and Co., 1875), pp. 104–5.
24. R. C. Richardson, *Household Servants in Early Modern England* (Manchester: Manchester University Press, 2010), p. 107.
25. HMC, *The Manuscripts of the Earl Cowper*, Vol. 3 (London: Eyre and Spottiswoode, 1889), p. 361.
26. "Advertisements", editorial, *London Gazette* Jan 20, 1670, p. 2; Ibid., Nov 21, 1687, p. 4.
27. Lady Newdigate-Newdegate, *Cavalier and Puritan in the Days of the Stuarts* (London: Smith, Elder, and Co., 1901), p. 309.
28. C. Roy Hudleston (ed.), *Naworth Estate and Household Accounts, 1648–1660* (Durham: Andrews and Co., 1958), pp. 153, 154; Thomson, *Noble Household*, p. 119.
29. Savile, *Advice*, pp. 83–4; Robert Parsons, *A Sermon Preached at the Funeral of the Right Honorable John, Earl of Rochester* (London: H. Hills, 1707), p. 16; Adam Littleton, *A Sermon at the Funeral of the Lady Jane* (London: John Macock, 1669), p. 55.
30. Newdigate, *Cavalier and Puritan*, p. 199; "Advertisements", editorial, *London Gazette* Apr 22, 1689, p. 2; Verney, *Memoirs*, Vol. 2, p. 276.
31. Philip Lee Ralph, *Sir Humphrey Mildmay: Royalist Gentleman: Glimpses of the English Scene, 1633–1652* (New Brunswick: Rutgers University Press, 1947), p. 115.
32. Newdigate, *Cavalier and Puritan*, p. 199; Verney, *Letters*, Vol. 1, p. 284.
33. Rev. Robert Isham (ed.), *The Journal of Thomas Isham of Lamport* (Norwich: Miller and Leavins, 1875), pp. 98–9.
34. Newton, *Lyme*, pp. 72–3.
35. Newdigate, *Cavalier and Puritan*, p. 198; Ralph, *Humphrey Mildmay*, p. 115; Verney, *Letters*, Vol. 1, p. 41.
36. Verney, *Memoirs*, Vol. 2, p. 276; Anon., *Hervey*, Vol. 1, pp. 241, 276.

37. Anon. (ed.), *Memoir of Lady Warwick* (London: The Religious Tract Society, 1847) p. 153; Ralph, *Humphrey Mildmay*, p. 116.
38. The will of Sir William Cowper, 1697, PCCRP: Will Registers, PROB 11/441/174.
39. Will H. Dircks (ed.), *The Autobiography of Edward, Lord Herbert of Cherbury* (London: Walter Scott, 1888), p. 96.
40. Bagley, *Nicholas Blundell*, Vol. 1, p. 207; Blake Tyson (ed.), *The Estate and Household Accounts of Sir Daniel Fleming of Rydal Hall, Westmorland, from 1688–1701* (Kendal: Cumberland and Westmorland Antiquarian and Archaeological Society, 2001), p. 75; Clifford, *Anne Clifford*, pp. 188, 205.
41. Fitzalan-Howard, *Lives*, p. 238.
42. Bagley, *Nicholas Blundell*, Vol. 1, pp. 119, 270.
43. Henry B. Wheatley (ed.), *The Diary of Samuel Pepys*, Vol. 1 (New York: Random House, pref. 1893), p. 697; Norman Egbert McClure (ed.), *The Letters of John Chamberlain*, Vol. 2 (Philadelphia: The American Philosophical Society, 1939), p. 155.

5 Attire and Appearance

1. Maurice Lee (ed.), *Dudley Carleton to John Chamberlain, 1603–1624: Jacobean Letters* (New Brunswick: Rutgers University Press, 1972), p. 237.
2. HMC, *The Manuscripts of His Grace the Duke of Portland*, Vol. 3 (London: Eyre and Spottiswoode, 1894), p. 293; George Savile, *Advice to a Daughter* (London: 1688), pp. 148–9.
3. Susan Vincent, *Dressing the Elite: Clothes in Early Modern England* (Oxford: Berg, 2003), pp. 13–21.
4. The will of Dame Elizabeth Beamount, 1608, PCCRP: Will Registers, PROB 11/111/485. A modernised spelling of the surname has been used in the text.
5. Rev. Kennet Gibson (ed.), *A Comment Upon Part of the Fifth Journey of Antoninus Through Britain* (London: John

Nichols, 1800), p. 251; Evelyn Philip Shirley (ed.), "An Inventory of the Effects of Henry Howard", *Archaeologia* 42, no. 2 (1870): p. 367; Anon. (ed.), *The Memorandum Book of Sir Richard Cholmley* (Northallerton: North Yorkshire County Record Office, 1988), p. 202; HMC, *The Manuscripts of His Grace the Duke of Rutland*, Vol. 2 (London: Eyre and Spottiswoode, 1889), p. 333.

6. Vincent, *Dressing the Elite*, pp. 21–3; The will of Sir Edmund Warneford, 1700, PCCRP: Will Registers, PROB 11/456/320; Gladys Scott Thomson, *The Russells in Bloomsbury, 1669–1771* (London: Jonathan Cape Ltd, 1940), p. 115.
7. Francis W. Steer (ed.), "The Inventory of Arthur Coke of Bramfield, 1629", *Proceedings of the Suffolk Institute of Archaeology and History* 25 (1951): p. 277.
8. Sarah A. Bendall, *Shaping Femininity: Foundation Garments, the Body, and Women in Early Modern England* (London: Bloomsbury, 2021), p. 258.
9. Vincent, *Dressing the Elite*, pp. 21–3; The will of Dame Ursula Sames, 1635, PCCRP: Will Registers, PROB 11/168/185; D. J. H. Clifford (ed.), *The Diaries of Lady Anne Clifford* (Stroud: Alan Sutton Publishing Ltd, 1992), p. 57.
10. Richard Griffin Braybrooke (ed.), *The Private Correspondence of Jane, Lady Cornwallis, 1613–1644* (London: S. & J. Bentley, Wilson, and Fley, 1842), p. 248.
11. Margaret Blundell (ed.), *Cavalier: Letters of William Blundell to his Friends, 1620–1698* (London: Longmans, Green, and Co., 1933), p. 110; "Mantua", *The Met*, https://www.metmuseum.org/art/collection/search/81809.
12. HMC, *Duke of Rutland*, Vol. 2, p. 31; Kirstin Olsen, *Daily Life in Eighteenth-Century England* (London: Greenwood Press, 1999), p. 96.
13. C. Willett and Phillis Cunnington, *The History of Underclothes* (Mineola: Dover, 1992), pp. 56–62.
14. Margaret M. Verney, *Memoirs of the Verney Family*, Vol. 1 (London: Longmans, Green, and Co., 1904), p. 479; HMC, *The Manuscripts of His Grace the Duke of Rutland*, Vol. 4

(London: Mackie and Co. Ltd, 1905), p. 472; Ibid., Vol. 2, p. 77.

15. Anon., *Richard Cholmley*, pp. 103, 210; Thomas Taylor Lewis (ed.), *Letters of the Lady Brilliana Harley* (London: The Camden Society, 1854), p. 50.
16. Margaret M. Verney, *Verney Letters of the Eighteenth Century*, Vol. 1 (London: Ernest Benn Ltd, 1930), p. 344. The letter is dated 1716, two years after the death of the last Stuart monarch.
17. HMC, *Duke of Rutland*, Vol. 4, p. 462; Clifford, *Anne Clifford*, p. 56; Anon., *Richard Cholmley*, pp. 92, 203.
18. Rev. Robert Isham (ed.), *The Journal of Thomas Isham of Lamport* (Norwich: Miller and Leavins, 1875), p. 21; J. J. Bagley (ed.), *The Great Diurnal of Nicholas Blundell of Little Crosby, Lancashire*, Vol. 1 (Liverpool: The Record Society of Lancashire and Cheshire, 1968), p. 45.
19. Henry Granville Fitzalan-Howard (ed.), *The Lives of Philip Howard, Earl of Arundel, and of Anne Dacres, His Wife* (London: Hurst and Blackett, 1857), pp. 271–2.
20. Shirley, "Henry Howard", pp. 348, 349; The will of Dame Alicia Greaves, 1684, PCCRP: Will Registers, PROB 11/378/65; The will of Dame Elizabeth Stampe, 1713, PCCRP: Will Registers, PROB 11/531/361; The will of Sir Edward Cleere, 1606, PCCRP: Will Registers, PROB 11/108/169.
21. The will of Dame Anne Seymour, 1695, PCCRP: Will Registers, PROB 11/428/322; The will of Dame Diana Warburton, 1694, PCCRP: Will Registers, PROB 11/419/266; Braybrooke, *Cornwallis*, p. 54.
22. R. Turner Wilcox, *The Mode in Hats and Headdress* (Mineola: Dover, 2008), p. 113; Steer, "Arthur Coke", p. 277.
23. Joan Nunn, *Fashion in Costume, 1200–2000* (Chicago: New Amsterdam Books, 2000), p. 62.
24. Lady Newdigate-Newdegate, *Cavalier and Puritan in the Days of the Stuarts* (London: Smith, Elder, and Co., 1901), p. 293.

25. Blundell, *Letters*, pp. 181–2.
26. Gladys Scott Thomson, *Life in a Noble Household, 1641–1700* (London: Jonathan Cape, 1950), p. 341.
27. Nunn, *Fashion*, p. 69; Georgine de Courtais, *Women's Hats, Headdresses, and Hairstyles* (Mineola: Dover, 1986), p. 70.
28. HMC, *Duke of Rutland*, Vol. 2, p. 21.
29. Braybrooke, *Cornwallis*, p. 89.
30. Todd Gray (ed.), *Devon Household Accounts, 1627–59: Part Two* (Exeter: Devon and Cornwall Record Society, 1996), p. 207; Clifford, *Anne Clifford*, p. 256; Blake Tyson (ed.), *The Estate and Household Accounts of Sir Daniel Fleming of Rydal Hall, Westmorland, from 1688–1701* (Kendal: Cumberland and Westmorland Antiquarian and Archaeological Society, 2001), p. 299; Bagley, *Nicholas Blundell*, Vol. 1, p. 181.
31. Nunn, *Fashion*, p. 62.
32. Austin Dobson (ed.), *The Diary of John Evelyn* (London: Macmillan and Co. Limited, 1908), p. 173; William Durrant Cooper (ed.), *Savile Correspondence* (London: The Camden Society, 1858), pp. 286–7.
33. Henry Morley (ed.), *The Spectator*, Vol. 3 (London: George Routledge and Sons, 1891), p. 708.
34. Ibid., Vol. 1, p. 191.
35. Ibid., Vol. 2, p. 421.
36. Andrew Clark (ed.), *The Life and Times of Anthony Wood*, Vol. 1 (Oxford: Clarendon Press, 1891), p. 509.
37. Susan North, *Sweet and Clean? Bodies and Clothes in Early Modern England* (Oxford: Oxford University Press, 2020), pp. 266–8; Gray, *Devon Household Accounts* 2, p. 140; Todd Gray (ed.), *Devon Household Accounts, 1627–59: Part One* (Exeter: Devon and Cornwall Record Society, 1995), p. 233; Lady Newton, *The House of Lyme: From Its Foundation to the End of the Eighteenth Century* (London: William Heinemann, 1917), p. 65; Morley, *Spectator*, Vol. 3, pp. 706–7.
38. James Orchard Halliwell (ed.), *Ancient Inventories of Furniture, Pictures, Tapestry, Plate, Etc.* (London:

J. E. Adlard, 1854), p. 3; Shirley, "Henry Howard", pp. 362, 363.

39. Thomson, *Noble Household*, p. 344; Steer, "Arthur Coke", p. 280.
40. James J. Cartwright (ed.), *The Wentworth Papers, 1705–1739* (London: Wyman and Sons, 1883), pp. 213, 279; Anon. (ed.), *The Memoirs of Sir Hugh Cholmley* (publisher unknown, 1870), p. 36.
41. Verney, *Memoirs*, Vol. 1, p. 156.
42. Cartwright, *Wentworth Papers*, p. 317.
43. Ibid., p. 320.
44. Ibid., pp. 274, 315.
45. James Orchard Halliwell (ed.), *The Autobiography and Correspondence of Sir Simonds D'Ewes*, Vol. 2 (London: Richard Bentley, 1845), p. 51; C. B. Phillips (ed.), *Lowther Family Estate Books, 1617–1675* (Gateshead: Northumberland Press Limited, 1979), p. 170; Richard Griffin Braybrooke (ed.), *The Autobiography of Sir John Bramston* (London: John Bowyer Nichols and Sons, 1845), p. 380.
46. C. H. Firth (ed.), *The Life of William Cavendish, Duke of Newcastle* (London: J. C. Nimmo, 1886), pp. 290–1.
47. Ibid., p. 292.

6 *Diet and Dining*

1. James J. Cartwright (ed.), *The Memoirs of Sir John Reresby* (London: Longmans, Green, and Co., 1875), p. 380.
2. James J. Cartwright (ed.), *The Wentworth Papers, 1705–1739* (London: Wyman and Sons, 1883), p. 42; Richard Brathwaite, *The English Gentleman; and the English Gentlewoman*, 3rd ed. (London: John Dawson, 1641), p. 183.
3. Todd Gray (ed.), *Devon Household Accounts, 1627–59: Part One* (Exeter: Devon and Cornwall Record Society, 1995), pp. 8, 230; George Ornsby (ed.), *The Household Books of the*

Lord William Howard (Durham: Andrews and Co., 1878), p. 172; Gladys Scott Thomson, *Life in a Noble Household, 1641–1700* (London: Jonathan Cape, 1950), p. 133.

4. Rev. F. R. Raines (ed.), *The Journal of Nicholas Assheton of Downham* (Manchester: The Chetham Society, 1848), pp. 54–5.
5. Elizabeth Cust, *Records of the Cust Family: Series 2* (London: Mitchell Hughes and Clarke, 1909), p. 148; Thomson, *Noble Household*, p. 134; C. Roy Hudleston (ed.), *Naworth Estate and Household Accounts, 1648–1660* (Durham: Andrews and Co., 1958), pp. 26–8.
6. Cust, *Cust Family* 2, p. 148; Ornsby, *Household Books*, pp. 353, 358.
7. Hudleston, *Household Accounts*, p. 40; Thomson, *Noble Household*, p. 152.
8. Emily Griffiths (ed.), *Through England on a Side Saddle: The Diary of Celia Fiennes* (London: The Leadenhall Press, 1888), pp. 97–8.
9. Catherine Parsons, "Horseheath Hall and Its Owners", *Proceedings of the Cambridge Antiquarian Society* 41 (1948): pp. 16–7; Francis Bamford (ed.), *A Royalist's Notebook: The Commonplace Book of Sir John Oglander* (London: Constable and Co. Ltd, 1936), p. 84.
10. HMC, *The Manuscripts of the Earl Cowper*, Vol. 3 (London: Eyre and Spottiswoode, 1889), pp. 73–4.
11. Bamford, *Oglander*, pp. 208–9; Margaret M. Verney, *Verney Letters of the Eighteenth Century*, Vol. 1 (London: Ernest Benn Ltd, 1930), p. 79.
12. Blake Tyson (ed.), *The Estate and Household Accounts of Sir Daniel Fleming of Rydal Hall, Westmorland, from 1688–1701* (Kendal: Cumberland and Westmorland Antiquarian and Archaeological Society, 2001), pp. 65, 215; Gray, *Devon Household Accounts 1*, p. xxxv; Rev. Kennet Gibson (ed.), *A Comment Upon Part of the Fifth Journey of Antoninus Through Britain* (London: John Nichols, 1800), p. 259.

13. Lady Newdigate-Newdegate, *Cavalier and Puritan in the Days of the Stuarts* (London: Smith, Elder, and Co., 1901), p. 18; Gray, *Devon Household Accounts 1*, pp. 33–4.
14. Gray, *Devon Household Accounts 1*, p. 191; Margaret M. Verney, *Memoirs of the Verney Family*, Vol. 1 (London: Longmans, Green, and Co., 1904), p. 525; Rev. W. D. Macray (ed.), *Beaumont Papers: Letters Relating to the Family of Beaumont* (London: Nichols and Sons, 1884), p. 19.
15. Verney, *Letters*, Vol. 1, p. 79; Lady Newton, *The House of Lyme: From iIts Foundation to the End of the Eighteenth Century* (London: William Heinemann, 1917), p. 319; Bamford, *Oglander*, p. 215.
16. Cust, *Cust Family* 2, p. 167; HMC, *The Manuscripts of His Grace the Duke of Portland*, Vol. 3 (London: Eyre and Spottiswoode, 1894), p. 416; Ibid., p. 379; Newton, *Lyme*, p. 266.
17. Anon. (ed.), *The Memorandum Book of Sir Richard Cholmley* (Northallerton: North Yorkshire County Record Office, 1988), p. 217; Griffiths, *Fiennes*, p. 168.
18. Christopher Hibbert, *The English: A Social History, 1066–1945* (London: Grafton Books, 1989), pp. 292–3.
19. Mark Girouard, *Life in the English Country House* (London: Book Club Associates, 1979), p. 88; J. T. Cliffe, *The World of the Country House in Seventeenth-Century England* (London: Yale University Press, 1999), pp. 24–8.
20. William Dougal Christie, *A Life of Anthony Ashley Cooper, First Earl of Shaftesbury, 1621–1683*, Vol. 2 (London: Macmillan and Co., 1871), p. 213.
21. Ornsby, *Household Books*, p. lii; Newton, *Lyme*, pp. 66, 70.
22. Austin Dobson (ed.), *The Diary of John Evelyn* (London: Macmillan and Co. Limited, 1908), pp. 288–9.
23. D. J. H. Clifford (ed.), *The Diaries of Lady Anne Clifford* (Stroud: Alan Sutton Publishing Ltd, 1992), pp. 78, 81, 241, 262; J. J. Bagley (ed.), *The Great Diurnal of Nicholas Blundell of Little Crosby, Lancashire*, Vol. 1 (Liverpool: The Record Society of Lancashire and Cheshire, 1968), p. 175.

24. Anon. (ed.), *Memoir of Lady Warwick* (London: The Religious Tract Society, 1847) p. 101.
25. Ibid., pp. 103–4.
26. Ibid., p. 123.
27. Richard Griffin Braybrooke (ed.), *The Private Correspondence of Jane, Lady Cornwallis, 1613–1644* (London: S. & J. Bentley, Wilson, and Fley, 1842), pp. 16, 54.
28. Cartwright, *Reresby*, p. 48; Rev. Robert Isham (ed.), *The Journal of Thomas Isham of Lamport* (Norwich: Miller and Leavins, 1875), p. 19.
29. Thomson, *Noble Household*, p. 194; HMC, *Duke of Portland*, Vol. 3, p. 381; Anon. (ed.), *Letter-Books of John Hervey, 1st Earl of Bristol*, Vol. 1 (Wells: Ernest Jackson, 1894), p. 245.
30. Cartwright, *Wentworth Papers*, p. 42.
31. Christie, *Cooper*, Vol. 2, p. 49; Bagley, *Nicholas Blundell*, Vol. 1, p. 196; Newton, *Lyme*, p. 357.
32. Bamford, *Oglander*, p. 48.
33. Cartwright, *Wentworth Papers*, p. 291; Cartwright, *Reresby*, p. 409; Philip Lee Ralph, *Sir Humphrey Mildmay: Royalist Gentleman: Glimpses of the English Scene, 1633–1652* (New Brunswick: Rutgers University Press, 1947), p. 67.
34. Raines, *Assheton*, p. 23; Margaret M. Verney, *Memoirs of the Verney Family*, Vol. 2 (London: Longmans, Green, and Co., 1904), p. 51.
35. J. C. Drummond and Anne Wilbraham, *The Englishman's Food: Five Centuries of English Diet* (London: Pimlico, 1994), p. 116.
36. Verney, *Memoirs*, Vol. 1, p. 483; Ibid., Vol. 2, p. 388; Hibbert, *The English*, p. 291; Bagley, *Nicholas Blundell*, Vol. 1, p. 239; Augustus Jessopp (ed.), *The Autobiography of the Hon. Roger North* (London: David Nutt, 1887), p. 225.
37. Drummond and Wilbraham, *Englishman's Food*, p. 117.
38. The will of Dame Johanna St John, 1705, PCCRP: Will Registers, PROB 11/480/286; Henry Morley (ed.), *The*

Spectator, Vol. 2 (London: George Routledge and Sons, 1891), p. 419; Cartwright, *Wentworth Papers*, p. 213.

39. HMC, *The Manuscripts of His Grace the Duke of Rutland*, Vol. 4 (London: Mackie and Co. Ltd, 1905), pp. 493, 546.
40. HMC, *Duke of Portland*, Vol. 3, p. 529; Verney, *Memoirs*, Vol. 1, p. 525; Newton, *Lyme*, pp. 71–2.

7 Animals and Amusements

1. HMC, *The Manuscripts of His Grace the Duke of Portland*, Vol. 3 (London: Eyre and Spottiswoode, 1894), p. 356.
2. Anon. (ed.), *Letters of Rachel, Lady Russell*, Vol. 1 (London: Longman, Brown, Green, and Longmans, 1853), pp. 91–2.
3. James J. Cartwright (ed.), *The Wentworth Papers, 1705–1739* (London: Wyman and Sons, 1883), pp. 55, 64, 284.
4. Cartwright, *Wentworth Papers*, p. 113; Margaret M. Verney, *Memoirs of the Verney Family*, Vol. 2 (London: Longmans, Green, and Co., 1904), p. 212; James Orchard Halliwell (ed.), *The Autobiography and Correspondence of Sir Simonds D'Ewes*, Vol. 2 (London: Richard Bentley, 1845), p. 77.
5. Augustus Jessopp (ed.), *The Autobiography of the Hon. Roger North* (London: David Nutt, 1887), p. 214.
6. J. J. Bagley (ed.), *The Great Diurnal of Nicholas Blundell of Little Crosby, Lancashire*, Vol. 1 (Liverpool: The Record Society of Lancashire and Cheshire, 1968), p. 291.
7. Ibid., p. 227.
8. William Waller, *Divine Meditations* (London: B. Griffin, 1683), pp. 63–4.
9. Will H. Dircks (ed.), *The Autobiography of Edward, Lord Herbert of Cherbury* (London: Walter Scott, 1888), pp. 74–5.
10. Joan Johnson, *The Gloucestershire Gentry* (Gloucester: Alan Sutton Publishing, 1989), p. 114; Cartwright, *Wentworth Papers*, p. 214.
11. Henry B. Wheatley (ed.), *The Diary of Samuel Pepys*, Vol. 1 (New York: Random House, pref. 1893), p. 373;

Lady Newton, *The House of Lyme: From its Foundation to the End of the Eighteenth Century* (London: William Heinemann, 1917), p. 74.

12. Cartwright, *Wentworth Papers*, p. 57.
13. Ibid., pp. 42, 306–7.
14. Guy de la Bédoyère (ed.), *The Diary of John Evelyn* (Woodbridge: The Boydell Press, 2004), p. 265.
15. D. J. H. Clifford (ed.), *The Diaries of Lady Anne Clifford* (Stroud: Alan Sutton Publishing Ltd, 1992), pp. 75, 76; Dircks, *Herbert*, p. 47.
16. Gottfried von Bülow (ed.), "Diary of the Journey of Philip Julius, Duke of Stettin-Pomerania", in *Transactions of the RHS*, New Series, Vol. 6, ed. anon. (London: Longmans, Green, and Co., 1892), p. 45.
17. G. Davies (ed.), *Autobiography of Thomas Raymond and Memoirs of the Family of Guise* (London: RHS, 1917), pp. 117–8.
18. Felicity Heal and Clive Holmes, *The Gentry in England and Wales, 1500–1700* (Basingstoke: Macmillan, 1994), p. 292; Rev. F. R. Raines (ed.), *The Journal of Nicholas Assheton of Downham* (Manchester: The Chetham Society, 1848), pp. 1, 8; HMC, *The Manuscripts of the Earl Cowper*, Vol. 2 (London: Eyre and Spottiswoode, 1888), p. 447.
19. HMC, *Earl Cowper*, Vol. 2, p. 386.
20. Nicholas Cox, *The Gentleman's Recreation: The First Part* (London: Freeman Collins, 1686), p. 42; and Cox, *The Hunter: A Discourse of Horsemanship* (Oxford: L. Lichfield, 1685), pp. 19–20.
21. HMC, *Earl Cowper*, Vol. 2, p. 383; Norman Egbert McClure (ed.), *The Letters of John Chamberlain*, Vol. 2 (Philadelphia: The American Philosophical Society, 1939), p. 259.
22. Cox, *Recreation 1*, p. 104.
23. Ibid., *The Gentleman's Recreation: The Second Part* (London: J. C. and F. C., 1686), pp. 32–3; Anon. (ed.), *The Memorandum Book of Sir Richard Cholmley* (Northallerton: North Yorkshire County Record Office, 1988), p. 176;

Gladys Scott Thomson, *Life in a Noble Household, 1641–1700* (London: Jonathan Cape, 1950), p. 228.

24. Anon., *Richard Cholmley*, p. 200; Charles Cotton, *The Compleat Gamester* (London: A. M., 1674), p. 49; William Dougal Christie, *A Life of Anthony Ashley Cooper, First Earl of Shaftesbury, 162–1683*, Vol. 1 (London: Macmillan and Co., 1871), p. 25.
25. Cotton, *Gamester*, p. 36.
26. Anon. (ed.), *The Life of Margaret Godolphin, by John Evelyn* (London: Alexander Moring Ltd, 1904), p. 84.
27. Rev. Robert Isham (ed.), *The Journal of Thomas Isham of Lamport* (Norwich: Miller and Leavins, 1875), p. 62.
28. M. Misson, *Memoirs and Observations in His Travels Over England* (London: 1719), p. 231.
29. George Sondes, *Sir George Sondes: His Plaine Narrative* (London: 1655), p. 16; Cotton, *Gamester*, p. 207; HMC, *The Manuscripts of His Grace the Duke of Rutland*, Vol. 4 (London: Mackie and Co. Ltd, 1905), p. 455.
30. Sondes, *Narrative*, p. 16; Philip Lee Ralph, *Sir Humphrey Mildmay: Royalist Gentleman: Glimpses of the English Scene, 1633–1652* (New Brunswick: Rutgers University Press, 1947), p. 41; Isham, *Thomas Isham*, p. 80.
31. C. H. Firth (ed.), *The Life of William Cavendish, Duke of Newcastle* (London: J. C. Nimmo, 1886), p. 308; Ralph, *Humphrey Mildmay*, p. 95.
32. Jerzy Limon, "The Masque of Stuart Culture", in *The Mental World of the Jacobean Court*, ed. Linda Levy Peck (Cambridge: Cambridge University Press, 2005), pp. 209–10.
33. Norman Egbert McClure (ed.), *The Letters of John Chamberlain*, Vol. 1 (Philadelphia: The American Philosophical Society, 1939), p. 255; Mary F. S. Hervey, *The Life, Correspondence, and Collections of Thomas Howard, Earl of Arundel* (Cambridge: Cambridge University Press, 1921), pp. 42–3; Thomas Park (ed.), *Nugæ Antiquæ*, Vol. 1 (London: J. Wright, 1804), p. 350.
34. HMC, *Duke of Portland*, Vol. 3, p. 294.

35. Ibid., p. 383.
36. Ralph, *Humphrey Mildmay*, pp. 48–9; Henry B. Wheatley (ed.), *The Diary of Samuel Pepys*, Vol. 2 (New York: Random House, pref. 1893), p. 414; Cartwright, *Wentworth Papers*, p. 280.
37. James J. Cartwright (ed.), *The Memoirs of Sir John Reresby* (London: Longmans, Green, and Co., 1875), p. 132.
38. White Kennett, *A Sermon Preached at the Funeral of the Right Noble William, Duke of Devonshire* (London: W. B., 1708), p. 53; Clifford, *Anne Clifford*, p. 37; Todd Gray (ed.), *Devon Household Accounts, 1627–59: Part One* (Exeter: Devon and Cornwall Record Society, 1995), p. xxxiii.
39. James Orchard Halliwell (ed.), *The Autobiography and Correspondence of Sir Simonds D'Ewes*, Vol. 1 (London: Richard Bentley, 1845), p. 235.
40. Malcolm Wanklyn (ed.), *Inventories of Worcestershire Landed Gentry, 1537–1786* (Worcester: The Worcestershire Historical Society, 1998), pp. 321–4; Clifford, *Anne Clifford*, p. 45.
41. Isham, *Thomas Isham*, pp. 25, 39.
42. Susan Jenkins, *Portrait of a Patron: The Patronage and Collecting of James Brydges* (London: Routledge, 2017).
43. Wanklyn, *Inventories*, pp. 152, 422.

8 Transport and Travel

1. Margaret M. Verney, *Verney Letters of the Eighteenth Century*, Vol. 1 (London: Ernest Benn Ltd, 1930), pp. 279–80.
2. D. J. H. Clifford (ed.), *The Diaries of Lady Anne Clifford* (Stroud: Alan Sutton Publishing Ltd, 1992), p. 255; HMC, *Report on the Manuscripts of Allan George Finch*, Vol. 1 (London: His Majesty's Stationery Office, 1913), p. 401.
3. Rev. F. R. Raines (ed.), *The Journal of Nicholas Assheton of Downham* (Manchester: The Chetham Society, 1848),

pp. 77–8; Anon. (ed.), *The Lady Falkland: Her Life* (London: Catholic Publishing and Bookselling Company Limited, 1861), p. 86.

4. Margaret M. Verney, *Memoirs of the Verney Family*, Vol. 2 (London: Longmans, Green, and Co., 1904), pp. 310–1; Ibid., Vol. 1 (London: Longmans, Green, and Co., 1904), p. 368.
5. Clifford, *Anne Clifford*, p. 30.
6. James J. Cartwright (ed.), *The Wentworth Papers, 1705–1739* (London: Wyman and Sons, 1883), p. 61.
7. Ibid., p. 57.
8. Joan Parkes, *Travel in England in the Seventeenth Century* (Oxford: Oxford University Press, 1925), pp. 64–5.
9. Verney, *Letters*, Vol. 1, p. 218; HMC, *The Manuscripts of His Grace the Duke of Portland*, Vol. 3 (London: Eyre and Spottiswoode, 1894), p. 310.
10. Verney, *Letters*, Vol. 1, p. 36; Anon. (ed.), *A Brief Historical Relation of State Affairs from September 1678 to April 1714 (Narcissus Luttrell)*, Vol. 5 (Oxford: Oxford University Press, 1857), p. 261; Ibid., Vol. 4, (Oxford: Oxford University Press, 1857), pp. 540–1.
11. HMC, *The Manuscripts of the Earl Cowper*, Vol. 3 (London: Eyre and Spottiswoode, 1889), p. 28.
12. Elizabeth Cust, *Records of the Cust Family: Series 2* (London: Mitchell Hughes and Clarke, 1909), p. 169; Gladys Scott Thomson, *The Russells in Bloomsbury, 1669–1771* (London: Jonathan Cape Ltd, 1940), p. 116.
13. HMC, *Duke of Portland*, Vol. 3, p. 505.
14. Ibid., p. 544.
15. Anon., *Luttrell*, Vol. 4, p. 57.
16. Rev. Daniel Parsons (ed.), *The Diary of Sir Henry Slingsby* (London: Longman, Rees, Orme, Brown, Green, and Longman, 1836), p. 59.
17. James Orchard Halliwell (ed.), *The Autobiography and Correspondence of Sir Simonds D'Ewes*, Vol. 1 (London: Richard Bentley, 1845), pp. 246–7.

18. Will H. Dircks (ed.), *The Autobiography of Edward, Lord Herbert of Cherbury* (London: Walter Scott, 1888), pp. 135, 139.
19. Anon. (ed.), *The Memoirs of Ann, Lady Fanshawe* (London: John Lane, The Bodley Head, 1907), pp. 138-40.
20. Dircks, *Herbert*, p. 58.
21. HMC, *Finch*, Vol. 1, p. 403.
22. Ibid., pp. 478, 479.
23. Verney, *Memoirs*, Vol. 1, p. 464.
24. Adrian Tinniswood, *The Verneys: A True Story of Love, War, and Madness in Seventeenth-Century England* (London: Vintage, 2008), pp. 259–65.
25. Clifford, *Anne Clifford*, pp. 202, 205, 212.
26. Verney, *Letters*, Vol. 1, p. 137.
27. Gladys Scott Thomson, *Life in a Noble Household, 1641–1700* (London: Jonathan Cape, 1950), p. 205.
28. Austin Dobson (ed.), *The Diary of John Evelyn* (London: Macmillan and Co. Limited, 1908), p. 265; Anon. (ed.), *Memoir of Lady Warwick* (London: The Religious Tract Society, 1847), p. 150.
29. J. J. Bagley (ed.), *The Great Diurnal of Nicholas Blundell of Little Crosby, Lancashire*, Vol. 1 (Liverpool: The Record Society of Lancashire and Cheshire, 1968), p. 316; Todd Gray (ed.), *Devon Household Accounts, 1627–59: Part Two* (Exeter: Devon and Cornwall Record Society, 1996), p. 5.
30. Anon. (ed.), *Letters of Rachel, Lady Russell*, Vol. 2 (London: Longman and Co., 1853), p. 114.
31. Ibid.
32. Thomson, *Noble Household*, p. 216.

9 Complaints and Cures

1. HMC, *Calendar of the Manuscripts of the Marquis of Salisbury*, Vol. 12 (Hereford: Hereford Times Limited, 1910), p. 633; Richard Griffin Braybrooke (ed.), *The Private Correspondence of Jane, Lady Cornwallis, 1613–1644* (London: S. & J. Bentley, Wilson, and Fley, 1842), p. 109.

2. Richard Griffin Braybrooke (ed.), *The Autobiography of Sir John Bramston* (London: John Bowyer Nichols and Sons, 1845), p. 381.
3. Ibid., p. 382.
4. Edward William Harcourt (ed.), *The Harcourt Papers*, Vol. 1 (Oxford: James Parker and Co., 1878), p. 193; Anon. (ed.), *The Memoirs of Sir Hugh Cholmley* (publisher unknown, 1870), p. 24.
5. James Orchard Halliwell (ed.), *The Autobiography and Correspondence of Sir Simonds D'Ewes*, Vol. 1 (London: Richard Bentley, 1845), p. 273.
6. D. J. H. Clifford (ed.), *The Diaries of Lady Anne Clifford* (Stroud: Alan Sutton Publishing Ltd, 1992), p. 25; Isaac Herbert Jeayes (ed.), *Letters of Philip Gawdy, 1579–1616* (London: J. B. Nichols and Sons, 1906), p. 135.
7. Dorothy Gardiner (ed.), *The Oxinden Letters, 1607–1642* (London: Constable and Co. Limited, 1933), p. 181. The name 'Oxinden' appears to have various spellings, including 'Oxenden'.
8. Alfred Morrison (ed.), *The Bulstrode Papers*, Vol. 1 (London: privately published, 1897), p. 6.
9. HMC, *The Manuscripts of the Earl Cowper*, Vol. 2 (London: Eyre and Spottiswoode, 1888), p. 429; Margaret M. Verney, *Verney Letters of the Eighteenth Century*, Vol. 1 (London: Ernest Benn Ltd, 1930), p. 26.
10. Lady Newton, *The House of Lyme: From its Foundation to the End of the Eighteenth Century* (London: William Heinemann, 1917), pp. 222–3.
11. HMC, *The Manuscripts of His Grace the Duke of Portland*, Vol. 3 (London: Eyre and Spottiswoode, 1894) p. 352.
12. James J. Cartwright (ed.), *The Wentworth Papers, 1705–1739* (London: Wyman and Sons, 1883), p. 40; Henry B. Wheatley (ed.), *The Diary of Samuel Pepys*, Vol. 2 (New York: Random House, pref. 1893), pp. 836, 839.
13. Halliwell, *D'Ewes*, Vol. 1, p. 373; HMC, *Duke of Portland*, Vol. 3, p. 305.

14. Rev. Daniel Parsons (ed.), *The Diary of Sir Henry Slingsby* (London: Longman, Rees, Orme, Brown, Green, and Longman, 1836), p. 40; T. Crofton Croker (ed.), *Autobiography of Mary, Countess of Warwick* (London: Richards, 1848), pp. 25–6.
15. Parsons, *Slingsby*, p. 40; Braybrooke, *Cornwallis*, p. 272; Francis Bamford (ed.), *A Royalist's Notebook: The Commonplace Book of Sir John Oglander* (London: Constable and Co. Ltd, 1936), p. 217.
16. Anon. (ed.), *Memoir of Lady Warwick* (London: The Religious Tract Society, 1847), pp. 121–2.
17. HMC, *Duke of Portland*, Vol. 3, p. 203.
18. Anon. (ed.), *The Memorandum Book of Sir Richard Cholmley* (Northallerton: North Yorkshire County Record Office, 1988), p. 204; HMC, *The Manuscripts of His Grace the Duke of Rutland*, Vol. 4 (London: Mackie and Co. Ltd, 1905), p. 530.
19. James J. Cartwright (ed.), *The Memoirs of Sir John Reresby* (London: Longmans, Green, and Co., 1875), p. 214; Harcourt, *Harcourt Papers*, Vol. 1, p. 181.
20. Anon., *Lady Warwick*, pp. 185–6; Croker, *Autobiography*, p. 34.
21. D. W. Hayton, *The House of Commons, 1690–1715*, Vol. 1 (Cambridge: Cambridge University Press, 2002), p. 751.
22. Bamford, *Oglander*, p. 218.
23. Ibid., p. 219.
24. Cartwright, *Reresby*, p. 214; Anon. (ed.), *Letter-Books of John Hervey, 1st Earl of Bristol*, Vol. 1 (Wells: Ernest Jackson, 1894), p. 144.
25. Anon., *Hervey*, Vol. 1, pp. 112–3.
26. Bamford, *Oglander*, p. 222.
27. HMC, *Duke of Portland*, Vol. 3, p. 373; Halliwell, *D'Ewes*, Vol. 1, p. 287.
28. Parsons, *Slingsby*, p. 70.
29. Braybrooke, *Cornwallis*, p. 296.
30. Parsons, *Slingsby*, p. 41.
31. Ibid., p. 47.

32. Braybrooke, *Cornwallis*, p. 145.
33. Anon., *Richard Cholmley*, p. 170; Parsons, *Slingsby*, pp. 47–8; J. J. Bagley (ed.), *The Great Diurnal of Nicholas Blundell of Little Crosby, Lancashire*, Vol. 1 (Liverpool: The Record Society of Lancashire and Cheshire, 1968), p. 144.
34. Margaret M. Verney, *Memoirs of the Verney Family*, Vol. 2 (London: Longmans, Green, and Co., 1904), p. 207.
35. Arthur Searle (ed.), *Barrington Family Letters, 1628–1632* (London: University College London, 1983), pp. 191–2.
36. Gladys Scott Thomson, *Life in a Noble Household, 1641–1700* (London: Jonathan Cape, 1950), p. 323.
37. Norman Egbert McClure (ed.), *The Letters of John Chamberlain*, Vol. 1 (Philadelphia: The American Philosophical Society, 1939), p. 351.
38. Verney, *Letters*, Vol. 1, pp. 187–8.
39. Ibid., p. 187.
40. William Durrant Cooper (ed.), *Savile Correspondence* (London: The Camden Society, 1858), p. 6.
41. Walter Scott (ed.), *Memoirs of the Court of Charles II, by Count Grammont* (London: George Bell and Sons, 1908), pp. 267–8.
42. HMC, *The Manuscripts of the Earl Cowper*, Vol. 3 (London: Eyre and Spottiswoode, 1889), p. 25; HMC, *Report on the Manuscripts of Allan George Finch*, Vol. 1 (London: HMSO, 1913), p. 208.
43. HMC, *Earl Cowper*, Vol. 3, p. 25; HMC, *Duke of Portland*, Vol. 3, p. 288; Durrant, *Savile*, p. 297.
44. Verney, *Memoirs*, Vol. 2, pp. 243–4.
45. Halliwell, *D'Ewes*, Vol. 1, p. 285.
46. Verney, *Memoirs*, Vol. 2, pp. 278–9.

10 Church and Charity

1. George Savile, *Advice to a Daughter* (London: 1688), p. 6.
2. Anon. (ed.), *The Memoirs of Sir Hugh Cholmley* (Ppublisher unknown, 1870), p. 34; Samuel Clark, *The Lives of Sundry*

Eminent Persons in This Later Age (London: Thomas Simmons, 1683), p. 114.

3. Elizabeth Hagglund, "Cassandra Willoughby's visits to country houses", *The Georgian Group Journal* 11 (2001): p. 186.
4. Richard Griffin Braybrooke (ed.), *The Autobiography of Sir John Bramston* (London: John Bowyer Nichols and Sons, 1845), p. 413; Margaret M. Verney, *Memoirs of the Verney Family*, Vol. 2 (London: Longmans, Green, and Co., 1904), p. 496; D. J. H. Clifford (ed.), *The Diaries of Lady Anne Clifford* (Stroud: Alan Sutton Publishing Ltd, 1992), p. 244.
5. Joanna Moody (ed.), *The Private Life of an Elizabethan Lady: The Diary of Lady Margaret Hoby, 1599–1605* (Stroud: Sutton Publishing Limited, 1998), p. 211; Anon. (ed.), *Memoir of Lady Warwick* (London: The Religious Tract Society, 1847), pp. 203, 246.
6. Clark, *Eminent Persons*, p. 111.
7. White Kennett, *A Sermon Preached at the Funeral of the Right Noble William, Duke of Devonshire* (London: W. B., 1708), pp. 54, 56.
8. Moody, *Hoby*, p. 194.
9. James Orchard Halliwell (ed.), *The Autobiography and Correspondence of Sir Simonds D'Ewes*, Vol. 1 (London: Richard Bentley, 1845), p. 363.
10. Lady Newdigate-Newdegate, *Cavalier and Puritan in the Days of the Stuarts* (London: Smith, Elder, and Co., 1901), p. 221.
11. Anon. (ed.), *The Lady Falkland: Her Life* (London: Catholic Publishing and Bookselling Company Limited, 1861), p. 54.
12. Rev. T. Ellison Gibson (ed.), *A Cavalier's Notebook* (London: Longmans, Green, and Co., 1880), pp. 214–5.
13. Joseph Jacobs (ed.), *The Familiar Letters of James Howell* (London: David Nutt, 1890), p. 106; HMC, *The Manuscripts of His Grace the Duke of Portland*, Vol. 3 (London: Eyre and Spottiswoode, 1894), p. 455.
14. Clark, *Eminent Persons*, p. 142.

15. Ibid.; Henry Granville Fitzalan-Howard (ed.), *The Lives of Philip Howard, Earl of Arundel, and of Anne Dacres, His Wife* (London: Hurst and Blackett, 1857), pp. 246–7.
16. HMC, *The Manuscripts of His Grace the Duke of Rutland*, Vol. 4 (London: Mackie and Co. Ltd, 1905), p. 518; George Ornsby (ed.), *The Household Books of the Lord William Howard* (Durham: Andrews and Co., 1878), pp. liv, 247; Gibson, *Notebook*, p. 160.
17. Todd Gray (ed.), *Devon Household Accounts, 1627–59: Part One* (Exeter: Devon and Cornwall Record Society, 1995), pp. xxxiii, xxxvi; Fitzalan-Howard, *Lives*, p. 211.
18. Clifford, *Anne Clifford*, p. 116; John Prince, *The Worthies of Devon* (London: J. McCreery, 1810, originally printed 1701), p. 696.
19. Angela Nicholls, *Almshouses in Early Modern England* (Woodbridge: The Boydell Press, 2017), pp. 73, 102.
20. HMC, *Duke of Rutland*, Vol. 4, p. 462; "History", *Sir William Borlase's Grammar School*, https://www.swbgs.com/page/?title=History&pid=12.
21. William Page (ed.), *The Victoria History of the County of Gloucester*, Vol. 2 (London: Archibald Constable and Company Limited, 1907), p. 352; Rev. Daniel Lysons, *The Environs of London*, Vol. 1, Part 1 (London: T. Cadell and W. Davies, 1810), p. 29.
22. Clark, *Eminent Persons*, p. 142.
23. Fitzalan-Howard, *Lives*, pp. 212–3.
24. Ibid., pp. 308–9.
25. Anon. (ed.), *The Life of Margaret Godolphin, by John Evelyn* (London: Alexander Moring Ltd, 1904), pp. 144, 148.

Epilogue

1. D. J. H. Clifford (ed.), *The Diaries of Lady Anne Clifford* (Stroud: Alan Sutton Publishing Ltd, 1992), p. 64.

BIBLIOGRAPHY

Primary Sources

Anon. (ed.), *A Brief Historical Relation of State Affairs from September 1678 to April 1714 (Narcissus Luttrell)*, Vols 3, 4, and 5 (Oxford: Oxford University Press, 1857)

Anon. (ed.), *Letter-Books of John Hervey, 1st Earl of Bristol*, Vol. 1 (Wells: Ernest Jackson, 1894)

Anon. (ed.), *Letters of Rachel, Lady Russell*, Vol. 1 (London: Longman, Brown, Green, and Longmans, 1853)

Anon. (ed.), *Letters of Rachel, Lady Russell*, Vol. 2 (London: Longman and Co., 1853)

Anon. (ed.), *Memoir of Lady Warwick* (London: The Religious Tract Society, 1847)

Anon. (ed.), *Memoirs of the Life of Colonel Hutchins*on (London: J. M. Dent and Co., 1913)

Anon. (ed.), *The Lady Falkland: Her Life* (London: Catholic Publishing and Bookselling Company Limited, 1861)

Anon. (ed.), *The Memoirs of Ann, Lady Fanshawe* (London: John Lane, The Bodley Head, 1907)

Anon. (ed.), *The Memoirs of Sir Hugh Cholmley* (Publisher unknown, 1870)

Anon. (ed.), *The Memorandum Book of Sir Richard Cholmley* (Northallerton: North Yorkshire County Record Office, 1988)

Bagley, J. J. (ed.), *The Great Diurnal of Nicholas Blundell of Little Crosby, Lancashire*, Vol. 1 (Liverpool: The Record Society of Lancashire and Cheshire, 1968)

Bamford, Francis (ed.), *A Royalist's Notebook: The Commonplace Book of Sir John Oglander* (London: Constable and Co. Ltd, 1936)

Bédoyère, Guy de la (ed.), *The Diary of John Evelyn* (Woodbridge: The Boydell Press, 2004)

Bond, Maurice F. (ed.), *The Diaries and Papers of Sir Edward Dering* (London: Her Majesty's Stationery Office, 1976)

Brathwaite, Richard, *The English Gentleman; and the English Gentlewoman* (London: John Dawson, 1641)

Braybrooke, Richard Griffin (ed.), *The Autobiography of Sir John Bramston* (London: John Bowyer Nichols and Sons, 1845)

Braybrooke, Richard Griffin (ed.), *The Private Correspondence of Jane, Lady Cornwallis, 1613–1644* (London: S. & J. Bentley, Wilson, and Fley, 1842)

Bülow, Gottfried von (ed.). "Diary of the Journey of Philip Julius, Duke of Stettin-Pomerania." In *Transactions of the RHS*, New Series, Vol. 6, edited by anon., pp. 1–67. (London: Longmans, Green, and Co., 1892)

Cartwright, James J. (ed.), *The Memoirs of Sir John Reresby* (London: Longmans, Green, and Co., 1875)

Cartwright, James J. (ed.), *The Wentworth Papers, 1705–1739* (London: Wyman and Sons, 1883)

Clark, Andrew (ed.), *The Life and Times of Anthony Wood*, Vol. 1 (Oxford: Clarendon Press, 1891)

Clark, Samuel, *The Lives of Sundry Eminent Persons in This Later Age* (London: Thomas Simmons, 1683)

Clifford, D. J. H. (ed.), *The Diaries of Lady Anne Clifford* (Stroud: Alan Sutton Publishing Ltd, 1992)

Cooper, William Durrant (ed.), *Savile Correspondence* (London: The Camden Society, 1858)

Cotton, Charles, *The Compleat Gamester* (London: A. M., 1674)

Cox, Nicholas, *The Gentleman's Recreation: The First Part* (London: Freeman Collins, 1686)

Cox, Nicholas, *The Gentleman's Recreation: The Second Part* (London: J. C. and F. C., 1686)

Cox, Nicholas, *The Hunter: A Discourse of Horsemanship* (Oxford: L. Lichfield, 1685)

Croker, T. Crofton (ed.), *Autobiography of Mary, Countess of Warwick* (London: Richards, 1848)

Davies, G. (ed.), *Autobiography of Thomas Raymond and Memoirs of the Family of Guise* (London: RHS, 1917)

Dircks, Will H. (ed.), *The Autobiography of Edward, Lord Herbert of Cherbury* (London: Walter Scott, 1888)

Dobson, Austin (ed.), *The Diary of John Evelyn* (London: Macmillan and Co. Limited, 1908)

Firth, C. H. (ed.), *The Life of William Cavendish, Duke of Newcastle* (London: J. C. Nimmo, 1886)

Fitzalan-Howard, Henry Granville (ed.), *The Lives of Philip Howard, Earl of Arundel, and of Anne Dacres, His Wife* (London: Hurst and Blackett, 1857)

Gardiner, Dorothy (ed.), *The Oxinden Letters, 1607–1642* (London: Constable and Co. Limited, 1933)

Gibson, Rev. Kennet (ed.), *A Comment Upon Part of the Fifth Journey of Antoninus Through Britain* (London: John Nichols, 1800)

Gibson, Rev. T. Ellison (ed.), *A Cavalier's Notebook* (London: Longmans, Green, and Co., 1880)

Gray, Todd (ed.), *Devon Household Accounts, 1627–59: Part Two* (Exeter: Devon and Cornwall Record Society, 1996)

Griffiths, Emily (ed.), *Through England on a Side Saddle: The Diary of Celia Fiennes* (London: The Leadenhall Press, 1888)

Halliwell, James Orchard (ed.), *Ancient Inventories of Furniture, Pictures, Tapestry, Plate, Etc.* (London: J. E. Adlard, 1854)

Halliwell, James Orchard (ed.), *The Autobiography and Correspondence of Sir Simonds D'Ewes*, Vols 1 and 2 (London: Richard Bentley, 1845)

Harcourt, Edward William (ed.), *The Harcourt Papers*, Vol. 1 (Oxford: James Parker and Co., 1878)

Hatton, Edward, *A New View of London*, Vol. 2 (London: 1708)

Hervey, Sydenham (ed.), *The Diary of John Hervey* (Wells: Ernest Jackson, 1894)

HMC, *Calendar of the Manuscripts of the Marquis of Salisbury*, Vol. 12 (Hereford: Hereford Times Limited, 1910)

HMC, *Report on the Manuscripts of Allan George Finch*, Vol. 1 (London: His Majesty's Stationery Office, 1913)

HMC, *Report on the Manuscripts of the Late Allan George Finch*, Vol. 2 (London: His Majesty's Stationery Office, 1922)

HMC, *The Manuscripts of His Grace the Duke of Portland*, Vol. 3 (London: Eyre and Spottiswoode, 1894)

HMC, *The Manuscripts of His Grace the Duke of Rutland*, Vol. 2 (London: Eyre and Spottiswoode, 1889)

HMC, *The Manuscripts of His Grace the Duke of Rutland*, Vol. 4 (London: Mackie and Co. Ltd, 1905)

HMC, *The Manuscripts of the Earl Cowper*, Vols 1 and 2 (London: Eyre and Spottiswoode, 1888)

HMC, *The Manuscripts of the Earl Cowper*, Vol. 3 (London: Eyre and Spottiswoode, 1889)

Hudleston, C. Roy (ed.), *Naworth Estate and Household Accounts, 1648–1660* (Durham: Andrews and Co., 1958)

Isham, Rev. Robert (ed.), *The Journal of Thomas Isham of Lamport* (Norwich: Miller and Leavins, 1875)

Jacobs, Joseph (ed.), *The Familiar Letters of James Howell* (London: David Nutt, 1890)

Jeayes, Isaac Herbert (ed.), *Letters of Philip Gawdy, 1579–1616* (London: J. B. Nichols and Sons, 1906)

Jessopp, Augustus (ed.), *The Autobiography of the Hon. Roger North* (London: David Nutt, 1887)

Kennett, White, *A Sermon Preached at the Funeral of the Right Noble William, Duke of Devonshire* (London: W. B., 1708)

Lee, Maurice (ed.), *Dudley Carleton to John Chamberlain, 1603–1624: Jacobean Letters* (New Brunswick: Rutgers University Press, 1972)

Lewis, Thomas Taylor (ed.), *Letters of the Lady Brilliana Harley* (London: The Camden Society, 1854)

Littleton, Adam, *A Sermon at the Funeral of the Lady Jane* (London: John Macock, 1669)

Lodge, Edmund (ed.), *Illustrations of British History*, Vol. 3 (London: John Chidley, 1838)

London Gazette, https://www.thegazette.co.uk/

Macray, Rev. W. D. (ed.), *Beaumont Papers: Letters Relating to the Family of Beaumont* (London: Nichols and Sons, 1884)

Magrath, John Richard (ed.), *The Flemings in Oxford*, Vol. 1 (Oxford: Clarendon Press, 1904)

Magrath, John Richard (ed.), *The Flemings in Oxford*, Vol. 2 (Oxford: Clarendon Press, 1913)

Margerison, Samuel (ed.), *Yorkshire Diaries and Autobiographies in the Seventeenth and Eighteenth Centuries* (Durham: Andrews and Co., 1886)

McClure, Norman Egbert (ed.), *The Letters of John Chamberlain*, Vols 1 and 2 (Philadelphia: The American Philosophical Society, 1939)

Misson, M., *Memoirs and Observations in His Travels Over England* (London: 1719)

Moody, Joanna (ed.), *The Private Life of an Elizabethan Lady: The Diary of Lady Margaret Hoby, 1599–1605* (Stroud: Sutton Publishing Limited, 1998)

Morley, Henry (ed.), *The Spectator*, Vols 1, 2, and 3 (London: George Routledge and Sons, 1891)

Morrison, Alfred (ed.), *The Bulstrode Papers*, Vol. 1 (London: Privately published, 1897)

Ornsby, George (ed.), *The Household Books of the Lord William Howard* (Durham: Andrews and Co., 1878)

Park, Thomas (ed.), *Nugæ Antiquæ*, Vol. 1 (London: J. Wright, 1804)

Parsons, Robert, *A Sermon Preached at the Funeral of the Right Honorable John, Earl of Rochester* (London: H. Hills, 1707)

Parsons, Rev. Daniel (ed.), *The Diary of Sir Henry Slingsby* (London: Longman, Rees, Orme, Brown, Green, and Longman, 1836)

PCCRP, Will Registers, PROB 11, The National Archives, Kew, London

Phillips, C. B. (ed.), *Lowther Family Estate Books, 1617–1675* (Gateshead: Northumberland Press Limited, 1979)

Plot, Robert, *The Natural History of Staffordshire* (Oxford: The Theatre, 1686)

Prince, John, *The Worthies of Devon* (London: J. McCreery, 1810, originally printed 1701)

Raines, Rev. F. R. (ed.), *The Journal of Nicholas Assheton of Downham* (Manchester: The Chetham Society, 1848)

Savile, George, *Advice to a Daughter* (London: 1688)

Scott, Harold Spencer (ed.), *The Journal of Sir Roger Wilbraham* (Publisher unknown, 1902)

Scott, Walter (ed.), *Memoirs of the Court of Charles II, by Count Grammont* (London: George Bell and Sons, 1908)

Searle, Arthur (ed.), *Barrington Family Letters, 1628–1632* (London: University College London, 1983)

Shirley, Evelyn Philip (ed.). "An Inventory of the Effects of Henry Howard", *Archaeologia* 42, no. 2 (1870): 347–378

Sondes, George, *Sir George Sondes: His Plaine Narrative* (London: 1655)

Steer, Francis W. (ed.), "The Inventory of Arthur Coke of Bramfield, 1629", *Proceedings of the Suffolk Institute of Archaeology and History* 25 (1951): 264–287

Tyson, Blake (ed.), *The Estate and Household Accounts of Sir Daniel Fleming of Rydal Hall, Westmorland, from 1688–1701* (Kendal: Cumberland and Westmorland Antiquarian and Archaeological Society, 2001)

Waller, William, *Divine Meditations* (London: B. Griffin, 1683)

Wanklyn, Malcolm (ed.), *Inventories of Worcestershire Landed Gentry, 1537–1786* (Worcester: The Worcestershire Historical Society, 1998)

Wheatley, Henry B. (ed.), *The Diary of Samuel Pepys*, Vols 1 and 2 (New York: Random House, pref. 1893)

Selected Secondary Literature

Beckett, J. V., *The Aristocracy in England, 1660–1914* (Oxford: Basil Blackwell Ltd, 1986)

Bendall, Sarah A., *Shaping Femininity: Foundation Garments, the Body, and Women in Early Modern England* (London: Bloomsbury, 2021)

Blundell, Margaret (ed.), *Cavalier: Letters of William Blundell to His Friends, 1620–1698* (London: Longmans, Green, and Co., 1933)

Boothman, Lyn, and Richard Hyde Parker (eds), *Savage Fortune: An Aristocratic Family in the Early Seventeenth Century* (Woodbridge: The Boydell Press, 2006)

Christie, William Dougal, *A Life of Anthony Ashley Cooper, First Earl of Shaftesbury, 1621–1683*, Vols 1 and 2 (London: Macmillan and Co., 1871)

Cliffe, J. T., *The World of the Country House in Seventeenth-Century England* (London: Yale University Press, 1999)

Courtais, Georgine de, *Women's Hats, Headdresses, and Hairstyles* (Mineola: Dover, 1986)

Cust, Elizabeth, *Records of the Cust Family: Series 2* (London: Mitchell Hughes and Clarke, 1909)

Devereux, Walter Bourchier, *Lives and Letters of the Devereux, Earls of Essex*, Vol. 2 (London: John Murray, 1853)

Drummond, J. C., and Anne Wilbraham, *The Englishman's Food: Five Centuries of English Diet* (London: Pimlico, 1994)

Edwards, Peter, *Horses and the Aristocratic Lifestyle in Early Modern England* (Woodbridge: The Boydell Press, 2018)

Girouard, Mark, *Life in the English Country House* (London: Book Club Associates, 1979)

Guerci, Manolo. "The Construction of Northumberland House and the Patronage of Its Original Builder, Lord Henry Howard, 1603–14." *The Antiquaries Journal* 90 (2010): pp. 341–400

Hagglund, Elizabeth. "Cassandra Willoughby's visits to country houses." *The Georgian Group Journal* 11 (2001): pp. 185–202

Hayton, D. W., *The House of Commons, 1690–1715*, Vol. 1 (Cambridge: Cambridge University Press, 2002)

Heal, Felicity, and Clive Holmes, *The Gentry in England and Wales, 1500–1700* (Basingstoke: Macmillan, 1994)

Hervey, Mary F. S. "A Lumley Inventory of 1609." In *The Sixth Volume of the Walpole Society*, edited by anon., pp. 36–46. (Oxford: Oxford University Press, 1918)

Hervey, Mary F. S., *The Life, Correspondence, and Collections of Thomas Howard, Earl of Arundel* (Cambridge: Cambridge University Press, 1921)

Hibbert, Christopher, *The English: A Social History, 1066–1945* (London: Grafton Books, 1989)

Jenkins, Susan, *Portrait of a Patron: The Patronage and Collecting of James Brydges* (London: Routledge, 2017)

Johnson, Joan, *The Gloucestershire Gentry* (Gloucester: Alan Sutton Publishing, 1989)

Kightly, Charles, *Berry Pomeroy Castle* (London: English Heritage, 2011)

Limon, Jerzy. "The Masque of Stuart Culture." In *The Mental World of the Jacobean Court*, edited by Linda Levy Peck, pp. 209–229. (Cambridge: Cambridge University Press, 2005)

Lysons, Rev. Daniel, *The Environs of London*, Vol. 1, Part 1 (London: T. Cadell and W. Davies, 1810)

Newdigate-Newdegate, Lady, *Cavalier and Puritan in the Days of the Stuarts* (London: Smith, Elder, and Co., 1901)

Newton, Lady, *The House of Lyme: From Its Foundation to the End of the Eighteenth Century* (London: William Heinemann, 1917)

Nicholls, Angela, *Almshouses in Early Modern England* (Woodbridge: The Boydell Press, 2017)

North, Susan, *Sweet and Clean? Bodies and Clothes in Early Modern England* (Oxford: Oxford University Press, 2020)

Nunn, Joan, *Fashion in Costume, 1200–2000* (Chicago: New Amsterdam Books, 2000)

Olsen, Kirstin, *Daily Life in Eighteenth-Century England* (London: Greenwood Press, 1999)

Page, William (ed.), *The Victoria History of the County of Gloucester*, Vol. 2 (London: Archibald Constable and Company Limited, 1907)

Parkes, Joan, *Travel in England in the Seventeenth Century* (Oxford: Oxford University Press, 1925)

Parsons, Catherine. "Horseheath Hall and Its Owners", *Proceedings of the Cambridge Antiquarian Society* 41 (1948): pp. 1–50

Ralph, Philip Lee, *Sir Humphrey Mildmay: Royalist Gentleman: Glimpses of the English Scene, 1633–1652* (New Brunswick: Rutgers University Press, 1947)

Richardson, R. C., *Household Servants in Early Modern England* (Manchester: Manchester University Press, 2010)

Sir William Borlase's Grammar School. "History", *Sir William Borlase's Grammar School*, https://www.swbgs.com/page/?title=History&pid=12

The Metropolitan Museum of Art (the Met), New York City. "Mantua", *The Met*, https://www.metmuseum.org/art/collection/search/81809

Thomson, Gladys Scott, *Life in a Noble Household, 1641–1700* (London: Jonathan Cape Ltd, 1950)

Thomson, Gladys Scott, *The Russells in Bloomsbury, 1669–1771* (London: Jonathan Cape Ltd, 1940)

Tinniswood, Adrian, *The Verneys: A True Story of Love, War, and Madness in Seventeenth-Century England* (London: Vintage, 2008)

Various, *Blenheim Palace World Heritage Site: Revised Management Plan 2017* (Norfolk: Historic Landscape Management Ltd, 2017)

Verney, Margaret M., *Memoirs of the Verney Family*, Vols 1 and 2 (London: Longmans, Green, and Co., 1904)

Verney, Margaret M., *Verney Letters of the Eighteenth Century*, Vol. 1 (London: Ernest Benn Ltd, 1930)

Vincent, Susan, *Dressing the Elite: Clothes in Early Modern England* (Oxford: Berg, 2003)

Walker, Matthew, *Architects and Intellectual Culture in Post-Restoration England* (Oxford: Oxford University Press, 2017)

Whyman, Susan E., *Sociability and Power in Late Stuart England* (Oxford: Oxford University Press, 2002)

Wilcox, R. Turner, *The Mode in Hats and Headdress* (Mineola: Dover, 2008)

Willett, C., and Phillis Cunnington, *The History of Underclothes* (Mineola: Dover, 1992)

Wilson, Richard, and Alan Mackley, *Creating Paradise: The Building of the English Country House, 1660–1880* (London: Hambledon and London, 2000)

INDEX